It's Friday, It's Crackerjack!

It's FRIDAY, It's CRACKERJACK!

The inside story of a teatime TV classic

Alan Stafford

fantom
publishing

First published in 2018 by Fantom Publishing, an imprint of Fantom Films
www.fantompublishing.co.uk

Copyright © Alan Stafford 2018

Alan Stafford has asserted his moral right to be identified
as the author of this work in accordance with the
Copyright, Designs and Patents Act 1988.

A catalogue record for this book is available from the British Library.

Hardback edition ISBN: 978-1-78196-315-9

Typeset by Phil Reynolds Media Services, Leamington Spa
Printed and bound by CPI Group (UK) Ltd, Croydon, CR0 4YY
Jacket design by Will Brooks

For Andrea

And the entire cast and crew of *Crackerjack*

CRACKERJACK!!!

Also by Alan Stafford and published by Fantom

TOO NAKED FOR THE NAZIS

The untold story of sand dancing legends Wilson, Keppel and Betty

Contents

Prologue

I T IS NOVEMBER 1978. Nicholas from Wandsworth School stands on a circular podium, raising him just a few inches above the floor. Held in his arms is a hotchpotch of bulky boxes and stuffed toys, piled to almost chin height. One hand grips a single cloth cabbage.

Nicholas is no idiot. True, he had no idea who wrote *Winnie the Pooh*. But he *did* know the colour of the road in *The Wizard of Oz*, what a seismograph is used for, and the two sides who fought the Wars of the Roses.

Now Ed Stewart approaches him once more:

What does the word 'crackerjack' mean?

Ed holds the microphone close to Nicholas' mouth. He thinks for a moment:

A firework, isn't it?

It isn't a stupid guess – firecracker, jumping jack – but it's a wrong guess. Ed puts him right:

No. A crackerjack is a thing or person of the highest excellence. So it's another cabbage for Nicholas.

Fortunately, Nicholas never receives that fateful third cabbage. He wins the game, chooses his prize, and returns the following week wearing the ornate peaked cap of a champion.

For anyone who grew up in the late 1950s, or the 60s, the 70s, or early 80s, *Crackerjack* means only one thing – a teatime TV show with games, pop songs and silly sketches. In America, *Cracker Jack* has a totally different meaning – a blend of caramel-coated popcorn and peanuts, popular for well over a hundred years and considered by many to be the world's first junk food. Every box contained a surprise gift – a plastic toy, a charm or a booklet. And the term '*Cracker Jack* prize' has come to mean something trivial and effectively worthless.

However, in Britain, a *Crackerjack* prize is a thing of legend. Something beyond mere monetary value. An object craved by the many and owned by the few. It is, quite simply …

… a pencil.

Introduction

I N JANUARY 2018 THE *Radio Times* revealed its list of The 50 Greatest Children's TV Shows, as decided by a panel of 30 children's TV experts. *Crackerjack* achieved a very respectable tenth place. All the more respectable when you learn that programmes like *Magpie* and *The Magic Roundabout* missed the list entirely.

The *Radio Times* summed up the show in a single paragraph. *Double or Drop* and the *Crackerjack* pencil both got a mention, but no namecheck for either Leslie Crowther or Peter Glaze. Max Bygraves headed a brief list of *Crackerjack* presenters, though he never actually hosted the show. He made a one-off guest appearance, that's all. But his name often crops up in lists of celebrities who appeared on *Crackerjack*. So it was inevitable (by the law of Chinese Whispers) that one day he would be promoted to presenter.

Around the same time, stand-up Stewart Francis announced his farewell tour: *Into the Punset*. This Canadian comic, who delivers a steady stream of wordplay one-liners in deadpan style, is about as far removed as you can get from frenetic funnyman Stu Francis. But Stewart's own publicity for the tour proclaims him 'the star of *Mock the Week*, *Live at the Apollo* and *Crackerjack*.' This typically low-key leg-pull by Stewart Francis (who has never knowingly crushed a grape) is just one further piece of misinformation destined to resurface in the press and online for years to come.

A quick trawl through the Internet will throw up any amount of erroneous information about *Crackerjack*. For instance, Vicki Michelle and Julie Dawn Cole were both apparently *Crackerjack* hostesses – which may come as something of a surprise to Jan Michelle and Julie Dorne Brown.

It would be a brave author who could claim his book was free from inaccuracies. All I can say is I've taken nothing at face value and, wherever possible, I've checked my facts. This is no academic tome – for the simple reason that I am no academic. Just a comedy writer who gets a teensy bit obsessive once in a while.

My previous book – *Too Naked for the Nazis* – was a biography of sand-dancing variety trio Wilson, Keppel and Betty. In the process of researching their story, I had to bone up on American vaudeville, British variety, European cabaret, two world wars and the small matter of the Nuremberg Trials. The time period for *It's Friday, It's Crackerjack* is the 1950s through to the 1980s – a rather more recent period of history. This has the added benefit that I could talk to many of the performers – whereas Jack Wilson, Joe Keppel and Betty Knox never returned any of my calls.

There are certain things you won't find in this book. Very few semi-colons, because I really don't understand them. Also it would be easy to fill a great many pages with episode listings, but what would be the point? You can find much of that information yourself on the BBC Genome Project website or on IMDb. Plus it's very difficult to guarantee total accuracy. *Crackerjack* was a live programme when it began and, later on, was almost always recorded a day or so before transmission. *Radio Times* listings are much like train timetables – accurate when they go to press, but prone to unavailable services, last-minute replacements or complete cancellation due to industrial action. And anyway, copious listings are just a little dull. So there you are. I possess neither a mortar board nor an anorak.

I have likewise not gone big on biographical information, other than when it has some relevance to the show. There are just too many personalities involved. Unfortunately, a good number of people who worked on the programme (including, sadly, a few of my interviewees) have since died. But, as this is a book about *Crackerjack*, deaths are generally only mentioned when they have some bearing on the story.

I freely apologise if you don't care for the term 'actress'. The problem for me is, if I call actresses 'actors', I also have to call hostesses 'hosts'. In the end I opted for the terminology of the period I am writing about. But I promise never to use that awful feminisation of the word 'comedian'. You have to draw the line somewhere.

The joy of writing this book has been the opportunity of talking to so many of the people involved in it. There's a full list of those I have interviewed in the back of the book. So, for the moment, I prefer not to spoil the surprise. But (unless I am clearly quoting from a book, newspaper or magazine article, or a broadcast) any quotation you read is the result of a personal interview, conducted by me, during 2017 and 2018. At times it felt like a global version of hide-and-seek, but it was one with a remarkably high success rate. A few people I contacted by email, rather more I interviewed over the phone, but many I met and talked to face-to-face. I can't quite believe the number of people who picked me up from the railway station, drove me to their homes, took pity on this impoverished author and fed and watered (and sometimes wined) him. And, if that wasn't enough, they then entrusted me with precious photos, scripts and DVDs. I am hugely, hugely grateful.

As a child, *Crackerjack* was a show that I loved. And, as it turned out, so did the people who worked on it. Everyone I talked to (even those who I feared wouldn't want to be reminded of it) spoke of the show and the team that helped put it together with genuine affection. For many, it was one of the happiest times of their lives.

I hope I've captured some of that happiness in the pages that follow.

Alan Stafford 2018

1
Rikki, the Baby Monkey

1955

I T WAS FIVE O'CLOCK on Wednesday 14th September 1955. Those fortunate youngsters whose parents owned a television (sales of which had dramatically soared after the coronation two years earlier) gathered round the set for their daily dose of 'Children's Television'. Earlier that afternoon, Bill and Ben the Flowerpot Men had flobbalobbed to the delight of their younger siblings. But the next hour was especially for them. They sat eagerly in front of that wooden box with its bulging glass screen as Sylvia Peters, their magic monochrome auntie, spoke to them and them alone:

> Today is a very special day, because we have the first of a new series of programmes from the Children's Television Theatre. It is called *Crackerjack* and stars Eamonn Andrews. But first of all we are going to begin with a film for the younger ones, which shows a day in the life of a baby monkey.

And a very special day it turned out to be. From 5.00 to 6.00 pm each day (weekends included) those 60 minutes were packed with a variety of illustrated stories, short films, dramas (often with a historical setting) and documentaries. Just two days ago there was the Monday Story told by Dorothy Smith; *A Plateful of Trouble*, with those three crazy guys, Morris, Marty and Mitch ('Marty' being a young Marty Feldman); how to plant a miniature garden; and a sports competition between champion gymnasts and children. On the Tuesday there was *The Little Painting* (a play by Stephen Mogridge) and a visit to Dudley Zoo. At the end of the hour, television would close down (a scheduling strategy known as the Toddlers' Truce) so that children could be put to bed, blissfully unaware that the goggle box would spring back to life an hour or so later.

Saturdays were a little more fun. Currently there was Gerald Campion in *Billy Bunter of Greyfriars School*. A few months earlier it had been *Jigsaw* – a magazine programme incorporating stories, music, magician Robert Harbin and the adventures of Mick and Montmorency (the latter, and shorter, of the two being Charlie Drake).

By and large, children's television was affordable, studio-based entertainment, often of an 'improving' nature. Most of the long-running classics of the genre had yet to appear. *Blue Peter* was three years away. It would be almost a decade before the stuffily titled *For Deaf Children* became the fast-paced animation-fest that was *Vision On*.

If the adventures of Rikki the baby monkey (the curtain-raiser to *Crackerjack*) were less than riveting, the young audience had no option but to sit it out. They couldn't turn over to another channel, because there *were* no other channels. Nor would there be. For at least another week.

On Thursday 22nd September 1955, something terrible happened. Grace Archer died in a fire. An estimated audience of 20 million heard it happen. At the time the BBC dismissed it as coincidence. But a 'strictly confidential' internal memo written several months earlier by H. Rooney Pelletier, Controller of the BBC Light Programme, said:

> The more I think about it, the more I believe that a death of a violent kind in *The Archers*, timed, if possible, to diminish interest in the opening of commercial television in London, is a good idea.

That very evening was the launch night of Associated-Rediffusion, the first Independent Television company, to be followed by 16 further regional companies over the next seven years.

It is a not unreasonable assumption that the BBC, in the months leading up to the launch of ITV, would have taken a long hard look at its current output, to ensure it would hold its own against whatever aggressive scheduling its new rival may throw at it. So any producer who fancied trying out something new – something that, if it took off, might *really* take off – could expect a sympathetic ear.

Johnny Downes, a wartime RAF pilot and recipient of the DFC, had gone on to become a stage manager in London's West End, a circus ringmaster, and eventually (in 1953, aged 33) a floor manager at the BBC. He won rapid promotion to television producer and, just two years later, he happened to be in the right place at the right time with the right idea.

Anna Home, who first joined children's television in the 1960s and rose through the ranks to become Head of Children's Programmes in the 1980s and 90s, documents *Crackerjack*'s origins in her book *Into the Box of Delights*:

> In 1955 there was a problem about finding a studio for forthcoming children's programmes as the traditional one, Studio E in Lime Grove, was to be out of service. Johnny Downes suggested doing a programme for children from the Television Theatre on Shepherds Bush Green. Freda Lingstrom, Head of the Children's Department, initially said 'no' to the idea, but changed her mind and suggested that Eamonn Andrews might be a good host.

Crackerjack is often credited with being the first live children's show. It certainly wasn't. There had been years of children's programmes, most of them broadcast live. But what every previous children's series had lacked was a live studio audience. Announcer Sylvia Peters may have given the impression that a brand-new theatre had been built especially for the show. But, in reality, the 'Children's Television Theatre' was still the Television Theatre, only now with an audience comprising 500 children.

The Television Theatre, although a recent BBC acquisition, was previously the Shepherds Bush Empire, a music hall and variety theatre designed by Frank Matcham and built in 1903. The BBC bought the theatre for £120,000 in 1953 and was broadcasting from there by October with the first of a monthly series *Variety Parade*, with a cast that included comparative newcomers Morecambe and Wise. At that time Wood Lane (the eventual site of the BBC Television Centre) was little more than a building site. So a ready-to-go theatre was a quick and logical solution to the BBC's lack of space. It soon became established as the home of many popular long-running comedy and variety shows.

Freda Lingstrom's choice of Eamonn Andrews as host would be crucial to the show's longevity. Dublin-born Eamonn was aged 32 and one of the best-known television personalities of the era. Initially he joined the BBC as a boxing commentator, but he was soon hosting a number of radio and TV shows. Most notable among these was TV panel game *What's My Line*, which started in 1951, in which panellists (including Dame Isobel Barnett and Gilbert Harding) had to guess the professions of members of the public from a brief mime and a series of 'yes/no' questions. In July 1955 Eamonn had become the presenter and first victim of *This is Your Life*, in which a celebrity is treated to a surprise retrospective of their life and career and a reunion with old friends and colleagues. From late 1955 onwards he would continue to present both shows alongside *Crackerjack*.

Eamonn was modest about his achievements. During his career he was voted Television Personality of the Year four times, but remained bemused by the phenomenon of personality:

> I became, almost overnight, a face. I acquired that new, meaningless description for people who can neither sing nor dance nor juggle nor play the harp – a personality. Television personality.

Eamonn didn't always appear the most relaxed of performers. He often looked a little awkward, slightly ill-at-ease. Later in his career, *Bestseller!* (a book by David Renwick and Andrew Marshall, writers of Radio 4 sketch show *The Burkiss Way*) poked fun at his tendency to perspire excessively, in a blurb to the imagined publication *Eamonn Andrews' Third Book of Perspiration*:

> … For when it comes to the inside workings of the TV and radio industries, Mr Andrews' thorough grounding and rich tapestry of experience would fill buckets. How is it done? According to the author the simplest method is to put on a heavy sweater, and of course this is just what his employers do.

But what Eamonn did have, as Terry Wogan had after him, was the gift of the gab. When required (and in live television you could never predict when it would be required, and in what quantity) Eamonn would be able to keep on chatting, in a natural, informal, though not always totally coherent manner. Marty Feldman (of the aforementioned Morris, Marty and Mitch) and co-writer Barry Took satirised his inconsequential and sometimes baffling utterings in the character of Seamus Android, portrayed by Bill Pertwee, in their late-1960s radio series *Round the Horne*:

> Hello. All right, well now – ha ha. All right. Well, I mustn't let my tongue run away with me. Now, I know you can't wait to and neither can I, so I won't, and with that – goodnight.

All of this is something of a cruel caricature of a man who was no actor, no egoist, but someone who could talk to the camera and who brought out the best of his fellow performers. There were plenty of TV presenters of the 1950s who would have been too stuffy and formal to front a variety show for children. Although future *Crackerjack* hosts may have had greater rapport with their audience, they came from a different era. For the mid-1950s, Eamonn was the right choice. He had two big things going for him. Firstly, his Irish brogue had no overtones of class and was a refreshing change from those traditional plummy BBC types. And secondly, he'd brought a game with him.

In his early career he had juggled an insurance job with broadcasts on the Dublin-based Radio Éireann. Then he took a big gamble. He gave up the security of the day job with the aim of establishing himself as a full-time broadcaster. Around this time he had been to the Dublin Theatre Royal to watch an evening of Cine Variety (a mix of films and live entertainers). One of the smash hits of the show proved to be a feature called *Double or Nothing* presented by fast-talking actor Eddie Byrne, as Eamonn recalled in his early autobiography *This is My Life*:

> This was a quiz in which members of the audience came up on the stage and were asked a series of four questions each. Prize for the first correct answer was half-a-crown, for the next, five shillings, the next ten shillings, and the last, one pound. After each question, the M.C. would say: 'Will you take the prize *now* and go away, or is it *Double or Nothing*?' If you chose to carry on, and answered correctly, you doubled your previous prize. If you failed, you got nothing.

Out of the blue, Eamonn was asked if he'd like to present *Double or Nothing* at the Savoy in Limerick. Having made a success of the show in this intimate theatre, he was then invited to be Eddie Byrne's successor at the vast Dublin Theatre Royal, one of the largest cinema theatres in Europe:

> When I spoke, I couldn't hear my voice coming back to me over the amplification system. It went out, away from me, and across the footlights and was lost. This was frightening. But at least I wasn't afraid of words, and spoke on. Presently, with the introductory patter over, I asked for four volunteers from the audience. There was a rush from the seats, and the commissionaires moved into action to control the stampede. The fear stayed with me as I introduced the first contestant. I was far more nervous than he.

I made a tentative wisecrack, and suddenly, from out there in the darkness a fantastic sound rolled down to me … the sound of an audience laughing. I knew then that, back in my own city, it was going to be all right.

Eamonn was soon established as a regular feature of the Royal's programme, alongside an ever-changing bill of big-name variety acts. When Joe Loss and his band came over from England for a fortnight's booking, Joe was full of praise for Eamonn. A few days into the run, Joe asked Eamonn to come round to his dressing room after the show:

> He said: 'Eamonn, you know I was saying the other night that I think the way you do *Double or Nothing* is great?'
> I nodded. Joe went on talking. 'Well, I've been looking at it a lot since. I still think it's great. I've got a proposition, my lad – how would you like to come over to England with the band show?'

During 1949 Eamonn toured England with the Joe Loss show, playing (amongst other venues) the Shepherds Bush Empire, in its final years as a variety theatre, before its transformation into the future home of *Crackerjack*. As Eamonn's BBC career began to take off he continued with *Double or Nothing*. As this June 1953 review (from theatrical newspaper *The Stage*) reveals, he had now developed the format almost beyond recognition. It was a brand new quiz, with a brand new name:

> Eamonn Andrews has a friendly way of presenting his *Double or Drop* quiz, and inveigles contestants on to the stage to win cabbages, balloons and cake-tins for their errors, and more delectable prizes for correct answers to unorthodox questions.

So this was what *Crackerjack* would be getting. A host who was rapidly becoming one of the BBC's hottest properties, plus a novel quiz, new to television, which would prove to be the backbone of the show. A month or so before the first programme, the BBC's copyright department wrote to Eamonn's agent, confirming their previous telephone conversation:

> The game will last for about 12 – 14 minutes and you confirmed that Eamonn Andrews or your office would be providing the BBC with the questions and we agreed that for the provision of the questions and the use of the programme lay-out the BBC should pay a fee of 12 guineas per television broadcast.

> We would be prepared to give a credit to the effect that the game is 'from a lay-out by Eamonn Andrews' or words to that effect, this being our standard practice in a case of this sort.

Eamonn's agent replied:

> With regard to *Double or Drop*, I have discussed the billing of this programme with Mr Andrews and we would prefer to use '*Double or Drop* devised by Eamonn Andrews' rather than 'from a lay-out by Eamonn Andrews.'

The reply was typed on paper headed 'Eamonn Andrews Ltd' – a clear indication of Eamonn's current celebrity status, and a hint of the shrewd businessman beneath the façade of the genial host. But shrewd only in the sense that he was nobody's fool. Five years later he would still receive just 12 guineas a show for *Double or Drop*.

As with Eamonn's stage shows, the game was only one element of the entertainment. If Johnny Downes was to mount a children's variety show, there were two other essential ingredients – music and comedy.

The music would be supplied by the Harry Parry Sextet. Harry was a jazz clarinettist, born in Bangor, Wales, whose playing was frequently compared to that of Benny Goodman. His sextet had regularly broadcast on BBC Forces radio during the Second World War, and at one time included pianist George Shearing in its line-up. After the war Harry continued both to play for and present jazz shows on the BBC Light Programme, and even had a stint hosting the popular record requests programme *Housewives' Choice*. He was a prestigious name to have on board and his photo accompanied a piece Johnny Downes wrote in the *Radio Times* to announce the start of *Crackerjack*. The same article had other exciting news:

> … we shall be introducing to you two brand new comics – Joe Baker and Jack Douglas, who always seem to be getting in trouble with Mr Grumble!

This would not be the last time that Johnny Downes would take a chance by casting two comparative unknowns in *Crackerjack*. They had only one previous TV appearance to their credit. Early the previous year they had appeared in the first episode of *Show Case*, in which Benny Hill introduced a succession of 'artists and acts new to television'. Though they were kept busy in the variety theatres, this appearance did little to kick-start their TV careers.

Jack Douglas would later achieve fame as Alf Ippititimus, the flat-capped buffoon with the nervous tic, but at this stage in his career he was straight man to Joe. Or rather, the lesser of two idiots. Jack was long and lanky, Joe was short and stout. They certainly had the looks for a comedy double-act.

Jack's father was a theatrical impresario, and Jack and his older brother Bill spent their early careers working in the family firm, producing stage shows and pantomimes. In 1948, Jack and Bill were touring Germany entertaining the troops with a Combined Services Entertainment's Unit variety show called *Hi There!* When he met Sergeant Joe Baker they immediately hit it off. Joe was coming up for demob, so Jack offered him a part in the panto he was directing at the Kingston Empire. Jack's autobiography *A Twitch in Time* (written with Sue Benwell) takes up the story:

> Joe played Mate in *Dick Whittington* and when the Captain, who was Joe's counterpart, took ill on dress rehearsal, I was the only one who knew the part. So, Joe and I rehearsed like mad for a couple of hours and the show opened to capacity business the very next day. We went on to do our bit and after the show a very famous agent of the day, Hyman Zahl, came backstage.
>
> 'How long have you two been a double act?' he asked.
>
> I glanced at my watch: 'About two hours and twenty minutes,' I told him.

Alan Fenton got to know Jack and Joe when he was one of the scriptwriters on their 1959 ITV series *New Look*. He told me about their onstage relationship:

> Jack Douglas was this big tall fellow, thick face, and he loved saying things like, 'I'll smash your face in.' Joe Baker was much shorter, very fat, not the most elegant in his manners, but he was funny. Jack Douglas was in control, he was the sort of master. And Joe Baker did what he was told and had these big eyes, you know, always looked upset. They were wonderful in cowboy sketches. Jack Douglas was the sort of man who kicked the doors open to come in and threatened everybody – and Joe would be cowering in a corner.

By the standards of television entertainment at that time, *New Look* was a pretty sophisticated blend of singing, dancing and comedy, with a cast that included Roy Castle and Lionel Blair's sister Joyce. Alan Fenton was naturally concerned whether the sketches he was writing were suited to Jack and Joe's style:

I was chatting to them once and I said, 'Look, you two have been together for a long time and I've only just joined. We're writing a certain kind of show, are you happy with the material?' And they said, 'Why don't you come and see us?' So I went to see them in this theatre, which was half empty. And it was this big, huge stage. Big proscenium arch. And I remember the big gag that they thought was so wonderful. Jack would stand at one side of the stage and he'd say to Joe, 'Look at this pillar. Isn't it funny?' And he'd describe it. And he'd say, 'What does that remind you of?' And Joe, standing the other side, says, 'Reminds me of this one here.' And this was the joke! So afterwards, they said, 'How did you enjoy it?' And I said, 'I enjoyed it very much, but I don't think *New Look* is music hall. I think you've got to adapt to it.'

Back to Summer 1955, and Johnny Downes had travelled down to Brighton to see Jack and Joe at work and to discuss *Crackerjack*. And the one thing he wasn't looking for was sophistication. Forget the stuffy old educational aspirations of children's programming. Everyone was in agreement that, just like variety shows for grown-ups, the primary purpose of *Crackerjack* was to entertain. As Eamonn wrote in the 1957 *BBC Children's Annual*:

> When Freda Lingstrom and Johnny Downes and myself got together to decide what we were going to do for Children's Television, we had no high and mighty plans. Already all the *important* things were catered for, and it was our job to find something *unimportant* that would pass pleasantly the hour or so between school and the evening exercises.

After their meeting in Brighton, Jack Douglas wrote to Johnny:

> Joe and myself will start work on the scripts some time this week and I will send you a draft as soon as it goes on paper. Is it okay for us to make the first one 'How to paint your rooms' and the second spot 'Joe's little brother breaks the radio.' We will work these out with a minimum of props and scenery as per our conversation.
>
> May Joe and I take this opportunity of thanking you for coming down to Brighton and here's hoping that your contract department and Sonny Zahl don't come to blows over the sordid question of salary.

Johnny Downes' assistant, Lois Singer, replied:

> The two sketches you mention will be most suitable, but Johnny has asked me to mention that the 'sound effects' in the radio sketch should keep away

from all war and other horrifying sounds! As far as props etc. are concerned, there's no need for you to be too stringent – anything reasonable we can usually supply easily – it's when special trick props, particularly large ones, have to be made that the trouble starts.

A week before the first show, Lois Singer wrote to the BBC copyright department to arrange a fee for a seven-minute sketch featuring Jack and Joe:

The idea for this sketch has been evolved from suggestions by the producer and comics themselves. These ideas have been put into script form for which we now request payment. This should be based on the minimum amount payable for a comedy script of seven minutes in length which is not the script writer's original idea, as I believe this is Mr Douglas' first script for Television.

The Mr Douglas in question was not Jack, but his elder brother Bill, who received seven guineas per show (five guineas less than Eamonn Andrews got for *Double or Drop* alone). So brother Bill was drafted in to make some kind of scripted order out of the chaotic invention of the trio of comics. I say 'trio' because there was also Mr Grumble – a cantankerous old man of about the same height as Joe, who would become the butt of most of their pranks. He was always billed as Mr Grumble, because using his real name might have led to some confusion. His actual name was Joe Baker.

Just as Jack Douglas came from a dynasty of theatrical producers, Joe Baker came from a dynasty of comics. The old-time variety act Joe Baker and Olga, who performed as a bickering henpecked husband and harridan wife, were in reality Joe Baker Junior's mother and father. So this creative quartet was very much a family affair – a father, a son and two brothers.

As Rikki the baby monkey came to the end of his busy day, the eager young audience still had a trailer to sit through before the main feature got under way. If they were getting fidgety, imagine the atmosphere in the TV Theatre control room. Although Freda Lingstrom had given *Crackerjack* the go-ahead, the budget would be modest, and Johnny Downes only had six shows to prove himself. If things didn't go well, by the end of the year *Crackerjack* would be a distant memory. The trailer finished and Sylvia Peters returned to the screen:

And now we are going to visit the BBC Children's Television Theatre to see *Crackerjack*, the first of a new series of programmes starring Eamonn

Andrews. So, if you are all comfortably settled, let us go straight over to the Television Theatre …

It wasn't Friday, it was Wednesday. It wasn't five-to-five, it was quarter past. But, sure as cabbages is cabbages, any minute now it would be … *Crackerjack.*

2
Lobster on Rear Business

1955 – 1957

A T BBC TELEVISION THEATRE, the hours leading up to the live broadcast of the first *Crackerjack* were the usual frenzied, but efficient, activity. A little more frenzied than usual, because variety shows would normally be broadcast in the evening, and this was going out at 5.15 pm. At least this meant a comparatively early finish for the crew but, on the downside, they would be working rather more intensely to get everything ready in time.

Eddie Stuart joined the BBC as a cameraman in 1955 and worked on *Crackerjack* regularly, including the first ever show:

> We used to start rehearsals at ten-thirty in the morning and we'd finish rehearsals by half past four. It was very quick. Johnny Downes used to, sort of – not make it up as he went along, that's wrong – sort of improvise, as it were. We would say, 'Would it be better if he did so-and-so?' And he would make his mind up from that. He was a good bloke. He was very easy to work with.
>
> The crew I was on – I later became the senior cameraman with that crew – I was the number 3 cameraman when I first worked on it, but gradually I worked my way up. Certainly on *Crackerjack* Camera 1 used to take the majority of the show.

In its early days *Crackerjack* had three cameras and two booms. (A boom was a telescopic arm with a microphone attached, mounted – along with its operator – atop a mobile platform.) Writing in *Eamonn Andrews' Book for*

Boys and Girls in 1956, producer Johnny Downes gave the young reader a glimpse behind the scenes:

> Two of the cameras are more or less stationary but the centre camera, Camera 1, is tracking – which means it is mounted on a Dolly (a kind of trolley) which runs far back into the auditorium for long-distance pictures and can push right up to the stage for close-ups.

Being previously a working theatre, the Television Theatre had to undergo some structural alterations to allow sufficient space for the movement of cameras and equipment, as Eddie Stuart explains:

> They took the right hand side of the stage and extended it out, right to the back of the theatre. And they made a runway for Camera 1 to go up and down the middle of the stage. And you had the audience sitting down on the left hand side of the camera. Otherwise it was just as it was. I mean, it was a perfectly normal studio set-up, except that you couldn't bring Camera 3 back too far, because he'd fall off the edge of the stage!

After working out how the cameras were going to shoot the show, and numbering each shot in the script, the aim was to run through the show twice before the audience arrived. Then around 500 children from nearby schools would descend upon the theatre. This was an invited audience and the two stipulations were that they must be over 12 years of age and be able to arrive at the Theatre by 5.00 pm without missing any of the school day. A theatre packed with children? Eddie had no horror stories to relate:

> They were all remarkably good actually. Johnny used to go out and lecture them! But no, they were very good. We never had the slightest bit of problem with them.

Here are the opening moments of the show, vividly described by Johnny Downes in the *Eamonn Andrews' Book*:

> And now comes the great moment ... a red lamp flashes in the control room ... stand by ... that's it – we're on the air!
>   'Fade up Camera 1.' Camera 1 is focused on part of the audience.
>   'Cue Music.' The floor manager signals to the band.
>   'Cut to 2.' The picture snaps over and we see our model theatre.
>   'BBC Children's Television Theatre presents ...' The model theatre's curtain goes up and we see CRACKERJACK. Another little curtain goes up ...

'Mix to Camera 1.' This time the picture gradually cross-fades from our model theatre to the real one and we see Eamonn Andrews coming through the curtains.

'Hello, boys and girls. Welcome to another edition of *Crackerjack*.'

'*Crackerjack*!' shouts back the audience, and the show has begun.

Crackerjack was an inspired choice of title, and apparently it was Johnny Downes himself who picked it. Even today, just utter the word and you invite the deafening Pavlovian response. There are few other long-running TV shows that can guarantee the same reaction. In the 1957 *BBC Children's Annual* Eamonn Andrews confirms it was ever thus:

> From the first day *Crackerjack* was born, it came back at us with a bang. The audience yelled back *Crackerjack* every time we said it, and from there on, that was the custom. In fact, it was often very funny to see somebody by mistake mention the word *Crackerjack* while they were talking about something else and then see them jump almost a couple of feet off the ground when the audience suddenly picked it up and yelled it right back at them.

Having introduced the show, Eamonn goes straight into the first game ever played on *Crackerjack* – schoolboys Victor Pond and Bill Wake take part in a banana-eating contest! The winner will go on to compete in *Double or Drop*.

The *Crackerjack* theme tune that started the show was composed by Harry Parry and played by his sextet. It's a jaunty little theme beginning with an upward arpeggio and then moving chromatically downwards to a dum-dee-dum-dee rhythm. Catchy, if not exactly singable. The Harry Parry Sextet returns now for a couple more numbers: *Blue Skies* and *Alabama Jubilee*. There follows another elimination round (also with boys), a balloon-blowing game – a particularly apt prelude to this week's special guest: Trevor Little, the Balloon Man.

Trevor Little's billing described not only his act but also his build. I remember seeing this genial rotund perfomer in Brighton, late in his career. After inflating a long white sausage-shaped balloon and releasing it, to soar, squeak, rasp, and finally flop lifeless into the fourth row, he implored the audience: 'If you find any, please pick them up – only they *do* upset the cleaners.' (A very adult gag that he would never have got away with on *Crackerjack*.)

The third elimination game (for girls) involves singing. Yes, speedy scoffing and hasty huffing-and-puffing were totally unacceptable activities for young ladies in the 1950s. Having selected the *Double or Drop* competitors, Eamonn now introduces the comedy sketch.

It is neither of the ideas that Jack and Joe had previously discussed with Johnny Downes. This first sketch of the series concerns Joe Baker being given a birthday cake to look after by Mr Grumble, who threatens that if anything happens to it, 'I'll 'ave your hide, young man, I'll 'ave your hide.' He exits, growling, and as Joe goes to close the door, Jack walks in and inadvertently pushes the cake into Joe's face. They then have no option but to bake a new cake, in a messy slapstick routine (with plenty of eggs and a soda siphon) that sets the tone for the whole series. If you're looking for clever wordplay, about the best it gets is Joe adding a flower (instead of flour) to the mix – and Joe running out of the door when Jack instructs him to beat it. Finally they admit defeat and Jack rushes off to buy a freshly baked replacement, but when Mr Grumble asks Jack to give him the cake, you can guess the rest! Not the finest of routines, but here are three masters of their art giving their all, to the sound of raucous childish laughter throughout.

And then into *Double or Drop*. Each child, standing on a small round podium, is asked a question in turn. A correct answer is rewarded with a prize or two. A wrong answer results in a cabbage being awarded, along with the prizes. The more questions the contestant gets right (or wrong) the more prizes they have in their arms. If they drop a prize, they also receive a cabbage. When a child has three cabbages, they are eliminated.

The prizes themselves weren't particularly special. They were chosen primarily for their bulkiness or unwieldiness. Typical prizes were cornflake packets, tinned fish, mops, buckets and sombreros. And the cabbages were made of cloth, stuffed and surprisingly heavy. The winner, however, got to choose a decent prize from a lavish display of books, board games and long-playing records.

Eamonn Andrews' one-page outline of *Double or Drop* (submitted to the BBC before the series began) is not unduly altered from the adult version he had previously toured theatres with. For instance, among the suggested list of prizes to heap upon the child is a cigarette case! There is also a proposed musical round, where children have to recognise an instrument played by someone in national dress hidden behind a screen – an idea which was never used. But there is absolutely no mention of cabbages, or indeed of penalty prizes of any sort. Cabbages had certainly been listed (along with balloons and cake-tins) as booby prizes in an earlier press review of Eamonn's stage show. In all probability, a cabbage pretty quickly came to symbolise a botched answer or a dropped prize (the latter always accompanied by the sound of a klaxon – to alert Eamonn, if his back was turned on the offending competitor at the time).

Live television has its pros and cons. There's a pace and excitement that is difficult to match in a stop-go recorded programme. On the other hand, there will be the odd slip that is impossible to correct. At one point in that first show (according to a 1962 interview in the *Radio Times*) Eamonn inadvertently said 'astrology' when he meant to say 'astronomy'. In the morning post he received an admonishing postcard from two 11-year-old schoolgirls:

> What a stupid man you are, to tell a fortune from a star.
> That, you see, sir, is astrology. You really owe us an apology

Actress and singer Barbara Burke was the first in a long line of attractive but ridiculously overqualified *Double or Drop* hostesses, whose job it was to pile the prizes on the schoolkids. The whole cast then joined together in a singalong medley of familiar songs, led by Jack, Joe and Mr Grumble.

As Eamonn attempts to close the show, he is interrupted by a couple of overgrown and overenthusiastic schoolboys (Joe Baker and Jack Douglas) who eagerly press a gift-wrapped parcel into his hands. As he starts to unwrap it, there's an electronic flash and the sounds of an explosion. The smoke clears, and a black-faced Eamonn bids a final farewell. The band plays the *Crackerjack* theme, the credits roll and the picture fades to black.

The original intention had been for Mr Grumble to be the victim of the exploding parcel, and for it to be a running joke throughout the series, but Eamonn (in his autobiography *This is My Life*) remembers discussing the idea with Johnny Downes and Freda Lingstrom (Head of Children's Television) who immediately objected:

> 'Why not?' I asked, 'It will make them laugh. And we'll point it so much beforehand they'll know it's a joke.'
> 'No,' Freda said, 'It's all right for the older ones, but very young children just will not accept that. They will not accept either very *young* people or very *old* people being blown up.'

It was a new thought to me.

Freda went on: 'They may not be upset if Mummy is blown up or Daddy is blown up – but *not* Grandpa or Baby Brother.'

*

Those three lofty Reithian principles are that the BBC should educate, inform and entertain. Episode one of *Crackerjack* really only scored in the last category, but score it did – and to entertain had always been Johnny Downes' sole aim. At the same time the following Wednesday, Eamonn was back on screen, presenting … *Playbox*.

No, *Crackerjack* hadn't been axed after one episode! It was always the intention that *Crackerjack* would be a fortnightly show, and it remained so for as long as Eamonn hosted it. *Playbox* seems largely forgotten, despite running for eight series and clocking up more than 100 episodes.

Like *Crackerjack*, *Playbox* initially ran from 5.15 to 6.00 pm. But it was a non-audience studio show, with a rather more educational bent and a budget more in line with that of standard children's programming. In *The Television Annual for 1958* Eamonn explains the differing aims of the two shows:

> *Crackerjack* and *Playbox* began as experiments and were by no means intended for long runs. That they have enjoyed long runs is my good luck. We created a Children's Television Theatre for light-hearted entertainment, and we balanced it by producing slightly more serious material from the *Playbox*.

Two future mainstays of children's television joined Eamonn on *Playbox*. There was a story from 'Hot Chestnut Man' Johnny Morris (later the popular host of *Animal Magic*) and illustrations from Tony Hart (a future presenter on *Vision On* and many other shows). There was also *Inter-Regional Quiz League*: a knockout quiz tournament between teams of schoolchildren from around the country, which ran throughout the series.

Playbox was the brainchild of busy producer and presenter Cliff Michelmore, who was still producing it in 1957 when he started hosting weekday early-evening magazine show *Tonight* (immediately following the abolition of the 6.00 pm Toddlers' Truce closedown). On Wednesdays he would spend 45 minutes in the gallery producing *Playbox*, then turn up in front of the cameras presenting *Tonight* a mere 20 minutes later.

The second edition of *Crackerjack* went out on Wednesday 28th September when, for the first time, there was something on the other channel – as ITV had started broadcasting the previous Thursday. The first edition of *TV Times* took a crafty swipe at the opposition:

> The people who run *your* programmes on the new Television channel think that you don't like to be called 'children' too often. So the hour between 5 and 6 o'clock on Mondays to Fridays is called Tea V Time – not Children's Hour.
>
> Tea V Time on Mondays will be called 'Venture' and will be for boys aged 9 to 15. Right through the week, the programmes will be aimed at special groups.
>
> Tuesday is for girls aged 9 to 15 and is called 'Elizabethan Fanfare'.

ITV may have been dead against talking down to young people, but sexual stereotyping was still very much in evidence:

> Wednesday has a general programme called 'Telebox'. It is the one day when they don't keep to the rule – 'Telebox' is for all ages (Mum and Dad, too).

It can be no coincidence that ITV chose to make Wednesday its family day, as *Crackerjack* was clearly one of few BBC children's shows to have a broader appeal. It also meant that a show called *Telebox* would play opposite one called *Playbox*. Seconds out … round one … the *box*-ing match had begun!

In fact, the first edition of *Telebox* was not so different from a typical BBC Children's Hour. There were four 15-minute shows: *Rumpus Point* ('a quarter of an hour of slapstick fun'), *Buddy Budgerigar* ('an unusual series of adventures which befall a small bird, aided and abetted by Peter Butterworth'), *Nat Temple and his Band* ('popular tunes of the moment') and *Round at the Redways* ('a weekly serial depicting the daily life of the Redway family'). It wasn't a particularly instructive hour, but then neither was *Crackerjack*. It had comedy and it had music, but it lacked a studio audience – and *Round at the Redways* would need to be pretty good to rival the excitement of *Double or Drop*. For the moment, the BBC had nothing to worry about. But as the years went on, and ITV spread beyond London to cover the whole country, the competition would grow fiercer.

Series one of *Crackerjack* continued with Jack Douglas and Joe Baker providing a slapstick sketch for every show – there was a Crazy House sketch, building a brick wall, a sea cruise, opening an old railway station. Sometimes (as with this seaside sketch from show three) they didn't even have time to commit the dialogue to paper, and we can only guess at the content from the stage directions:

> JOE undresses to go swimming – long shirt business.
> GRUMBLE falls. Lobster on rear business.
> Cut to Camera 2: Close up GRUMBLE'S rear and lobster.
> Throwing lobster from one to another. JOE goes to breakwater.
> Water thrown over JOE business.

Each week there was a guest speciality act – Kodell (magician), Ravic and Babs (roller skaters), Tommy Elliott (concertina). Show six boasted a future star turn – Terry Hall with Lenny the Lion. Terry was one of the best ventriloquists in the business, and his camp companion with the trans-atlantic twang was one of the best dummies. In just over a year they would be fronting their own Children's Hour show.

If the bold experiment of *Crackerjack* had failed, then show six would have been its swansong. Perhaps, in order to keep Eamonn Andrews in full employment, *Playbox* would have become a weekly show. However, *Crackerjack* continued for another nine programmes, taking its fortnightly run from 14th September 1955 to 28th March 1956. The only change to the line-up was that the Harry Parry Sextet was superseded by Eddie Mendoza and his Band.

This upped the comedy content of the show, because Eddie 'Tash' Mendoza was a true eccentric. Born Edward Middleton in Aberdeen, he progressed from solo accordionist to fronting accordion band El Cubanos. He subsequently moved to comedy in the Spike Jones mould, fronting bands that were both musically and visually bizarre, such as The Archer Street Spivs and Eddie Mendoza's Crazy Loonies. Eamonn Andrews provided this neat description of Eddie in the 1957 *BBC Children's Annual*:

> Eddie Mendoza, the band leader with the Scottish accent and a moustache as long as one of the R's he rolls, has been a great hit. Eddie is more likely to appear on *Crackerjack* wearing a 'Davy Crockett' hat and conducting with a bow and arrow than he is in any conventional guise.
>
> In fact, I'll never forget the last programme on which he arrived wearing the Davy Crockett Hat, but for some odd reason dressed up in white flannels and shirt and carrying a cricket bat. Joe took one look at him and said 'Davy Cricket'.

21st December 1955 saw the first *Christmas Crackerjack* (extended from 45 minutes to an hour) with return bookings for Tommy Elliott, Terry Hall and Lenny the Lion, and balloon man Trevor Little, together with a debut from trick cyclist Bernard Riley.

The show starts with a group of boys and girls pulling a giant cracker, from which Eamonn Andrews emerges. Joe Baker, Jack Douglas and Mr Grumble ad lib some Christmassy chat, including the inevitable *Crackerjack* puns. (Presumably along the lines of 'Are you going to pull that cracker, Jack?') Later on in the show Jack and Joe do a rather neat crosstalk routine which, as a nice change, is fully scripted:

JACK: How did you get to this party anyway?
JOE: I came in with my brother's ticket.
JACK: Well, where's your brother?
JOE: He's outside looking for his ticket.

Jack proceeds to rehearse a recitation of 'Little Miss Muffet Sat on her Tuffet', with interruptions from Joe:

JACK: '… eating her curds and whey.'
JOE: What's curds and whey?
JACK: Well, it's er – it's er –
JOE: Like tripe and onions.
JACK: No, it's not like tripe and onions – it's a sort of milk.
JOE: So she was eating her milk and drinking her fish and chips, I
        suppose.
JACK: To continue – 'There came a big spider who sat down beside her,
        and –'
JOE: Have you or anyone you know ever seen a spider sit down?
JACK: Well no, I don't think so.
JOE: And yet you say Miss Muffet saw a spider sit down.
JACK: Yes.
JOE: Then it was something stronger than milk she was drinking.

At the end of the show (just before the entrance of Santa) the three comics, plus bandleader Eddie Mendoza, hostess Barbara Burke and Lenny the Lion perform a variation on the old seaside show favourite: *If I Were Not Upon the Stage*. In this case the words are 'If I were in a pantomime'. Each enters in turn, in full costume, and sings a verse about their character, concluding with a piece of dialogue and accompanying actions – like 'rub the lamp' for Abanazar and 'washing clothes' for Widow Twankey. Last to enter is Joe Baker as Fairy Bluebell, and the song ends with all six in a line, singing and gesticulating simultaneously. A surefire showstopper earning Jack's brother Bill an extra 30 shillings for writing it.

The remainder of the series had the usual comedy content – one big sketch (cowboys, detectives, etc.) and a finale singalong in appropriate costume – for instance, dressed as tramps, with *The Man Who Broke the Bank at Monte Carlo* sung by Mr Grumble, and *We're a Couple of Swells* by Jack and Joe.

Joe Baker had a reputation as a practical joker – he was one of the first British comedians to make a long-playing record of hoax phone calls to unsuspecting tradespeople. One *Crackerjack* sketch was set in a police station with Jack Douglas playing the sergeant. During a rehearsal break, he went outside the stage door (still in costume) for a puff on his pipe. As Jack relates in his autobiography, Joe had rounded up a few stage hands to play a prank:

> Suddenly, out came the nine stagehands and, before I could say a word, they had started a mock street fight with me as their pretend punch bag. I went along with the make-believe scrap by reacting to their 'blows' and groaning in all the appropriate places.

Unfortunately a woman passer-by noticed what appeared to be a helpless policeman being beaten up. She dashed off to a phone box and dialled 999:

> As soon as the stagehands heard the police siren, they bolted back inside the theatre again like frightened rabbits. I was just picking myself up off the pavement when the cavalry screeched to a halt beside me and even they mistook me for a real police officer.
>
> 'Excuse me, Sergeant,' said the concerned constable leaping out of his patrol car. 'We've had the report of a fight down here.'
>
> 'No, no, Constable,' I explained breathlessly, brushing the dirt off my uniform and bending down to retrieve my pipe from the gutter. 'We were just rehearsing a scene from *Crackerjack*.'

In the *Radio Times* in 1956, Eamonn Andrews recalled one onscreen jape that not everyone appreciated:

> During one programme I picked up from the stage floor what appeared to be a large sword and flung it into the wings. Immediately bandleader Eddie Mendoza walked out wearing one of those trick swords that fasten round the

body and give the impression of going right through. The whole *Crackerjack* audience laughed. We laughed. Eddie laughed. Everyone laughed. Or so it seemed.

Next morning's post brought the equaliser. Was I quite, quite mad? Did I realise there were thousands of young children preparing to run through thousands of other young children with carving knives because *Crackerjack* had proved it didn't hurt?

Writing in the *BBC Children's Annual*, Eamonn detailed the spectacular finish to the series. The first show had ended with an explosion, but this was nothing compared with the closing moments of the final show. As before, Jack and Joe, dressed as a pair of mischievous schoolboys, entered with a gift for Eamonn:

> Each time I took one of these presents or passed them on to someone else, there was always an explosion. They arrived back with another parcel, but this time I passed them on to Producer Johnny Downes.
>
> They disappeared in the direction of the control room where Johnny was supervising all the pictures that were coming from his three cameras on the stage. Inevitably there was a tremendous explosion, the picture went lopsided and I believe I looked like the way you look when you see yourself in a distorted mirror. Then we said goodbye and the captions showing the names of the people who had taken part in the last edition were rolling across a screen with blackened and charred edges, smoke swirling upwards as if there was a most awful conflagration just beneath the camera lens.
>
> Needless to say, it was no more and no less than a smoke candle held underneath the camera, creating apart from the smoke that peculiar, pungent smell so common on Guy Fawkes Night, when you light your fireworks and your crackers and your catherine wheels.

And this was how the first series ended, with a pair of comedians blowing up the BBC. Michael Bentine did it in the 1960s, the Goodies in the 1970s – but this was 1956! What's more, it was part of Children's Hour, which traditionally closed to the strains of *Twinkle Twinkle Little Star*. When Jack Douglas and Joe Baker had started preparing sketches for the series, they had been warned to 'keep away from all war and other horrifying sounds'. But, as *Crackerjack* got into its stride, Johnny Downes seemed to have few qualms about spicing up the slapstick with a healthy dose of anarchy and arson. It was a novel way of getting the show noticed. Or perhaps a novel way of handing in his notice. Only time would tell.

*

Six months later *Crackerjack* was back for a fortnightly run of 14 shows – from September 1956 to March 1957. It was the same team but a different location. The Television Theatre in Shepherds Bush had closed – not due to fire damage after the last series, but for extensive renovation that would take more than a year to complete. During this period, all audience variety shows moved to the King's Theatre Hammersmith, another magnificent old music hall that the BBC acquired briefly, putting it on the market again once they were able to return to Shepherds Bush.

The only change in the line-up was new hostess Vikki Hammond who stayed for two series. During her second series she also appeared on cinema screens as one of the disturbingly alluring sixth-formers in *Blue Murder at St Trinian's*. A few years later she'd achieve even greater success in Australia, hosting her own variety show and becoming a regular in Aussie soap *The Sullivans*. Yet again, *Crackerjack* had chosen a performer with huge potential and given them little to do except smile, do the odd bit of singing and hand out cabbages.

Vikki wasn't available for the first show of the series and was replaced by singer Barbara Whiting. Bearing in mind the show already had a father and son and two brothers, it was only logical for Johnny Downes to offer the job of hostess to his own wife.

The series begins with Joe reading a fan letter:

Dear Joe Baker, since you first appeared on television, I can assure you that television sales have increased one hundred percent. My mother sold hers, my uncle sold his, my auntie sold hers. P.S. Can you get me a good offer for *my* set?

After the third elimination game, Eamonn introduces the sketch:

And now it's time to hear from Joe Baker and Jack Douglas. During their summer holidays, the boys were forced to sunbathe in the public libraries and took to reading books on history. Their first tale concerns the famous Spanish Armada …

It had been a very cool, very wet summer, which explains the sunbathing joke. But, more importantly, Eamonn's introduction heralds *Crackerjack's* very first historical sketch. After the slapstick theme that ran through series one, this series would contain a strong historical vibe – including Cavaliers and Roundheads, the Norman Conquest, and the Great Fire of London. Custard pies and costume drama: two essential ingredients of *Crackerjack* – and both originated with Jack and Joe. Their Spanish Armada script is a little more polished than previous offerings:

JACK: We're forty leagues out to sea.
JOE: Forty what?
JACK: Leagues. You know what a league is, don't you?
JOE: Yes, that thing that Chelsea are always at the bottom of.

The slapstick isn't totally dispensed with – naturally if a bucketful of slops is to be thrown overboard in a strong wind, it won't be the last you see of them. Having no cannonballs to defeat the Spanish, their only option is to use ship's cook Mr Grumble's plum duffs, though the only ship they succeed in sinking belongs to Sir Francis Drake.

Their talent for lunacy is also acknowledged in a return booking for guest star Terry Hall with Lenny the Lion:

TERRY: Lenny, how can you be so stupid?
LENNY: I've been taking lessons from Baker and Douglas.

It's a mark of Terry Hall's expertise that the word 'Baker' proved no obstacle. Although the majority of guest stars were magicians and acrobats, *Crackerjack* was starting to secure the odd big name, including Norman Wisdom and Petula Clark. And when Jack and Joe weren't rewriting history, they were anticipating future events by piloting a space rocket:

JOE: You know I don't like space ships, they make me dizzy. I wonder why that is.
JACK: The reason you get dizzy is because your celebrial membrane comes into contact with your vertebrae purging the blood through the left and right oracle not letting it flow through the common cococtus. Therefore causing an altitude complex. Now do you understand?
JOE: Yes, but why do I get dizzy?

The final show of the series finishes with a song – either confident of the show's return or dropping a heavy hint to BBC management – with an audience refrain of: '*Crackerjack, Crackerjack*, in the Autumn we'll be back.' The last verse of the song is left to Mr Grumble:

You've tried to blow me up, it's true. But this time I'm too smart for you.

Mr Grumble makes a rapid exit, the audience repeats the chorus, there's a loud explosion, and Mr Grumble re-enters (as the script puts it) 'blown up'. Last series they'd blown up the theatre, this time it was the ultimate taboo (and expressly against Freda Lingstrom's wishes) – they'd blown up an old man! Once again it was anarchy that had the last laugh.

In fact, Freda Lingstrom was no longer Head of Children's Television. She'd been superseded by Owen Reed, who perhaps was more amenable to the idea of geriatric combustion. By now the BBC ratings had begun to decline, as ITV stations proliferated across the country. A month or so after the end of the series, Eamonn addressed this issue in a letter to Owen Reed:

> To meet growing competition and to provide an additional sprat, it will be most valuable if we can provide for a big name guest on each programme, in addition to the *act* we have up to now named as 'guest'.
>
> This celebrity spot to last, say, five minutes and to be a performance and not an interview. If the guest is such as not to have an act, then to be incorporated in a sketch or a game. At any rate, to *do* something.

As the song said, 'in the Autumn we'll be back'. But when the third series started in October 1957, the only cast members to return would be Eamonn and hostess Vikki Hammond.

3
Little Wormhole-Under-Sludge

1957 – 1960

W HEN EAMONN HAD WRITTEN to Children's TV boss Owen Reed about the future of *Crackerjack* he also said:

> My vote is for no substantial change where possible. I can ask for no more than the enthusiasm, the care, the planning and the downright ability of Johnny Downes as producer. I look forward with the greatest pleasure to working with him again.

Although it was to be a largely new team, the show would still be in the safe hands of Eamonn in front of camera and Johnny in the gallery. Jack Douglas and Joe Baker helped ensure a strong debut for *Crackerjack*, but working on a midweek fortnightly show for half a year at a time had its pros and cons. Because of the early transmission time, it was still possible to fit in a twice-nightly variety engagement, or even a pantomime, provided the venue was in the London area. But any venue much more than an hour away just wouldn't be possible. Leaving *Crackerjack* enabled Jack and Joe to spend the lucrative 1957-58 panto season in *Dick Whittington* at the Alexandra Theatre, Birmingham.

In May 1958, Jack, Joe and Mr Grumble were back on children's TV in the single-episode sitcom *Ignorants Abroad*, before Baker and Douglas went to

ITV (and a later timeslot) with *New Look*. And then, in the early 1960s, Joe decided to go solo. He subsequently moved to America and was a frequent voice artist in Hanna-Barbera cartoons, including The Thing in the bizarre Marvel Comics/Flintstones mash-up: *Fred and Barney meet The Thing*.

A straight man without a comedy partner – this could have spelled the end of Jack Douglas' career. But Alan Fenton (who wrote material for Jack and Joe in *New Look*) had observed that Jack wasn't your run-of-the-mill stooge:

> There was a bit more to it than that, because you could see he was also quite funny. He was *playing* the straight man, you know. You could see he was playing the straight man. And he was a very likeable chap.

Jack took the highly unusual move of going from straight man to comic. His twitchy Alf Ippititimus came about as a spontaneous space-filler one night on stage, when Joe was late making his entrance. A couple of years after his split with Joe, Jack found himself in a new double-act, with Des O'Connor acting as feed. By the 1970s he was enjoying big-screen success as one of the *Carry On* regulars.

For the next *Crackerjack* comic, Johnny Downes again took a chance on a new name with little previous TV exposure. A barman, working at the Buckstone Club in London, recalls a conversation between Digby Wolfe, a fast-talking comedian and scriptwriter, and actor Harry Fowler:

> Digby happened to mention, quite casually in the course of conversation, that he reckoned he could get anybody on to television if they were clever enough. So Harry Fowler said: 'How about Ronnie?'
>
> Anyway, Digby took on the challenge and he did get me into television, but more importantly perhaps, he got me into Winston's night-club in Mayfair.

The name of that barman was Ronnie Corbett. In his autobiography *High Hopes* he acknowledged the boost Digby Wolfe gave to his career. Digby was writing the current show at Winston's and gave Ronnie a part in it. The resident star of Winston's was female impersonator Danny La Rue, but Danny was away for a couple of months being a glamorous pantomime dame:

> So anyway, Danny La Rue returned to Winston's from pantomime, saw the show and decided to keep me on.

Digby also cast Ronnie as his valet in a TV sitcom announced each week as: 'Digby Wolfe in *Sheep's Clothing*.' The scriptwriters were Sid Green and Dick Hills, who later wrote for (and often appeared with) Morecambe and Wise.

Writer Alan Fenton first met Ronnie when they did national service together:

> I was a new pilot officer and I was posted to RAF Hornchurch. I walked into the office and there was this chap, little fellow, sitting in the chair with his feet on the desk. As I recall, this was probably the Squadron Leader's office, who was the boss. And from that moment we became friends. He was extraordinarily relaxed and he really didn't care. And he was very friendly, as Ronnie always was.
>
> At the same station was Cedric Hardwicke's son, Edward. We were kids – what was I? – I was probably 18.

Sir Cedric Hardwicke was a distinguished character actor on stage and in film. In the late 1940s he emigrated to America and subsequently remarried. His son Edward would later become a familiar face as Doctor Watson to Jeremy Brett's Sherlock Holmes:

> Meeting Edward Hardwicke was very significant for Ronnie, because Edward took him back to his mother's house. And she loved him, as many people did, and was very, very kind to Ronnie, very good to Ronnie. And he stayed there, I think, for some months. And she introduced him to all sorts of people. He met *everybody* in show business. And it helped, to an extent. But Ronnie *worked*. He did jobs. As long as they were honest, he didn't care what they were. They were the most menial things – he worked for Mecca, he would cook, he would clean, he would whatever. But he never deviated – he wanted to be a success. And he wanted that to be in comedy, in the theatre, and so on. This is what he wanted.
>
> We used to go out quite often in those days. And we were sitting in – I think – some Indian restaurant. It must have been around Knightsbridge somewhere. Some cheap place. And we started talking about what we wanted to do with our lives. And I said I had no idea. And I said, 'What about you, Ronnie? What's the one thing you most want?' And he said, 'If someone would open that restaurant door, right now, and say, "That's Ronnie Corbett!"'

Ronnie had a few minor film roles, and even fewer TV appearances, to his credit when Johnny Downes signed him up as *Crackerjack's* new resident comic. Pretty soon he'd be recognised up and down the country. Thinking, no doubt, of the physical contrast between Joe Baker and Jack Douglas, Johnny paired Ronnie with Michael Darbyshire, a lean lanky beanpole of an actor. Michael was particularly associated with the Players' Theatre in London, which specialised (and still does) in recreating Music Hall and Victorian entertainment. In the late 1970s, he would become well known as Hubert Davenport, a prissy Victorian spook in the children's sitcom *Rentaghost*.

Series three of *Crackerjack* ran for 12 episodes, every other Wednesday, from October 1957 to March 1958. Writing in the *Radio Times* at the start of the series, Eamonn Andrews admitted:

> We make no secret of the fact that we are ever so slightly swollen-headed when we hear that adults, who being free at that time of the evening, choose to look at what is officially titled as a Children's Programme. Swollen-headed, but not surprised. You see we've always maintained that *Crackerjack* is an adult programme for minors.

He also addressed the thorny issue of sexism:

> Yours truly is ready and waiting for the equally divided it's-not-fair mail that begins – 'We think you're too easy on the boys,' and 'We think you give the simple questions to the girls.' We've been thinking of putting all the boys and girls in a great revolving drum on Wednesday and picking them out at random to avoid discrimination.
>
> In this series we shall have new and resplendent settings in the Children's Television Theatre.

The renovations were complete and they were back where it all began at Shepherds Bush. The stage had been extended forward and there was now a band room for the musicians. Patrick Heigham, a junior sound assistant with the BBC who worked at the Television Theatre in the early 1960s, explains:

> The band room was constructed under the circle of the TV Theatre, on the right hand side of the audience, at the same level as the extended stage floor, which was fitted over the old orchestra pit.
>
> The band room was designed to give isolation of the band 'noise'. Otherwise it would have leaked onto any stage or boom mikes, and made both the programme balance and the PA feed to the audience somewhat unmanageable.

Being a theatre, there was not a lot of room in the wings. So having a band offstage, in the area beyond the proscenium arch, would not have been possible. Also, how do you keep the band quiet, when they are not actively playing?!

The occupants of the band room were Bert Hayes and his Sextet, who had provided the music for another Johnny Downes production – *The Lenny the Lion Show* – while *Crackerjack* was off the air. Bert Hayes was, for many years, resident musical director at Butlin's Cliftonville holiday hotels in Margate, which became his home town. This was the start of a very long association between Bert Hayes and BBC children's television, and he would commute from Margate to BBC Shepherds Bush several times every week.

Ron Prentice played bass guitar in Bert Hayes' band in the mid-60s and remembers the band room well:

> The band played in a separate room and listened on headphones. There was a television set, I think – a screen somewhere – that we could watch when we weren't playing if we wanted to. Most of the time we didn't bother.

There was a small window in the band room, giving Bert Hayes visual contact with the performer on stage when required. Otherwise he'd direct the band from the piano, listening for his cues on headphones:

> He'd be getting two lots of cues. One from the stage and probably one from the producer. He didn't conduct us, he used to just nod and we played. He'd sit at the piano and play his notes and nod at the same time, and we'd all start. Bert was a really nice guy. I never had a hard word from him all the time I worked with him.

The pairing of Ronnie Corbett and Michael Darbyshire worked remarkably well – because it wasn't quite as you'd expect. In spite of Michael's height, he wasn't the Jack Douglas figure, taking command and ordering Ronnie around. He was amiable, posh, softly spoken, quite camp, and really rather dim and naïve. Ronnie was brash, slick, fast-talking. He was the brains of an outfit where brains were in very short supply. Each man wore a smart suit, of the type a stand-up comic of that era might wear on stage. Michael's had wide stripes and Ronnie's had big checks. Ronnie was 26 when he joined *Crackerjack*, and Michael was 40. But they looked and acted the same age and, if anything, it was Ronnie who played the grown-up.

As previously, there was one main sketch per show. But other bits and pieces were scripted by Ronnie and Michael themselves, like this exchange from their second show when Ronnie brings on a mail bag:

MICHAEL: Did you make it yourself? I say, Eamonn, he's jolly clever, isn't he?
RONNIE: No, of course I didn't make it. It belongs to the GPO and it's full of letters.
MICHAEL: Oh I see. You've become a postman.

In fact, the bag contains letters from their fans – all three of them! Eamonn helps read them out:

EAMONN: 'Dear Ronnie Corbett and Michael Darbyshire, I don't think that play you did last time was very good.'
MICHAEL: Oh?
RONNIE: Oh well, never mind, it was the play they didn't like. They didn't say they didn't like us.
MICHAEL: Read us another one, Eamonn.
EAMONN: 'Dear Michael Darbyshire and Ronnie Corbett, I liked the play you did last time …'
RONNIE: There you are, what did I tell you?
EAMONN: '… but I didn't like either of you in it.'
RONNIE: Oh!

Soon after the series had started, Ronnie Corbett contacted his good friend Alan Fenton:

Ronnie came to me one day – God knows why – and said, 'I'm in this show *Crackerjack* and I'm not very happy with the stuff. Could you write me a sketch?' So I said, 'Ronnie, I don't, you know …' I'd written auditions for him to go to the Palladium which were appalling, I mean, terrible things. But he knew I was interested in comedy. And he knew I had some funny ideas. And he knew that was one of the things I would rather like to do. So I said, 'Okay, but I warn you!' Anyway, I wrote him a sketch. I can't remember what the sketch was. I think it was something fairly physical.

Although Alan has no clear recollection of the sketch, the first show that credits him as writer features a routine set in an Antiques Shop. Michael picks up a bugle and blows it:

MICHAEL: What a beautiful Stradivarius.
RONNIE: You never told me you were a musician.
MICHAEL: I don't put all my eggs in one glasshouse, you know.
RONNIE: No. And people who live in baskets shouldn't throw eggs.
MICHAEL: Except in February which has 28 days clear.
RONNIE: And 29 each leap frog.
MICHAEL: A stitch in time saves nine.
RONNIE: And 29 each leap year.
MICHAEL: Mary had a little lamb.
RONNIE: And 29 each leap year.

Alan's first sketch was written under his real name of Felsenstein, which he translated into Rockstone for subsequent shows. For the next series, by which time he was a regular contributor, he abbreviated his name to Alan Fell. Other writers for Ronnie's first series were Gordon Snell and Maurice Browning (colleagues of Michael Darbyshire from the Players' Theatre) and Myles Rudge, scriptwriter and lyricist of many a Bernard Cribbins hit single, including *Right Said Fred*.

Between series, Eamonn had been lobbying for more big-name guest stars to help the show hold its audience against commercial television opposition (which, at the start of this series, was 30 minutes of *Zoo Time* with Desmond Morris, and 30 minutes of *The Count of Monte Cristo*, a lavish serialised British/American co-production). ITV was already becoming a serious threat, but Eamonn's pre-series article in the *Radio Times* indicated that Children's Television head Owen Reed had taken his concerns seriously:

> The first of a long line of glittering guests will be the scintillating Miss Jill Day, who will visit our new Backstage Club.

The Backstage Club was a regular feature, enabling Eamonn, Ronnie and Michael to interact with the guest celebrity, and incorporate them fully into the show. Each programme in the series now had two guest spots – the speciality act and the big name. In addition to singer Jill Day, there would be subsequent appearances from children's favourite Mr Pastry (Richard Hearne), Max Bygraves, comedian Ted Ray and his son Robin, and husband-and-wife singing team Pearl Carr and Teddy Johnson.

The main sketch usually had a supporting actor or two, including a few familiar faces. When Ronnie and Michael enter a waxwork competition organised by Sir Rupert Sandwich, they end up masquerading as waxworks themselves, with Michael as Charles II and Ronnie as Nell Gwyn. The children would have instantly recognised Sir Rupert – because the actor, Ivan Owen, was also a regular in *Playbox*, the show that alternated with *Crackerjack*. Ivan played Inspector Bruce in *The Playbox Detective Agency*, a feature where viewers could try to crack the clues before the villain was revealed.

The upper-crust tones of Sir Rupert Sandwich would return to *Crackerjack* in the early 1980s, though by then Ivan Owen had become extremely camera-shy. He would often be found crouching under a desk with only his right hand visible. Yes, Ivan Owen and Basil Brush were hand in glove.

The earliest complete edition of *Crackerjack* to be preserved in the archives is the final episode of Ronnie Corbett's first series. It is of particular interest because the vast majority of Eamonn Andrews' utterings were totally unscripted (other than when he introduced or participated in a sketch). So this is an early opportunity to see how he ran the games and quizzes, and generally held the show together.

The first image, accompanying the theme tune, is a rather jolly cartoon version of the Shepherds Bush Theatre and surrounding buildings. The moon and stars are overhead. A large sign on the front of the theatre flashes on and off with the words: BBC CHILDREN'S TELEVISION THEATRE and there are silhouetted crowds gathered outside. The word CRACKERJACK is gradually revealed from left to right on the theatre marquee – which then flashes in time with the sign above it. Eamonn's voice is heard saying: 'Yes, it's *Crackerjack*' – and a camera 'wipe' from the centre of the screen outwards (like parting theatre curtains) reveals an audience of children yelling their response.

Bert Hayes and his Sextet (onstage rather than cooped up in the band room) kick off the show with a raucous polka, very much in the Eddie Mendoza tradition, with squealing clarinet and rasping bass sax. Eamonn conducts the games briskly and efficiently, but fusses rather a lot when a boy in a human wheelbarrow race lets his school blazer come in contact with the dusty studio floor. ('Oh, look at your clothes! Oh, my goodness! Would you ask someone to get a brush? Don't go home that way or I'll be in great trouble!') It's also apparent that the children are required to say nothing other than their names and the answers to the quiz.

The first guests are Pinky, Perky & Company, making an early appearance in a career that would see them fronting a number of series on both BBC and ITV. Married couple Jan and Vlasta Dalibor operated the marionette pigs, and a speeded-up tape gave the pair their distinctive singing style.

Ronnie Corbett and Michael Darbyshire's first sketch (which they also wrote) involves them planning their holidays. It's full of whimsical nonsense, played totally deadpan. They are hoping for a more glamorous holiday than last year's trip to Little Wormhole-under-Sludge:

MICHAEL: Where do you want to go to?
RONNIE: Well, a little further afield.
MICHAEL: Oh, you mean Greater Wormhole-under-Sludge!
RONNIE: No, foreign parts. You know, like the Bahamas and
           Birmingham.
MICHAEL: Bahamas? That's somewhere near Aylesbury, isn't it?
RONNIE: Yes, that's right. It'll mean catching a train.

They have been saving money each week with Eamonn, but when they ask how much it all adds up to, he tells them that due to breakages (in sketches from previous weeks) they actually owe *him* money. They depart, grumbling that now they'll have to take in lodgers (signposting their main sketch later in the show). Eamonn performs well in the sketch but, as Ronnie and Michael walk off, he unwisely attempts to adlib some comic material, which makes very little sense and is met with total audience silence. Comedy was never Eamonn's strong suit:

Oh well, we'll let them take in lodgers. I think we'll put them with the Dalibors. That'll teach them. Then they'll have to learn a dance like the two little piggies there. Weren't they very good? They really were.

At the end of each elimination game, Eamonn makes sure that nobody goes home empty-handed. There is now a rather special consolation prize. You might expect it to be as old as *Crackerjack* itself, but there was no mention of it when Eamonn wrote in the *BBC Children's Annual* after the first series:

There are no big and important prizes because that would spoil the whole thing. And every boy and girl seems to have been quite happy to go off, if only with a box of sweets or two.

But now every child who competed, win or lose, had a lasting souvenir of the event … the *Crackerjack* pencil. It was an inspired choice. Just the mention of it would spur the audience into an ear-piercing shriek of *Crackerjack*! Thousands must have been handed out over the years, but they rarely turn up on eBay. A treasured possession beyond compare. If you own a wooden pencil with *Crackerjack* printed on the side, it is but a worthless forgery. The genuine article is an elegant Burnham propelling pencil with a green marbled design and the word *Crackerjack* in gold lettering, complete in its own case. In time it would be superseded by the *Crackerjack* pen, which sounded more special but somehow wasn't. Who'd want a *Crackerjack* pen when they could have a *Crackerjack* pencil?

In the closing moments of the show, the cast join with star guest, pianist Winifred Atwell, in a chorus of *See You Later, Alligator*, heralding the show's return in the autumn. But there were two cast members who wouldn't be returning – hostess Vikki Hammond and comic Michael Darbyshire.

It may have been theatrical commitments that prevented Michael Darbyshire from rejoining the show. But it was a great pity. Their partnership (both writing and performing) brought out the best of Ronnie. He was the one in control, and Michael merely followed, though neither of them had a clue where they were going. It was a creative double-act reminiscent of Richard Murdoch and Kenneth Horne in *Much-Binding-in-the-Marsh*. A likeable pair of chums, who never seemed to argue, and didn't really care which one got the laughs. It was arguably Ronnie Corbett's most successful *Crackerjack* pairing.

Michael Darbyshire's subsequent career included a number of appearances on *The Good Old Days* (the BBC's long-running celebration of music hall) as part of the Players' Theatre chorus. He returned to children's television in 1976, playing Hubert Davenport in four series of *Rentaghost*. He died suddenly – in his theatre dressing room during a performance of the farce *Chase Me Comrade* – aged 62.

*

There were 14 more episodes of *Crackerjack* between September 1958 and March 1959. Credited as writer for half of those episodes was Alan Fenton (billed as Alan Fell) who had rapidly become established in the profession, thanks to his friend Ronnie Corbett:

Ronnie's agent was Jimmy Grafton, who also wrote, and Ronnie introduced me. He must have said, you know, 'Alan wants to write comedy.' And I went to see Jimmy in the pub and he said, 'Oh, you want to be a comedy writer?' And I said, 'Well, yes, I'll have a go at it.' And he said, 'Well, go home and write me something funny and bring it back tomorrow.' So I went home and wrote something funny – it probably wasn't very – and mostly verbal. And from then on I was a comedy scriptwriter. I was writing for television. It was amazing!

Jimmy Grafton ran the family pub – the Grafton Arms – in Strutton Ground, Victoria Street, London. He was an important figure in the formation of radio comedy team The Goons. The four of them (including, in those early days, Michael Bentine) used an upstairs room at the Grafton Arms to meet up and work on ideas. Jimmy Grafton was the script editor on their first few radio series, and also became Harry Secombe's agent.

Another of Jimmy Grafton's protégées was Jeremy Lloyd – who, with David Croft, later created and wrote *Are You Being Served?* and *'Allo 'Allo!* Whereas Alan Fenton had a talent for verbal humour, Jeremy's strength was in visual gags. The two worked (separately and in collaboration) on a number of Jimmy Grafton projects, including *Crackerjack* and ITV's *New Look.* As Jeremy recalled, 'I still couldn't type, but I paid friends who could.' Writing in his autobiography *Listen Very Carefully, I Shall Say This Only Once*, Jeremy describes an early encounter with ex-army major Jimmy Grafton:

Major Grafton would like you to report to the pub at Strutton Ground. You are one of the writers on the new show, *New Look* to be made at the Wood Green Empire every Saturday night. Boy, I had arrived. I walked through the crowded bar of the Grafton Arms, up the smoky stairs, into the Major's office. Papers were everywhere. The Major was on the phone, making a frantic call. Was it to Harry Secombe, one of his clients? No, it was the bookmakers. The Major was a keen backer of horses. 'Be with you in a moment, Jeremy – just managed to get on the two-thirty with a Yankee double.' I was to find out that the Major spent more time placing bets than writing, and that doing the show in his presence was a laborious business, interrupted by the television set going on just as they were going up to the post, or the radio, or a call directly to the track. A lot of writing was done in the attic.

Jeremy soon became a familiar face as an actor, initially cast as a 'chinless idiot' in one of Billy Cotton's TV series. Jeremy, a refined stick-thin giant, was the perfect antithesis of this rotund cockney bandleader.

With Jeremy Lloyd as regular scriptwriter and Alan Fell (Fenton) as semi-regular, *Crackerjack* embarked on a fresh series with a new partner for Ronnie. But this was no fresh-faced new discovery. Eddie Leslie had been Norman Wisdom's first straight-man in the late 1940s. In Norman's autobiography *My Turn* he tells of their first meeting, in the pantomime *Robinson Crusoe*:

> We hit it off straight away. Eddie proved to be a natural foil, a man who would go along with my most outrageous ideas. He was built like a bouncer, with a face carved out of granite – and it stayed that way despite all my efforts to 'corpse' him in rehearsals.
>
> For a gag Eddie once took on the undefeated ju-jitsu champion Yukio Tani at the London Palladium – and was thrown about so much that afterwards he claimed to have seen the theatre from more angles than anyone else in show business.

Eddie Leslie excelled in physical comedy (the more physical the better), which was ideal for a performer like Norman Wisdom who delighted in pratfalls and stunts. A typical Norman and Eddie routine would be a boxing match, where Eddie would continually get the better of Norman, but the little man would triumph in the end.

Eddie couldn't have been a greater contrast to Ronnie's previous co-star, Michael Darbyshire. Inevitably the relationship changes when your stooge is now a gruff-voiced older man of thuggish appearance (Eddie was 55, about twice Ronnie's age). It didn't suit Ronnie's style and was to cloud his memories of the show. In his autobiography *High Hopes*, Ronnie gives hardly a mention of *Crackerjack* apart from his experiences with Norman Wisdom's former feed:

> Eddie was the straight character who was always twisting Norman's ear or giving him a punch. This was something I spent quite a lot of my early career trying to avoid.
>
> Because I was little, the general idea among show-business agents was to turn me into a sort of Norman Wisdom or a Charlie Drake type of performer who was always being put upon and persecuted with flour and water and hit with rubber hammers, and that sort of thing.

All the time, I felt that wasn't me at all. It didn't feel right to be put upon. There was something about the way I worked which meant I didn't actually *feel* small. It may sound odd, but throughout my career, I have been the last person to realise that I was diminutive.

It's not uncommon to read the direction 'EDDIE HITS RONNIE' in the scripts of this series, which would be standard fare for many a double-act. But it only really works for a comedian with an element of pathos, who can milk a reaction from a sympathetic audience. And Ronnie wasn't that kind of comic.

This is a typical piece of slapstick from *Christmas Crackerjack* of December 17th:

> EDDIE: Here's a chance for you to win a shilling. (TAKES ONE FROM POCKET.) Now I put this funnel here like this! (PUTTING IT DOWN RONNIE'S TROUSERS.) And all you have to do is to balance the shilling on your forehead – that's it. And without using your hands drop it into the funnel.
>
> AS RONNIE BALANCES THE SHILLING, EDDIE POURS JUG OF WATER DOWN RONNIE'S TROUSERS. RONNIE REACTS AND EDDIE LAUGHS.

The biggest problem with this double-act is the lack of onscreen chemistry, which is an inevitable hazard of putting together two people who have never previously worked together. Johnny Downes was taking no such risk with his other new *Crackerjack* double-act, which proved a truly inspired choice. Pearl Carr and Teddy Johnson had made a guest appearance the previous series, and now they were regulars. This husband-and-wife singing act made an enormous contribution to the show – in addition to their music spot, they took part in the sketches, and even acted as host and hostess during *Double or Drop*. In many ways they helped shape *Crackerjack* into the show we all remember.

Pearl and Teddy both had excellent comedy credentials. Pearl had been resident singer with the radio show *Breakfast with Braden*, scripted by Frank Muir and Denis Norden. Her character was rather gauche and totally infatuated with the show's star Bernard Braden – as in this excerpt where she turns up wearing a man's shirt and suit:

BERNARD:	But how come this urge to look like me?
PEARL:	Well, somebody told me you were in love with yourself, so I thought that perhaps if I dressed like you I might remind you of you.
BERNARD:	But Pearl – you're wearing high heels.
PEARL:	Yes, they said –
BERNARD:	It's a lie!

Teddy Johnson also had a track record in comedy – having acted as feed to legendary American comedian (and master of the 'slow burn') Jack Benny. After a London Palladium appearance in 1952, Jack had been offered two further weeks in variety at Manchester and Glasgow. His Palladium straight man had other commitments, so Teddy stepped in as stooge:

> Lew Grade chose me to 'feed' Benny, which was a wonderful experience. And Jack was most complimentary. He was very kind in assessing what my feeding had done to him. He said, 'You've really excelled.' I didn't see any reason why he should exaggerate. He didn't have to tell me that I was so 'bloody good', which was the compliment he virtually paid to me.

As they were so integral to *Crackerjack*, Pearl and Teddy would rehearse during the week with Ronnie Corbett, Eddie Leslie and producer Johnny Downes. As Eamonn's contribution was largely unrehearsed, he would only be required on the day of transmission. Teddy has fond memories of those rehearsals:

> I loved *Crackerjack*. It was one of the most enjoyable experiences in my life. Ronnie was absolutely wonderful. He would listen to anything you said. 'Should I – ? Should I do that? It might be a bit better, you know.' He was always thoughtful, Ronnie. And he was an absolute two years of delight to work with.
>
> Eddie Leslie was quite egotistical, in a way. He had that forceful personality. He had it in his feeding to Norman Wisdom. He was very forceful.

Overseeing the proceedings was producer Johnny Downes:

> Johnny was conducive to any suggestion we made for the show. And he used to go into ecstatic squeals of delight when we came up with some funny stuff. I've never seen such childish awareness. And he wasn't a childish man. Quite the opposite. Any comedy that really clicked, he loved. Unusual for a comedy producer to do that. And he was most delightful to work for, because, as I

say, he was enjoying most of the things that we did. And it was nice to hear his squeals of delight. He was very demonstrative about enjoying what he was seeing.

The most significant change that Pearl and Teddy helped bring about was the final sketch. There were now two sketches in every show – a slapstick sketch and a musical finale. Rather than a general singalong, this was the main sketch of the show, in which the dialogue would be interspersed with a few appropriate songs. This was a forerunner to the mishmash of costume drama and top twenty hits that has come to be everyone's iconic memory of *Crackerjack*.

Another essential ingredient (which began during this series and continued for many years to come) was the arrival in the closing moments of a heavily disguised Eamonn, who would then reveal his true identity and close the show.

The finale sketches in this series are all introduced by Eamonn as tales from his 'upside-down' book of fairy stories. A typical sketch is a retelling of pantomime *Cinderella* in early January 1959. After the ball, Cinderella (Pearl) is still thinking of her prince – *Am I Wasting My Time?* The ugly sisters (Ronnie and Eddie) banish Cinderella to her room – *Sisters*. The Prince (Teddy) describes the girl he's lost – *Eyes of Blue*. He is reunited with Cinderella and asks her to marry him – *From This Moment On*. The Fairy Godmother enters, reveals herself as Eamonn, and says goodbye – *We'll All Go Riding on a Rainbow*.

Again there was a strong line-up of guests throughout the series, including singers Dennis Lotis, Lonnie Donegan, Alma Cogan and future *Record Breaker* Roy Castle.

In the final show of the series (again preserved in the archives) Eamonn precedes Pearl and Teddy's musical spot with this introduction:

> I'm sure that everybody in *Crackerjack*, both in the theatre and at home, would like to join me in saying congratulations for that wonderful success, when they just got second at Cannes in the European song contest for their famous dicky-bird song.

Crackerjack was still being broadcast on alternate Wednesdays, and you can achieve a lot in a fortnight. The previous Wednesday, Pearl and Teddy had performed *Sing Little Birdie* at the Eurovision Song Contest in Cannes, achieving a creditable (and nowadays scarcely credible) second place. It was a catchy tune but, as Teddy admits, not to everyone's taste:

> Everybody had turned it down. Nobody wanted to know. None of the other singers – Lita Roza, Dennis Lotis. They all said no. Lita Roza, it was anathema to her. She said, 'Another bloody march tune!' We'd heard several songs – none of which had done anything for us. And as soon as he started playing this one – *Sing Little Birdie* – Pearl and I looked at each other, 'Yeah, that's it.'

A week after Eurovision, Pearl and Teddy were back on *Crackerjack*, without missing a show. Surprisingly they perform a different song – *Sweet Elizabeth* – complete with a touch of physical comedy, when Pearl repeatedly and 'inadvertently' clobbers Teddy. The show is the usual hectic round of activity, with Teddy playing two different roles in a lighthouse sketch before immediately joining Pearl to assist in *Double or Drop*, still attired in his naval uniform from the previous sketch.

The best gag of the lighthouse sketch (in which Ronnie is punched, has slops thrown over him, and is chucked out to sea) is when lighthouse keeper Eddie asks Ronnie to identify a distant ship, seen through the porthole-shaped window:

EDDIE: What is it? A dreadnought or a destroyer?
RONNIE: A destroyer. (REACHES THROUGH PORTHOLE AND
            HANDS EDDIE THE SMALL MODEL SHIP) Look!
EDDIE: Put it back! The admiral will do his nut!

After one of the games, Eamonn seems positively grumpy with the unresponsive studio audience. 'They're very, very much asleep, our audience here today. That's twice I've said *Crackerjack* and they never noticed.' There are eager shouts of *Crackerjack*, but Eamonn is in an unforgiving mood. 'Ahh no. Too late, too late now.'

Special guest Dickie Valentine takes the title role of Pied Piper of Hamelin in the final sketch of the series – another tale from Eamonn's 'Upside-Down Book.' Thankfully, this version gives a happy twist to the bleak ending. The Piper agrees to return the children if the Mayor of Hamelin will pay for them all to have ice creams. The ice-cream seller then removes hat and wig (which is glued to the hat) and, to no one's astonishment, turns out to be Eamonn all along.

Jeremy Lloyd and Alan Fell (Fenton) both moved on to other projects, including writing for *The Dickie Henderson Show* with Jimmy Grafton. Jeremy continued scriptwriting for the rest of his working life but, after a few years, Alan started to have second thoughts:

> In those days, I could make enough money to pay my rent. I could run a car, take a girl out occasionally, but you couldn't make the kind of money that you can make today, *if* you're successful. I'm not saying I would have been that successful, but I could see a ceiling here.

Alan subsequently went into business, travelled the world and made far more money than your average comedy writer, before eventually packing it in to become a novelist.

Pearl Carr and Teddy Johnson would return to *Crackerjack* in the autumn. They spent the summer season at Torquay Pavilion with Terry Hall and Lenny the Lion. Of course they were now stars of *Crackerjack*, and the reception they got took Teddy by surprise:

> We went to Torquay in '59 and it was fantastic. In those days you used to do two shows a night. And we would come out of the dressing room door, and the stage door outside would be crowded with children waiting for our autographs. And between the shows we couldn't have any rest. We had to sign the autographs, bless them. And we did so. And they were grateful. And, let's face it, *we* were grateful. We had them as customers at our show. It filled the first houses. So we had a great season there in Torquay. I don't think we had hardly an empty seat for the whole season.

*

A new 14-show run of *Crackerjack* began on 1ˢᵗ October 1959, but on a different day. Thursday instead of Wednesday – one step closer to the weekend. The change of day had very little effect on *Crackerjack* – but delayed the start of *Playbox* because of that periodic Thursday scheduling hiatus known as a general election. Nothing much else had changed, apart for one small detail. Eamonn talked us through the line-up in *Radio Times* including:

> Ronnie Corbett with newcomer (to this show, though not, of course, to television) Raymond Rollett.

Raymond Rollett was already a familiar face on children's TV. He had been Squire Trelawney in *three* serialisations of *Treasure Island*. He had also voiced a number of puppet shows. The grown-ups may also have seen him as the Chief Constable in *Blue Murder at St Trinian's* (also starring former *Crackerjack* hostess Vikki Hammond). And he was one of those 'turner-uppers' who played a variety of roles in *Hancock's Half Hour*.

Raymond Rollett was the archetypal authority figure. He was pompous and rotund with poached-egg eyes. He was the perpetually exasperated boss, sitting behind any number of desks in any number of sitcoms. Chris Boxall (author of *Raymond Rollett: The Forgotten Actor*) asked many of Raymond's friends and colleagues for memories of the man. Actor Graham Crowden (who had performed with Raymond at the Regent's Park Open Air Theatre) thought the name Raymond Rollett suited him perfectly, 'a genial Roly Poly man – with chins!!'

Ronnie Corbett was yet again paired with a somewhat mature straight man. Raymond was 52, a few years younger than Eddie Leslie but looking a good deal older. The relationship with Ronnie this time round was less bullying and more in keeping with Raymond's own avuncular personality. In fact he was avuncular in the literal sense of the word, playing Uncle Raymond to young nephew Ronnie.

After the previous series of *Crackerjack* ended, its place in the schedules had been filled by *The Lenny the Lion Show* (another Johnny Downes production). The scriptwriter for that series was Frank Roscoe, who Johnny then re-engaged for this series of *Crackerjack*. Frank, from Chorley, Lancashire, first got into writing after reading a newspaper article bemoaning the shortage of radio comedy writers from the North. He was soon writing for many of the great Northern comics of the day – Dave Morris, Jimmy James and Norman Evans.

Although the slapstick element was still present in Frank's *Crackerjack* scripts, Ronnie was now cast as inept clown rather than persecuted victim. It was an improvement, but not a great one. The relationship with Uncle Raymond foreshadowed his role in future sitcoms, such as *Sorry!* Ronnie, being short, was required to act like a child. It was, perhaps, no coincidence that Frank Roscoe was also currently writing the Light Programme's long-running family sitcom *The Clitheroe Kid*, starring adult schoolboy Jimmy Clitheroe.

Teddy Johnson recalls Raymond Rollett's presence in the rehearsal room as being a total contrast to his predecessor, Eddie Leslie:

> He was just very quiet and very withdrawn. He wasn't unpleasant to anybody – or surly. But he just, sort of, seemed to realise he was just an extra. I don't remember Raymond Rollett being a good feed. He was okay. But Eddie Leslie was forceful. Raymond Rollett was just an actor doing a part.

Raymond wasn't like the previous *Crackerjack* regulars. He was a theatre actor, not a variety turn. Sketches had generally developed during the week as everyone chipped in with suggestions for gags and physical business. Raymond learnt his lines and gave a good performance – but couldn't be expected to match the creative input of Ronnie's previous stooges.

A typical sketch involves Uncle Raymond, a schoolmaster, rehearsing for the end-of-term play. He's been cast as a spy, complete with dummy bomb, plotting to blow up a factory. Naturally, Ronnie overhears him and becomes convinced his uncle really is a deranged terrorist. After Uncle Raymond finally explains, they both have a laugh about it:

RONNIE: We ought to give those children a real Christmas treat. (LAUGHS)

RAYMOND: What do you mean?

RONNIE: Instead of using a dummy bomb to blow up a factory, we should have a real bomb, and blow up the school.

RAYMOND: (CHUCKLING) Oh yes. Very amusing. Blow up the school!

RONNIE: (LAUGHING) Yes. Then the school would really have broken up for Christmas!

In a final twist they discover that the person who made the prop bomb has (due to a misunderstanding) built a real bomb. It makes slightly uneasy reading today, but this Tom-and-Jerry attitude to explosives was present in *Crackerjack* right from the start.

In another sketch, Ronnie and Uncle Raymond are at a railway station:

RONNIE: We've got bags of time. Just enjoy yourself in this buff-ett.

RAYMOND: Ronald! Buff-ay. The 'T' is silent.

RONNIE: Not the way you drink it.

RAYMOND: By the way, is it a mail train?

RONNIE: I don't know. Could be male – could be female.

Making his first guest appearance on the series is Harry Secombe, and the final show features Cliff Richard. The last sketch of this show is the customary mini-musical in costume. The setting is fairyland, with Pearl Carr as the Fairy Queen and Ronnie as court jester Percy the Pixie, cracking a gag especially pertinent to Eamonn:

RONNIE: Only the other day, I did devise a television programme for all the caterpillars in the glade.

TEDDY: A television programme for caterpillars! What was it called?

RONNIE: This Is Your Leaf.

After many more terrible jokes, the Queen sacks Percy the Pixie and appoints Eamonn as the new jester, granting him three wishes. His first is to wish the wee folk well. His second is to wish a happy summer for all the boys and girls at home. And his third (perhaps acknowledging his traditional look of discomfort during the show's final moments) is shyly whispered to Ronnie, who then tells the Queen:

RONNIE: He wishes he hadn't such a rotten voice when he has to sing in *Crackerjack*!

The audience shouts back *Crackerjack* and (not for the first time) they end on a chorus of *Riding on a Rainbow*.

After that final show, nearly everybody rode straight over the rainbow never to be seen again. Teddy Johnson and wife Pearl were faced with a difficult choice:

We did two years on *Crackerjack* and I think we could have done a third, but I was too impatient. ITV were offering us a series, albeit only six, whereas *Crackerjack* were 13. And it was going to be a better proposition – after all, ITV was just emerging. They were just becoming popular. They were establishing a foothold. And I don't think anyone took them seriously enough. Obviously ATV, if they've got a series which they've got to cast, they're going to do it as soon as possible. So I got a bit panicky and took the opposition. And I think that upset the BBC a little bit. I don't know if they *did* hold it against us. But there were such things being said as, 'You'll never work for us again.'

Teddy and Pearl subsequently made regular guest appearances on such ITV variety shows as *The Arthur Haynes Show* and the Morecambe and Wise series, *Two of a Kind*. A couple of months after I met and interviewed Teddy, he celebrated his 98th birthday.

Ronnie Corbett also moved on to other things. As he confessed to Roy Plomley on *Desert Island Discs* in 1971, he hadn't been happy in *Crackerjack* for some time:

> I always had the feeling it never quite worked. I'm not extremely fond of having flour put over my head, or falling a lot, or things like that.

His friend Alan Fenton has a pretty good idea why Ronnie stayed on *Crackerjack* for so long:

> I think probably that Ronnie regarded it as a very low sort of platform for him to climb the comedy mountain. I don't think he was particularly happy or fulfilled in *Crackerjack*. And I'm sure he was still fitting in all sorts of jobs by the way.

One job that easily fitted around *Crackerjack* was late-night cabaret at Winston's nightclub:

> I remember going there and seeing Ronnie there with Danny La Rue, and it was fun. That was a big thing. They were frequented by quite a mix of people. There were a few who had some familiarity with the insides of prisons. There were people who were extremely well known in show business. And he met them all. And got on with them all.
>
> He was a hard worker, Ronnie. I used to go down to Buckstone's Club, opposite the stage door entrance of the Haymarket Theatre. You went down the stairs and there was this club full of mostly out of work actors and comics. And there was Ronnie Corbett standing behind the bar – on a box, so that he could be seen. And he enjoyed it. You didn't get the impression that he was doing it for the money and it was a bore. He conveyed pleasure, which is a great thing that he had. It's why people liked him.

For Raymond Rollett it was a sad ending. He continued to play the odd role in children's television – including a schoolmaster in *The Lenny the Lion Show* – and appeared in a couple of episodes of Harry Worth sitcom *Here's Harry*, co-written by Frank Roscoe. But insufficient work was coming his way and, in December 1961, he was fined £25 for shoplifting two shirts from an Oxford Street store.

His last TV appearance was in *Crackerjack's* sister show *Playbox*. He played Edward Grimstone (described by the show's producer as a 'double-dyed villain') in regular feature *The Six-Clue Challenge* – with detective Ivan Owen, the future Basil Brush. The show was pre-recorded on 15th December 1961. Between that recording and the show's transmission (on 21st December) Raymond booked himself into a hotel and took an overdose of barbiturates. The headline in the *Daily Express* read: TV COMIC CROOK DIED OF SHAME AFTER STEALING.

Writing in 1987 to Chris Boxall (Raymond's biographer), Ronnie Corbett said:

> I did three seasons of *Crackerjack* and worked the third time round with dear Raymond. It wasn't really very long after this piece of work that Raymond sadly died. He was always a very dear, sweet person.

Like Jack Douglas, Ronnie Corbett was equally capable of playing both straight-man and comic. Far more fulfilling than playing funny man in *Crackerjack* was his role as stooge to Danny La Rue in witty topical late-night cabaret. And, with an audience frequently more star-studded than the cast, it was a great way to be seen by those who could further your career. As Ronnie told Roy Plomley, the big break came courtesy of TV satirist David Frost:

> David had seen me in Winston's Club, and at Danny La Rue's own club where I moved on to after Winston's. And he rang me up one day and said, 'I've seen you in the club and I'm going to do this series for BBC television. I would like you to be in it.'

That series was *The Frost Report*, which paired him for the first time with Ronnie Barker. And thus a legendary double-act was born.

Crackerjack would be back in September 1960. Johnny Downes had only a few months to find himself a new cast. Of his previous three straight-men, no one had stayed beyond a single series. Would his next choice of stooge be any different?

4
Wheelbarrows with Square Wheels

1960 – 1964

THE PREVIOUS SERIES HAD straddled the decades, but series six was firmly planted in the 1960s. And it showed. Commencing in September 1960, this 16-part series bristled with energy from the get-go. After a breezy opening number, there's a tribute to all those hard-working individuals behind the scenes:

EAMONN: For instance, there's the carpenter who makes the scenery …

(We see a man hammering a door in place. Second man flings open door, closes it again, and we see first man's cut-out silhouette on the wall.)

EAMONN: When the scenery is knocked together, it has to be painted …

(We see a man mixing paint in a large zinc bath. He struggles to put it on a cloth-covered table. Bath crashes through table onto the floor as man watches in astonishment.)

EAMONN: Then of course we have the scriptwriter …

(We see a man typing. Stops typing, laughs at joke, laugh builds. Beckons Eamonn – straight face, shakes head and exits. Man starts crying, tears up paper and eats it.)

EAMONN: And now let's meet the man who's been doing all these jobs for us. Our Jack of all Trades, Leslie Crowther!

Hotfoot from those three visual gags (all performed live, of course) Leslie then launches into a fast-paced, gag-packed monologue:

Phew! What a day I've had. I got up nice and early, jumped into my bath … then jumped out again. I still had my pyjamas on! I got dressed, dashed out of the house, got on a bus … got off again. No money. So I ran all the way behind the bus and saved fourpence. Wish it had been a taxi, I'd have saved half a crown!

While he rabbits on, someone enters with a rope and hook and attaches it to Leslie. He's still talking as he's whisked upwards out of view.

It's one hell of an opening routine! From those first few minutes it would seem that *Crackerjack* was now The Leslie Crowther Show. It suggests a giant leap of confidence from producer Johnny Downes, because (as with previous discoveries) Leslie was far from a household name. His early stage career included a number of minor Shakespearean roles at the Regent's Park Open Air Theatre, some of them alongside previous *Crackerjack* stooge Raymond Rollett. He later wrote of Raymond: 'We were very pally. He was always very kind to young actors, and encouraged them in their careers. He was a lovely man!!'

For the past five years Leslie had toured on-and-off with the *Fol-de-Rols* – a seaside concert party (an institution that, by then, was virtually extinct) performing intimate revue for all the family. By the start of 1960 he'd been married for nearly six years, and he and wife Jean had twin daughters.

Jean Crowther recalls one special night when Leslie was on stage and a brace of BBC talent-spotters were in the audience:

He was in *The Fol-de-Rols* up in Edinburgh and both George Inns and Johnny Downes had gone up to have a look at shows, and were looking for people. And because our twins were by this time coming up to school age, we knew we had to stop touring. And they both offered Leslie work. George Inns offered him *Hi Summer* which featured Kenneth Connor, and Johnny offered him *Crackerjack* starting in the September. Leslie finished *The Fols*, I think, in March, and did the television with Ken Connor in the summer, and then started *Crackerjack*.

Also new to *Crackerjack* was Vivienne Martin. Early in her career Vivienne played Arabella, daughter of bookmaker Clarence Fritton (Alastair Sim), who enrols at a disreputable girls' school run by her aunt Millicent Fritton (also Alastair Sim), in the movie *The Belles of St Trinian's*. She starred in numerous stage musicals and revues – and later appeared on TV with comics Benny Hill and Dick Emery. Possessing one of the broadest smiles in the business, she was to become a familiar face as Lionel Hardcastle's chatterbox secretary Gwen Flack in the sitcom *As Time Goes By*.

Vivienne started each *Crackerjack* with a song (usually from a musical) accompanied by Bert Hayes and his Octet – yes, the budget now allowed him the luxury of two extra musicians. Vivienne also became the first female performer to be fully integrated into the sketches, in an assortment of roles that made the most of her comedic talents and versatility.

The series was scripted by Stan Mars who (like Jeremy Lloyd and Alan Fell) was another jobbing writer from Major Jimmy Grafton's attic. Stan Mars was the pen name of Stan Marshall, a Scottish comedian and writer who used to supply material for Stanley Baxter. The two of them invented the *Parliamo Glasgow* routines, in which Glaswegian dialect was taught phonetically by a tutor with a cut-glass English accent, as if it was a foreign language. Stan Mars also wrote many *Francie and Josie* sketches for Stanley Baxter and Rikki Fulton (and later Rikki and Jack Milroy) which were a huge success north of the border, both on stage and television. *Crackerjack* was one of Stan's first jobs after he moved south, and later he worked with Jimmy Grafton on *The Dickie Henderson Show*, and on TV and stage material for Harry Secombe.

There is something decidedly odd about the first show of this series. In Leslie Crowther's opening monologue he makes a few jokes about Vivienne, but not a mention of the third member of the team, who is never announced, but appears in one of the visual gags at the start of the show, and also fixes the hook to Leslie at the end of the monologue. In a later safe-breaking sketch, for most of the script Leslie's accomplice has the character name JOE, until halfway down the last page when it abruptly changes to PETER. All of this suggests Peter Glaze may have been something of a last-minute booking. There is certainly none of the Leslie/Peter crosstalk which would soon become a staple of the show.

Writing in the 1966 *BBC Book of Crackerjack* Leslie describes his first encounter with Peter:

Peter was playing with the Crazy Gang at the Victoria Palace, and the producer of *Crackerjack* took me along to meet him, to see if we'd get along all right. There he was on stage, dressed up as the mother-in-law in a wedding scene, and at the end of it he fell through a trapdoor. I guessed that anyone who didn't mind doing all that must be all right.

When Leslie joined *Crackerjack* he was 27, while Peter Glaze was 43. Peter's father was actor-manager Will H. Glaze, and Peter's stage debut was in one of his father's productions, aged nine. He continued to perform in touring revue – and, in January 1939, after the Wednesday evening performance of *Cinderella*, he eloped to Gretna Green with the principal boy and was back in time for the next day's show. The principal boy (female, of course!) was his first wife Mary. They had two children, a boy and a girl. However, the marriage lasted only slightly longer than the Second World War and the couple divorced in 1946.

In the last years of the war, Peter joined the cast of the Windmill Theatre (the one London theatre that 'never closed'), performing in tasteful adult revue with scantily clad dancers and motionless nudes. An early *Stage* review observed, 'he gives one the impression of working too hard'. But less than a month later they'd revised their opinion: 'Mr Glaze has much improved, and is now right in the front rank of revue comedians.'

Windmill archivist (and former Windmill Girl herself) Jill Millard Shapiro has kept in contact with several girls who worked with Peter, all now in their late 80s and 90s. In early 2017 she asked for their recollections, starting with Margaret McGrath:

> I did a duet with Peter in 1944, just the two of us on stage. It was called *Any Casting Today* and was a funny little scene about a stage-struck girl. I do remember Peter always wore his glasses. I think his eyesight was poor.

Googie Cooney:

> Peter was more than just a Windmill comedian. He was part of the ensemble. He worked with us. He was on stage with the girls and the Windmill boys for many of the production numbers, but usually in a comedy role.

And finally, Winifred Hodge:

> It was difficult to keep a straight face when we were on stage with Peter Glaze. He was funny even when he wasn't trying to be.

In 1949 Peter married his second wife, who would also become his agent, April Young. Tony Glaze, Peter's son from his first marriage, met up with them occasionally in the 1950s:

> I actually went to stay with Peter and April. They kindly put me up when I first left school, because I was looking for work. I worked for April's agency as an office junior and delivered the odd messages and answered the odd phone call. I had to take a message to Jimmy Edwards at the London Coliseum. And he said, 'Are you Peter Glaze's boy?' I said, 'Yes.' He said, 'Good God, I didn't know he was old enough!'
>
> Peter was understudy for the Crazy Gang at the Victoria Palace. He understudied literally all of them. Whoever was off, he was covering for them. That's the way it worked. I mean, he had bits to do in the show himself as well. You can't just have understudies hanging around the place, can you? No, he was quite a *tour de force* really.

The Crazy Gang, an enduring and unpredictable troupe of comedians who first got together in the early 1930s, consisted of three double acts (Flanagan & Allen, Nervo & Knox and Naughton & Gold) plus cod-French comic 'Monsewer' Eddie Gray. Peter's involvement with them started in 1950 when Charlie Naughton was taken ill 48 hours before the out-of-town opening of their latest revue *Knights of Madness*, as April Young wrote in a potted biography in 1999:

> Peter learned the entire show and played it throughout its Oxford run, and was asked to stay for a week or so after it opened at the Victoria Palace. In the end he stayed for five consecutive shows, running some ten years, playing in the show but also playing, often for two weeks at a time, for every member of the Gang. He was regarded as their Spare Part.

The Eamonn Andrews Crackerjack Book tells of the night Peter received a message that he was urgently needed to deputise for Teddy Knox:

> Eight minutes later he found himself walking on stage to discover Teddy Knox standing there in front of him. Teddy, a great practical joker, had played yet another trick. Peter Glaze could think of nothing else to say than, 'Fancy meeting you here,' and retreating once more to his dressing room.

On another occasion Peter rushed into the dressing room for a quick change, to find Jimmy Nervo had put all his makeup in the dressing-table drawer and nailed it shut.

There was little evidence of a Crowther and Glaze double-act in the first *Crackerjack* of the series, and it took quite a while for it to become firmly established. Like Joe Baker and Jack Douglas there was the comic contrast between the tall thin one and the short fat one – only this time it was the tall one who was the comic and the short one who was the stooge.

A later show opens with Peter as a magician and Leslie as his inept assistant. And, in the main sketch, Leslie enrols in the Peter Glaze Charm School:

LESLIE: This is your school for deportment and elocution, isn't it?
PETER: Yes.
LESLIE: Well, I want to be deported and elocuted.

Although there are certain words a writer really can't use in a children's show, Stan Mars takes full advantage of the fact that the audience will never get to read the stage directions:

ENTER VIVIENNE LOOKING LIKE A RIGHT SCRUBBER.

PETER: You can always tell a girl. They smell nice.
LESLIE: Oh yes? (SNIFFS AT VIV)
PETER: Do you recognize the perfume? Is it Paris Temptation, worth ten guineas an ounce?
LESLIE: No, St Pancras Station, tenpence a gallon.

The musical finale was still in the process of evolving. The idea, this series, was that Eamonn would pick a word (supposedly at random) from the producer's dictionary and the cast would perform a series of songs on that theme, for instance 'Travel' or 'Fashion'. They have particular fun when previous regulars Pearl Carr and Teddy Johnson guest on an episode with the theme: 'Bananas'. First Peter Glaze performs *Yes, We Have No Bananas* as a cockney market trader, then Leslie and Teddy reinterpret it as a pair of histrionic Russian Cossacks, followed by Pearl as a Japanese geisha, and finally Vivienne as an overdramatic operatic soprano.

As Pearl and Teddy were no longer on hand to help out with *Double or Drop*, the job of *Crackerjack* hostess was reinstated. When she joined at the start of the series, Patricia Michael (a recent graduate of the Guildhall School of Music and Drama) had only a few chorus-line appearances to her credit. By Christmas she'd won the title role in *Robinson Crusoe* at Windsor, and had to leave *Crackerjack* mid-series. In the years that followed she played leading roles in a variety of stage musicals – everything from *The Desert Song* to an all-singing all-dancing version of *Gone With the Wind*.

Dancer and actress Jillian Comber was at home looking after three very young daughters from a marriage that unfortunately hadn't worked out, when she got a call from her agent:

> And she said, 'You can't just laze around.' She said, 'The girl who gives the cabbages and everything in *Crackerjack* is going off to do pantomime and she'll be away for three shows. And all that Johnny Downes wants is somebody to do the cabbages. You just go up there on the day, do the cabbages and the pencils behind Eamonn Andrews and that's all you do. It'll get you out of the house, dress you up, get you smart.' I went along, and after two shows Johnny Downes said, 'Would you stay on until the end of May?'

It wasn't very long before Jillian's agent was back on the phone:

> 'Johnny Downes would like to build you more into the show.' And so, gradually, I went up to two days' rehearsal and then I went to five days. Rehearsals were wonderful! They were ten o'clock to two o'clock every day. So I actually could look after my children, get them to school, be back in time to pick them up. It sounds as if I was a terribly ambitious type of person. But I had the children and I managed to do the show as well. I was very, very lucky and I thoroughly enjoyed my time.

One reason rehearsals finished early was that Leslie Crowther had now become one of three resident comics on BBC's *The Black and White Minstrel Show* alongside Stan Stennett and trombonist George Chisholm. Leslie would make a prompt exit from *Crackerjack* rehearsals and spend the rest of the afternoon in a different venue, rehearsing for the *Minstrels*.

In the recent Pearl and Teddy *Crackerjack* Jillian had played a rather more refined pupil at Peter Glaze's charm school, and duetted with Pearl Carr as a Japanese geisha girl. She soon became an established member of the comedy quartet in many of the sketches.

Jillian Comber first met Leslie Crowther and his future wife Jean at drama school, and through the years they worked together on and off:

> I did *The Ovaltineys* on Radio Luxembourg, and I did a bit of *Accent on Youth* which was another radio programme. And really I've been connected with Leslie and Jean – schooldays, *Ovaltineys*, *Accent on Youth*, then in pantomime with Leslie in Leeds, then into *Crackerjack*. And, of course, when

I walked into the rehearsals of *Crackerjack*, Leslie said, 'My God! Schooldays! It's Jilly.'

Although Leslie Crowther and Jean had worked together very little at drama school, they were cast as host and hostess of *The Ovaltineys Concert Party of the Air*, recorded in front of an audience at the Abbey Road studios for Radio Luxembourg, with a cast that included Jillian Comber. Leslie and Jean presented this bedtime-drink-sponsored show (with a theme song still sung by those far too young to remember it) for three years. As Jean Crowther describes it, it seems something of a *Crackerjack* prototype:

> There was singing, there was a quiz, there was Les and I doing gags which were pretty drear. But we finished up with a story, one of those Enid Blyton-type adventures: 'I say, Leslie, look at this!' And that was when he'd started pursuing me. And he used to bring me bunches of violets to the studio, which I quite often left behind.

As the *Double or Drop* newcomer, Jillian Comber became Eamonn Andrews' right-hand woman:

> He was basically like a Mr BBC, in a way. All I can think of Eamonn is – he was never out of a suit. Always wearing a suit. He was very much in command of everything. He was an absolute gentleman. But you didn't get close to him. He *did* tell me about his children, and how he lived in Sussex. But he was more like a father figure, to be really honest.

Because of the unpredictable nature of *Double or Drop*, Jillian quickly learnt a useful trick of the trade:

> There used to be a person at the side of me, when we were first doing it. If you had a clever child, or two of them that were really going to parry, then I had to put things in very difficult positions, so that they would drop. Because the timing on the live shows had to be so precise, with the children and the cabbages. And I can always remember the chap saying, 'Go and work on that one.' It was very unfair. But it was just because of being a live show.

Towards the end of the series there's a wonderfully ingenious wordplay routine. It begins with Peter Glaze reciting a poem about his mother:

PETER: I dearly love my mother, she really looks quite topping.
              She walks so very daintily, when she does the weekend shopping.

Vivienne Martin also has a poem, entitled *My Lamb*:

VIV: She loves to nibble clover, as she gambols on the soil
         Her eyes are soft and mellow, and she's wonderfully loyal.

Jillian Comber's offering is called *My Dog*:

JILL: When I take her out each day, I take her in the park
         She's got the sweetest little nose, but she doesn't like the dark.

Finally Leslie Crowther wades in with *My Car*, letting his cultured tones slip a little in the last line:

LESLIE: I wash her down all over, and I top her up with oil.
         She's painted blue and yellow, and she conks aht every moil.

They decide they don't really like any of them. So they try it a different way – taking a line at a time from each poem, and getting huge laughs in the process:

PETER: I dearly love my mother,
VIV: She loves to nibble clover,
JILL: When I take her out each day,
LESLIE: I wash her down all over.

PETER: She really looks quite topping,
VIV: As she gambols on the soil,
JILL: I take her in the park,
LESLIE: And I top her up with oil.

PETER: She walks so very daintily,
VIV: Her eyes are soft and mellow,
JILL: She's got the sweetest little nose,
LESLIE: It's painted blue and yellow.

PETER: When she does the weekend shopping,
VIV: And she's wonderfully loyal.
JILL: But she doesn't like the dark.
LESLIE: And she conks aht every moil.

Subsequent series of *Crackerjack* contain other neatly-constructed transposable poems. It's not been possible to identify the author, though Leslie Crowther himself is a possible candidate.

The series ends with the traditional farewell song. This time it is Vivienne Martin who sings, 'Now it's goodbye to *Crackerjack*. We hope that we will soon be back …' to the tune of *There is a Tavern in the Town*. Vivienne left at the end of the series and, the following year, was on the West End stage as Nancy (replacing Georgia Brown, who created the role) in smash-hit musical *Oliver!*

A month after *Crackerjack* finished its run, Peter Glaze recorded perhaps his most famous TV sitcom role. In episode two of the final series of *Hancock's Half Hour*, Tony Hancock plays Joshua Merryweather in daily radio soap opera *The Bowmans* (a thinly veiled spoof of Walter Gabriel in *The Archers*). The actors stand around the studio microphone, scripts in hand. As Tony strays ever further from his lines (and his original accent) the ferocious yapping of his dog attempts to return him to the script. Several times the animal impersonator (played by Peter Glaze) and Tony almost come to blows. After the decision is made to 'kill off' Joshua Merryweather, Tony milks his death scene for all that it's worth, finally adding, 'I'd like my dear old dog to be buried alongside of me.'

This series of *Hancock's Half Hour* (its title shortened simply to *Hancock*) was the first to lack the presence of Sid James. In its opening episode, Hancock is alone in his bedsit for the entire programme. The only other actor, appearing fleetingly as a BBC announcer on Hancock's telly, is Michael Aspel – someone destined to work alongside Peter Glaze in the years to come.

*

Crackerjack was back in October 1961, with new resident singer Pip Hinton. Pip, again, came from a background of musical theatre and revue. Her big TV break had happened two years earlier. *On The Bright Side* – a television revue starring Stanley Baxter and Betty Marsden – ran for two series. Producer Jimmy Gilbert had seen Pip Hinton onstage in *Where's Charley* (a musical version of the farce *Charley's Aunt*) starring Norman Wisdom:

> I was his leading lady. Yes, I got a lot of fans from being with Norman. Just after him, I went to see the producer Jimmy Gilbert. And he was in a caravan, because they hadn't built White City. And I had my interview with him in a caravan!

By the time Pip joined *Crackerjack*, the BBC Television Centre at White City was fully up and running – though, by and large, *Crackerjack* would continue to be transmitted from the Television Theatre. Pip, although a newcomer to the team, found it easy to fit in:

> Johnny Downes was a wonderful director, who didn't seem to direct at all. He was just there, telling you where to come in. But he was wonderful – booted and suited like they were in those days. Booted and suited and looked like a very ordinary bank manager. But he used to keep the show going.

Like Vivienne, Pip would provide an opening number for the show, accompanied by Bert Hayes and his Octet:

> Every Sunday night he would phone me and ask me what I was going to do. And what arrangement would I like? And he would take it down on the telephone and deliver it to the band. And they used to rehearse it before I got there. I chose what I sang – always one of the Top Ten. I remember I did *Downtown*. He'd set the key, and I'd give him the arrangement I wanted – a long arrangement, a slightly shorter one, double the ending, things like that. And every Sunday night the telephone would ring. I'd say, 'That's Bert!'

The 1962 *Eamonn Andrews Crackerjack Book* detailed the line-up of Bert Hayes' Octet – all top-rate highly versatile session musicians drawn from some of the top bands:

> Session Trumpet is Alan Moorhouse, who among other sidelines is arranger to Keith Prowse Music Company. Alto Saxophone is Peter Hughes, who also plays Bass Clarinet and Flute, and had four years with Cyril Stapleton. Denis Watts plays another Alto Sax, Flute and Clarinet. Before joining Bert, he had a long period with Ted Heath. The Clarinet is played by Ted James, who can also take a part with the Tenor Saxophone, Piano and Violin. The Tenor Saxophone comes from Charles Palmer, who again is a Violinist, and plays the Clarinet. The Beat for the Group is provided by Peter Vandike on the Double Bass, and Frank King on the Drum and Timpani.
>
> Bert has never failed to produce some of the odd sounds Johnny Downes calls for. When a special hubble-bubble sequence was asked for, Peter Hughes improvised with some rubber tube and a jar of water.

Incidentally, *The Eamonn Andrews Crackerjack Book* of 1962 was the sole result of a number of requests from Eamonn's agent for exclusive *Crackerjack* merchandising rights. Initially the proposal was for a boxed game with Eamonn's photo on the lid. In the end, Eamonn's other show *Playbox* was produced as a boxed game, though just a bog-standard games compendium. Such a pity that no one took the time and trouble to devise a *Crackerjack* board game, where you had to collect as many pencils as possible without landing on a cabbage, and everything was decided on the roll of a Peter Glaze.

Stan Mars turned down the offer to write a second series of *Crackerjack* and left to pursue other projects. His replacement for the first half of the series was someone *en route* to a highly illustrious career – Dick Vosburgh. A few years earlier, on a writing team that included Sid Green and Dick Hills, he'd scripted *Pantomania: Babes in the Wood* – the BBC's annual Christmas pantomime packed with celebrities, including Tony Hancock as Robin Hood, Sid James as Friar Tuck, and Eamonn Andrews in the unlikely role of Merry Man.

Of all the *Crackerjack* writers during Leslie's time on the show, it is Dick Vosburgh who stands out most vividly in Jean Crowther's memory:

> He was very tall, very dishevelled and American. He was one of the new breed, rather like Alan Bennett and Jonathan Miller, except they'd all been to public school. I think he wasn't *quite* what the BBC was expecting. He didn't conform with the pattern. He used to write on lavatory paper sometimes when he couldn't find any paper.

Dick Vosburgh, born in New Jersey, became a renowned writer and lyricist, particularly on *The Frost Report* and *The Two Ronnies*. His stage musical *A Day In Hollywood, A Night in the Ukraine* featured a recreation of the Marx Brothers. He had six children, which sometimes made writing at home difficult. He came up with this novel solution: 'I often write scripts going endlessly round the Circle Line.'

Dick was in his early 30s when he joined *Crackerjack*, and this would be something of a baptism of fire. The second show of the series went out on 2nd November 1961, 25 years to the day since the first BBC television broadcast. To celebrate this anniversary, Queen Elizabeth II was to visit BBC Television Centre – and the final stop on her itinerary would be Studio 3, to see a broadcast of *Crackerjack*.

Studio 3 at Television Centre had been in use for just over a year. Other studios opened in the months that followed, and some were yet to be completed. Numerous shows had broadcast from TV Centre, but never

Crackerjack. However, as it was known to be a favourite of the Royal Family, for this one occasion *Crackerjack* upped sticks from its regular home in Shepherds Bush and prepared to meet its monarch.

Eamonn's autobiography *This is My Life* gives a good impression of the pre-show atmosphere:

> Before the transmission, I was conscious of shadowy figures moving around, pacing out how many steps it would take from here to there, mumbling gallant replies in mimed rehearsal lest Her Majesty should happen to ask them a question. I watched one important executive traversing and re-traversing six yards of studio space round a camera and back again vainly trying to work out how he could do it without turning his back on the Queen and obviously getting impossibly tangled up. The more he tried it over to himself, the more he began to look like someone not quite right in the head, rehearsing, with an invisible partner to an invisible Victor Silvester tune, an impossible dance. I pretended not to notice.

However, the royal visit to TV Centre wasn't totally stiff and starchy. The *Daily Sketch* reported that the Queen was introduced to comedian Jimmy Edwards, chairman of the Variety Artistes' Federation which was currently in dispute with ITV:

> 'I see you are on strike there,' she told Jimmy, referring to ITV. Then she added, 'But I see you are still working here.' Replied Edwards: 'Well, it could happen here.'
>
> 'They can't afford it after building all this, can they?' joked the Queen.

For the royal *Crackerjack*'s opening crosstalk spot (scripted by Dick Vosburgh) Leslie Crowther enters dressed as a schoolboy. It's a cunning ploy to get himself a prize on *Double or Drop*. Peter Glaze tests his general knowledge and Leslie's answers are littered with references to TV shows and personalities of the day:

PETER: I'll give you the first line of a nursery rhyme and you complete it. 'Hickory Dickory Dock …'
LESLIE: The mouse played Beat the Clock!
PETER: Give me an example of wasted energy.
LESLIE: Telling a hair-raising story to David Nixon.

One of the actual competitors, though she didn't make it through to *Double or Drop*, was Margaret Gidman (now Maggie Bernstein) from nearby Hayes County Grammar School:

> I remember that we were suddenly, one afternoon, put on a coach and taken to the BBC TV Centre. And found ourselves on *Crackerjack* on the day the Queen was visiting. I assume they must have somehow notified our parents that we were going, but I don't remember them saying it to *us*. I just remember them announcing to the class, 'Right, we're off to *Crackerjack*.' And, of course, we were all thrilled to bits.
>
> For one of the games we were given little wheelbarrows with square wheels, and we had to run back and forth across the stage trying to collect crockery which, of course, kept falling off and breaking. And whoever collected the most got through to the next little game.

The show's main comedy sketch is a Western. It not only plays to Dick Vosburgh's strengths, he even manages to blag himself a walk-on part. Here Pip is teaching Leslie to dance:

LESLIE: One, two, three … One, two, three … Gosh! This is fun! I've never done this before.
PIP: What – dance?
LESLIE: No – count up to three! Let me take you to the Rodeo tonight.
PIP: How do you know there's a Rodeo on?
LESLIE: I read about it in the Rodeo Times.
DICK: (ENTERS) Miss Kitty! Miss Kitty!
LESLIE: Who's that?
PIP: Why, it's Billy the Goat.
LESLIE: Billy the Goat?
PIP: Yes, he's the father of Billy the Kid.

At the end of the sketch, a menacing stranger enters with his hat pulled down over his eyes and a bandana masking his face. The others draw their guns:

LESLIE: I'm aimin'.
PETER: And I'm aimin'.
PIP: And I'm aimin'.
LESLIE: (LIFTS EAMONN'S BANDANA OFF) And he's Eamonn!

After *Double or Drop*, Eamonn picks a London guide book from the prize hamper, giving the theme to the musical finale. An appropriate backdrop incorporates all the familiar landmarks. Leslie and special guest Harry Secombe, as police constables, perform *We Run Them In*, Pip and Jillian (in Pearly Queen outfits) sing *Knock'd 'Em in the Old Kent Road*, Pete (as a Pearly King) sings *Any Old Iron* – and the whole cast finishes with *Let's All Go Down the Strand*. This was the part of the show that the Queen was scheduled to see during her visit to the studio.

Jillian Comber remembers the meticulous preparations for this moment, with the help of a BBC continuity announcer:

> We rehearsed it. Polly Elwes played the Queen. And anyone who wasn't to meet the Queen was put in a cupboard, practically. And we were told the Queen will come in, in the middle of the performance, and she will just come in quietly at the back. And will you please go on with the show, exactly as it is. Well, the Queen came, and about 75 bodyguards seemed to walk in. And every child turned round and stared at her!

As the finale concludes, Eamonn steps forward:

> If you detected a very special note of excitement in the audience, it is because *Crackerjack* has had its most distinguished visitor ever. (BOWS) Your Majesty, we are extremely honoured to say 'Welcome to the *Crackerjack* studio.'

It *was* the *Crackerjack* studio, but only for the day. The Television Theatre was their true home, and they'd be back there for the rest of the series and beyond.

Brian Johnston provided the commentary for the viewer at home, while Eamonn introduced Her Majesty to the cast, starting with Leslie Crowther, who later wrote in *The Bonus of Laughter*:

> When it was my turn to be introduced she told me that she always watched the programme with Prince Charles and Princess Anne. I was so flabbergasted that I burst out loudly: 'You don't!'
>
> 'Yes we do,' the Queen replied, and when we both realised my breach of royal formality we laughed like mad!

Pip Hinton, still attired in her finale costume, was next in line:

I had a wonderful outfit that we'd borrowed from somewhere. A *real* Pearly Queen outfit. Hundreds and hundreds of buttons on it. And I remember what she said to me. She said, 'Did you sew them on yourself?' 'No ma'am,' I said.

Standing next to Peter Glaze was Jillian Comber:

She said, 'What a very nice dress.' I mean, look at it, it was absolutely ghastly! 'Thank you, ma'am.'

The Guardian told how everyone on the studio floor was presented to the Queen, with six exceptions:

The exceptions were the six schoolchildren who had taken part in the show. They were left to stand uneasily in a line, studying their toecaps, waiting to give a shy, inexpert, respectful bob or bow.

And one of those six was Margaret Gidman:

The Queen appeared in a sort of yellow silk coat with a brooch – she always seemed to have one of those brooches on her left side at the top. And a matching hat. I was amazed at how old she looked, to me, as a 13-year-old. We all had to curtsey. She came and just, sort of, said hello to us. And then they gave her these gifts.

Eamonn reached into the pile of *Double or Drop* prizes and gave the Queen two silver *Crackerjack* pencils, one each for Prince Charles and Princess Anne, and an Andy Pandy doll for Prince Andrew. The Queen told Eamonn how she and her children were regular viewers: 'I watch it. It moves quickly, I enjoy it.'

The closing moments of the broadcast (which, rarely for *Crackerjack*, was recorded about an hour-and-a-half before transmission) are detailed in the camera script:

THEREAFTER THE QUEEN MAY BE SEEN TALKING TO A CAMERAMAN ON HIS 'CRANE' FOLLOWED BY FADE OUT AND APPROPRIATE CLOSE BY BRIAN JOHNSTON.

Senior cameraman Eddie Stuart (who'd been with *Crackerjack* from the start) was seated on one of the BBC's newest pieces of equipment, which used hydraulic foot-pedals to raise both him and his camera. He was the only person in the studio permitted to converse with the Queen while sitting down:

> I explained how the camera worked. We had quite a chat actually! That camera was, in fact, called a Heron. There was one pedal made you go left or right when you pressed it down. When you pressed it down with your *heel* it went the other way. And when you pressed the other pedal with your foot it went *up*, and with the heel it went *down*. And I could go up and down and round and round if I wanted to.
>
> But that camera was specially for the Queen's visit. Normally we would have a Mole Crane, which was the one at the TV Theatre – which was one chap driving it, one chap swinging it, and going up and down and left and right, and me trying not to fall off at the front.

Before the Queen left the Television Centre, she told Head of Light Entertainment Eric Maschwitz, 'I didn't realise what a busy factory this was.'

For the second half of the series, commencing January 1962, the scriptwriting duties were passed to Maurice Wiltshire, yet another writer to have Jimmy Grafton and *Goon Show* connections. He had co-written four episodes of *The Goon Show* with Larry Stephens, when Spike Milligan was indisposed – and he wrote (often with Larry) over 40 episodes of ITV sitcom *The Army Game*. After *Crackerjack* he went on to write an episode of ITV's *Dickie Henderson Show* with Jimmy Grafton and Jeremy Lloyd, and script-edit *The Telegoons* (a glove-puppet *Goon Show*), before moving permanently to Australia. Maurice stayed with *Crackerjack* through to the last show of the series which, by a happy coincidence, was their 100th show.

Eamonn (writing in *The Eamonn Andrews Crackerjack Book*) recalled that *Crackerjack* had begun around the same time as rock-and-roll. To keep the show bang up to date, they rounded off Edition 100 with The Twist:

> The whole gang came twisting on to the stage – Leslie and Pip, Peter and Jillian and the rest. But, of course, they insisted I should come on too, because they knew I couldn't dance for toffee and it gives them a great kick to see me about ten miles behind the beat!
>
> During rehearsal, I got one of the dancers to give me some quick tuition in twisting. Although I say it myself, I wasn't doing too badly and was all set to shake the *Crackerjack* gang. Then I made my mistake. I asked guest star Adam Faith to come down with me in the finale. Adam twisted so niftily that beside him I must have looked like a retriever shaking himself after a swim.

A fortnight after the series ended, Martin Jackson of the *Daily Express* had good news for the future of the show:

> Commercial television has lost its fight to lure Eamonn Andrews from the BBC. He is to sign an exclusive two-year contract with the corporation, guaranteeing him at least £30,000 a year.
>
> It is 35-year-old Andrews' first exclusive contract, and makes him TV's highest-paid compere.

Apparently Eamonn had rejected four different offers from commercial stations in recent months:

> Said his agent, Mr Edward Sommerfield last night: 'It's not the money. It is that the BBC have promised us new programmes, and the right type of programmes.'
>
> Andrews will continue to compere *This Is Your Life*, *What's My Line?* and *Crackerjack* until the new shows are ready for the screen.

Strangely, these 'new shows' never materialised. The next two years were to look virtually identical to the previous half dozen.

Not only did Eamonn stay in place for the next two series, but so did the whole team – Leslie, Peter, Pip and Jillian – plus Bert Hayes and Johnny Downes. The odd writer came and went, but this was the longest period with no cast changes to date.

*

There were more shows in Series Eight than any previous series – 17 fortnightly episodes running from September 1962 to April 1963. It started, as the previous one had ended, with Adam Faith as guest star.

Previously, Leslie Crowther had juggled TV appearances on both *Crackerjack* and *The Black and White Minstrel Show*. Now he was in a long run of the *Minstrels'* stage show at the Victoria Palace. As he wrote in *The Bonus of Laughter*, every Thursday, the minute *Crackerjack* was over, it was the same hectic routine:

> I would dive into a taxi, standing outside with the engine throbbing, for the race to Victoria through the rush hour. Many times I would get out of the taxi, walk through the stage door, hear my entrance music and walk straight on to the stage. Once the traffic jam in Victoria was so bad that I leaped out

of the taxi and ran to the theatre. All I could do when I eventually got on to the stage was to look at the audience and pant heavily for a minute or two until I'd got my breath back. They must have thought I was bonkers!

The third show of the series is one of only half-a-dozen or so complete Eamonn Andrews *Crackerjack*s preserved in the film archives. There are some excellent comedy routines, commencing with a reprise of the mixed-up poems first performed with Vivienne Martin two series ago. After Egyptian magician Gally-Gally performs the classic 'cups and balls' illusion, using live baby chicks, Eamonn (at the speedy pace of one of those TV commercial disclaimers) banishes any concerns about animal cruelty. Though it's not hard to detect a cynical edge to his final two words:

> And those little chickens he has in lovely warm incubators in the dressing room and when they're finished working with Gally-Gally they go back to a farm and grow up to be happy little chickens, I'm sure.

The first sketch is provided by the series' new scriptwriter Eddie Maguire, who had an impressive track record in radio comedy, writing for *Ray's A Laugh* (with Ted Ray), *Archie's the Boy!* (with ventriloquist Peter Brough and Archie Andrews), and domestic sitcom *Meet the Huggetts* (with Jack Warner and Kathleen Harrison). It's a Cleopatra sketch that not only predates the Eric Morecambe, Ernie Wise and Glenda Jackson routine by nearly a decade, it even (as Eamonn makes clear in his introduction) predates the Elizabeth Taylor movie:

> I'm sure many of you have read, as we all have, about this film *Cleopatra*, which has been going on for years and years and years, it seems to me, and apparently still is not finished. Well, Peter got fed up with this and decided to write his own script and try and persuade a BBC cameraman to film it for him.

Peter naturally casts himself in the main role of Mark Antony, with Pip as Cleopatra and Leslie in the minor role of a Roman soldier, with nothing to do but continually interrupt:

PIP: Why are you so late?
LESLIE: He's just got out of bed.
PETER: I have *not* just got out of bed!
LESLIE: Then why are you wearing this sheet?

PETER: It's not a sheet, it's a toga.

PIP: I can see you're noble, Mark Antony.

LESLIE: (EXAMINES SHEET) And I can see your laundry mark, Antony!

PIP: Tell me Antony, I believe you have conquered the world.

PETER: Ah yes, I conquered Sicily, I conquered France, I conquered Egypt!

PIP: And then?

LESLIE: He ran out of conkers.

Double or Drop has a couple of refinements. The winner of the previous week comes back (adorned in a champion's hat) to defend their title against two new contenders. And outgoing champions receive an extra-special *Crackerjack* prize – a pen *and* pencil set.

The final sketch is another innovation for this series, and a major landmark in *Crackerjack* history. Announced by Eamonn as the first stone-age musical, *I Tawt I Taw a Dinosaur* has it all – skimpy costumes for Jillian and Pip (who still remembers the coarse hessian skirt), shaggy wigs and polystyrene clubs for Peter and Leslie, and … pop songs! They're not quite as up-to-the-minute as they would become in later years, but a couple (*Rock with the Caveman* and *Ape Call*) are from the late 1950s, and *Tower of Strength* was a Number One hit just the previous year for Frankie Vaughan.

Almost as soon as he'd joined *Crackerjack* Leslie Crowther had got involved with the writing of the show. He would often tinker with a script, adding the odd gag or bit of business. But the 'history goes pop' finales were all Leslie's idea and (while Eddie Maguire wrote the earlier part of the show) Leslie scripted and compiled the finales himself. He rarely received a writer's credit, but those finales soon became the highlight of the show.

*

In September 1963 *Crackerjack* started another run of 17 shows. Reminiscent of his very first appearance three years earlier, Leslie makes a spectacular entrance. One by one Eamonn introduces the cast, but when he announces Leslie there is no sign of him. We then see a speeded-up Leslie (on film with silent-movie piano accompaniment) running frantically through studio corridors, intercut with shots of a slovenly tea lady pushing her trolley. Leslie dashes through a swing-door, there is an enormous crash, and we see the stunned tea lady on the floor surrounded by upturned urn and crockery. Leslie, seated astride the trolley, rapidly disappears down the corridor before bursting through a studio wall and confronting Eamonn.

Leslie's wife Jean has good reason to remember that stunt:

> It was me being the tea trolley lady, because nobody had turned up, and Johnny said, 'Oh, Jean, would you do that?' And Leslie runs, and I'm pushing, and he knocks into the tea trolley. I never got paid. I just got hauled into it. Our children were most amused when they realised it was me.

The final sketch has a distinctly topical edge. *Moonstrike*, a BBC drama series about the French Resistance, had finished just a month ago. Leslie's version is called *Sunstroke* and incorporates two recent pop hits: *If You Gotta Make a Fool of Somebody* by Freddie and the Dreamers, and *Do You Want to Know a Secret?* by The Beatles.

It was still a few months before the launch of *Top of the Pops* at the start of 1964. And pop acts were starting to feature more frequently as *Crackerjack* guests, including Brian Poole and the Tremeloes, The Searchers and The Swinging Blue Jeans. But Jillian Comber recalls that not everybody was welcome:

> We did get a following of slightly older people and even young mums with children that loved the pop groups, because at that time the pop group was really something. And I can always remember Johnny Downes saying, 'We could have The Beatles, but I can't have them with *that* hairstyle. Not on *Crackerjack*.' That's true! That was in January, February. In September they were so big we couldn't have them.

Earlier that year (in May 1963) The Beatles had sung at teatime on Thursday. But not on *Crackerjack*. Johnny Downes may have refused them, but Peter Whitmore (later to become Johnny's successor) snapped them up for the Lenny the Lion show: *Pops and Lenny*. A couple of years later, The Beatles were special guests on Eamonn Andrews' ITV chat show. Eamonn announced, 'Ladies and gentlemen, it's The Beatles!' Straightaway John Lennon shouted back, '*Crackerjack!*'

Patrick Heigham was a sound assistant who worked on *Crackerjack* during this period. His duties included rigging the boom mikes as well as miking the pop groups:

> The day started at nine a.m. as I recall. We looked on it as a short day, as when it came off the air, after de-rigging, we could go home!

As the TV Theatre was still licensed as such, there could be no cables crossing from the stage area to the extended stage beyond the proscenium arch, since the safety curtain (the Iron) had to be lowered and raised in the presence of the audience. If there was a pop group, then it was a standard rig for Lead/Rhythm/Bass guitars and drum kit. Some of the mike feeds had to be plugged to wall boxes situated above the flies (theatre, remember) with extension cables dropped to the stage floor.

I believe the kids loved it! Every mention of the word *Crackerjack* was loudly echoed by the audience. I did hear a story of our usual Sound Supervisor attending a high-powered meeting when *Crackerjack* was mentioned, and he reacted in the same way!

Another sound assistant at this time was Eric Wallis:

> For audio people the most challenging part was trying to reproduce the sound recorded on the disc of the many popular artists that the producer had booked. The controlled conditions of a sound studio are very different to a multi-camera television studio.

Eric had also worked on the *Pops and Lenny* show with The Beatles. He remembers the biggest problem with top-name groups was not their *own* sound, but that of their fans:

> This was a time when the groups' on-stage sound equipment was pretty basic compared to today. When we rehearsed them, the groups' speaker levels were set to suit both the sound mixer and the artists. However, when it came to transmission, the audience was so loud the group had difficulty hearing themselves. So they promptly turned their speakers to maximum, causing some consternation in the sound control room.

And there was more consternation just around the corner. Those within the BBC had long seen it coming but (in January 1964) Eamonn Andrews, celebratory glass in hand, beamed out from the pages of the *Daily Mirror*:

> Eamonn Andrews has finally been wooed over to ITV – after fourteen years as a key BBC personality.
>
> He goes to ABC TV, the Midlands and North weekend programme company, at a fee which makes him the highest paid commentator on the small screen.
>
> His three-year contract will pay him about £120,000.

It was inevitable that there would come a day when ITV would offer more money than the BBC could hope to match. And, to be fair, the BBC hadn't been making the best use of him. *What's My Line?* had finished the previous year, leaving Eamonn with only *This Is Your Life, Crackerjack* and *Playbox*.

Playbox had been in existence for as long as *Crackerjack*. Both shows were fortnightly, with Eamonn hosting *Crackerjack* one week and *Playbox* the next. *Playbox* always had a quiz element to it, usually a knockout quiz between regional school teams, running throughout the series. Once there was even an international quiz with a Dutch team via the Eurovision link. For its present series (which would turn out to be its last) the faintly infantile title *Playbox* had been dropped in favour of *Top Score*. It was now virtually a variety show, and (though lacking a resident comedy team) had grown increasingly similar to *Crackerjack*. There was Nat Temple and his band, two hostesses, singer and zither player Shirley Abicair, and magician and origami expert Robert Harbin.

Eamonn wasn't going anywhere just yet. His contract with ABC didn't start until September, so he would remain to see out the current series of *Top Score* and *Crackerjack*. Over the next few months *Crackerjack* began to receive a certain amount of criticism in the press. The first salvo, appropriately enough, was fired by Brian de Salvo of *The Stage*. It missed Eamonn entirely, because Eamonn was missing from the show:

> I now invite early death by catapult in suggesting that *Crackerjack* talks down to the children. During the games I couldn't help thinking that the con-
testants were behaving more like adults than Leslie Crowther, deputizing as quizmaster for Eamonn Andrews.

Brian de Salvo had canvassed the opinions of some South London schoolchildren, who thought both *Double or Drop* and pop guests The Bachelors were 'smashing'. But there was one item that totally divided critic and child:

> After The Bachelors I thought Pip Hinton's opening song the best thing in the show. Sad to relate my guinea pigs were not very thrilled with 'ladies that sing'.

A more vitriolic attack came from *The Guardian* in the aftermath of the recent restructuring of BBC children's programming. *Crackerjack* had always been made by the Children's Department but, in 1964, the Children's

Department was merged with Women's Programmes into Family Programmes. However, *Crackerjack*, along with other children's audience shows (of which there were now several) plus children's drama, now became the responsibility of the BBC Light Entertainment department. The various department names within the BBC gave Jillian Comber cause for amusement:

> I believe, when I came into it, we were under a thing called Family Planning. And then we went into Light Entertainment. But only the BBC could put us into something called Family Planning! I've lived off that story – I may be telling a complete falsehood – but when they said, 'Your contract is with Family Planning.' 'What?! I've done it – I've got three children!'

The move to Light Entertainment would prove hugely beneficial to *Crackerjack*. It was already attracting a family audience, and Light Entertainment would provide the kind of budget that children's television would struggle to match. But this was a cause of concern. Many people feared that the quality element of weekday children's programming (such as drama, which was more expensive to produce) would be hit hardest by this restructuring. Judith Cook's opinion piece in *The Guardian* of March 30th 1964 pulled no punches:

> Fifth-rate westerns, sixth-rate variety, and tenth-rate pop programmes, interspersed with cartoons, would appear to be our fare for the future. Those jolly adults in the depths of the planning department, who think that children fold up and hoot with laughter week after week at *Crackerjack* and *Tich* must be simple-minded to a degree.

(*Tich* was a creation of ventriloquist Ray Alan. A schoolboy dummy perhaps more suited to children's television than Lord Charles – a monocled aristocrat with a drink problem.)

In the *Guardian* letters page, Stuart Hood, BBC television's Controller of Programmes, was quick to defend *Crackerjack*:

> I do not know where Judith Cook gets her information about children's audiences. The evidence that comes my way shows that *Crackerjack* is immensely popular and that children get a good deal of pleasure out of it.

Judith Cook responded:

> As to *Crackerjack*, apart from children of my friends who find it boring, a quick poll round some of the children attending my daughters' junior school

revealed that practically all of them watch *Robin Hood* on the other channel while it is being shown.

Despite the odd journalistic barb and the imminent departure of its host, *Crackerjack* kept calm and carried on, with sketches that (both in writing and performance) stood comparison with those of any evening show.

In May, the final show of the series starts with *Where There's You There's Me* sung and effortlessly tap-danced by Pip and Leslie. This is followed by more of their mixed-up verse. Peter Glaze's poem is a tribute to Pip: 'Her healthy skin just glows and glows, she has the cutest turned-up nose.' And Leslie praises her taste in clothes: 'She has a summer dress that's new, it's pale pink and drip-dry too.' Of course, the verses become less flattering when the lines are alternated:

PETER: Her healthy skin just glows and glows.
LESLIE: She has a summer dress that's new.
PETER: She has the cutest turned-up nose.
LESLIE: It's pale pink and drip-dry too.

One of the elimination games is a relay race in which boys and girls, seated on rugs, use legpower to slide themselves across the floor. Eamonn's commentary acknowledges that perhaps this is not the most decorous pose for a girl in a skirt: 'We did tell the ladies they could have tracksuits, but they decided not to spoil the fashion.'

Next up is slick pickpocket Vic Perry. This was an era when a grown man could rummage freely through a couple of schoolboys' pockets without causing comment. Similarly no one seemed overly concerned about the lyrics of *Leave My Woman Alone* by pop duo Peter and Gordon, who threaten a rich rival with a flashy car that if he ever offers their girl a lift, 'I'm going to do some work on you.'

The finale is not only highly topical, it's downright cheeky. The current BBC Sunday teatime drama was a serialisation of *Rupert of Hentzau* (the sequel to *The Prisoner of Zenda*) with Peter Wyngarde in the title role. It was only halfway through its run when *Crackerjack* decided to send it up rotten with their own version of this Ruritanian romance, entitled *The Prisoner of Fender* or *Leslie of Eyesore*.

Leslie and Peter make their entrance to The Mojos' recent hit *Everything's Alright* and take a swig of beer from their authentic looking 'steins'. (Leslie's has TVC in large letters on the base – presumably meaning it comes from the Television Centre props department!) Pip Hinton is brooding and Garbo-esque, while Leslie's tongue and lips continually struggle with those torturous Ruritanian vowels. Finally, Leslie persuades the villain's henchman to switch his allegiance by offering to double his fee:

FRITZ: Double your money? Who taught you zis trick?
LESLIE: Hughie Green.

Eamonn enters, fully costumed, and delivers the usual one line of dialogue. As he starts to say goodbye, both to the series and to his own association with the show, Leslie interrupts him and presents him with a silver salver inscribed with the initials of cast and crew. Over the closing music and credits, Eamonn (who was never totally at ease with the concept of smiling) puts on a brave grin, though he seems genuinely touched by this affectionate gesture.

To many, Eamonn Andrews was Mr *Crackerjack*. His departure marked the end of an era. *Crackerjack* would never be the same again. But then, maybe, it was time for a change.

5
My Dear Mr Crowder

1964 – 1968

W
ITH THE EXCEPTION OF Eamonn Andrews, everybody returned in October 1964 for the new series. In many ways it was the same show as before. But there was one big change that had nothing to do with Eamonn.

The children's magazine show *Blue Peter* had made its debut in 1958, three years after *Crackerjack*. In September 1964 *Blue Peter* changed from a weekly show to twice-weekly, with an episode every Monday and Thursday. As *Crackerjack* had gone out on a Thursday for the previous five series, it was going to have to make a move. So, for the first time in its history, *Crackerjack* went out on Fridays.

Apart from the occasional live edition, *Crackerjack* was now recorded earlier in the week: initially on Wednesdays, then later on Thursdays. This was doubtless due to the Television Theatre being more heavily used by light entertainment shows at the weekends. It made no real difference to the cast, because editing was virtually impossible. So it was 'recorded live' and any fluffs and mistakes were left in, just as they would be in a live transmission.

Also, because there was no longer *Playbox* or its equivalent to alternate with, *Crackerjack* became a weekly show – apart from the Friday following show one, which was devoted to coverage of the general election results.

So *Crackerjack* was back for 23 weekly shows. A punishing schedule for one person in particular, the new host – or not so new as it turned out – Leslie Crowther. Leslie had deputised for Eamonn once before. Now he would regularly double the duties of comic and host. For any lesser mortal it might have been a case of 'double *and* drop'.

In fact *Double or Drop* was one feature of the show that Leslie would never have to deal with. When Eamonn moved to ITV, the game he had devised went with him. Not that he ever used it again. Over the years *Crackerjack* tried out any number of final games, none of which worked as well or made any great impression on the viewers. Most people believe that *Double or Drop* was with *Crackerjack* from beginning to end – but it was about to take a 14-year sabbatical.

The only additional cast member, who appeared on a semi-regular basis throughout the series, was flamboyant comedy conjuror Harold Taylor, who (like Bruce Forsyth) made his entrance with a pose reminiscent of Rodin's *The Thinker*. Harold's self-contained magic spot gave Leslie the chance to catch his breath or, if nothing else, made a quick-change a little less frenetic.

Someone who assisted Leslie with some of those lightning costume changes was dresser Tony Hare:

> I was looking after Leslie Crowther and, on this occasion, the finale sketch, Leslie was Long John Silver. And he was dressed in the full bit, with the leg strapped up and the peg-leg and everything. And I had to get him out of the Long John Silver gear into a dinner suit in just over a minute. He had a quick change while something else was going on onstage. But anyway we did a couple of rehearsals. And we made it!

Johnny Downes still produced but Peter Whitmore came in as director, and would take over as producer the following series. Jillian Comber believes the combination of Peter Whitmore as director and Leslie Crowther as host brought new energy to the show:

> It couldn't have been done without Johnny Downes, because Johnny had that flair for what *Crackerjack* should be. He set this pattern. And it evolved from his pattern. He was a very nice man, but quite set in his ways. He didn't have as much flexibility in him. We were practically like the end of the pier when we were with Leslie and Peter Whitmore. It was just one of those wonderful shows.
>
> Eamonn had one way of standing. One way of presenting his words. He was the schoolmaster in *Crackerjack* really. When Leslie took over, he became the sixth-form naughty boy. When it was Eamonn it was, 'Hello there, children everywhere.' When it was Leslie it was, 'Cor, here we are again, innit great?'

The feel of the show changed because Leslie was such a wonderfully relaxed, funny, friendly person to work with. He was one of the nicest men you could ever meet. And he used to say, 'I'm starstruck, I'm stagestruck, I love it!'

At the start of the series, Leslie told the *Radio Times*:

Entertaining children started simply as a job, but now I find I have a real affection for *Crackerjack* and what it does. I find you get to like children more and more – you have to or you leave the programme.

Of course, adults watched *Crackerjack* too, and the *Radio Times* listed amongst its viewing audience 'retired people, bank managers, night-shift workers and publicans'. But the majority of Leslie's fan mail came from children:

He has a host of fans who are devoted letter-writers. 'Most of the children seem to write without being prompted by parents, because I've had letters simply addressed to "Leslie, BBC",' he said.

Leslie's wife, Jean, has kept some of these letters, including this neatly written and imaginatively spelt example:

My dear Mr Crowder I think you are beautyfull and I wood like a foto of you if you cud spare me won please I am six years old ond go to school
   Lost of luv from Rosemary Ann Deighton xxxxxxxxxxxxxxxxxxxxxxxx
   I am looking forward to CrakJak to see you I luv you but I have promist to marriy Jefry Clark

Jean also remembers one of Leslie's most regular correspondents:

There was one lady – she always signed, even her Christmas cards, Elsie Julie Day 'Constant Viewer'. And she thought Leslie could see out of the television into her room. She would say, 'I've moved your photo, do you like where it is now?'
   I think one of the best compliments was when somebody said to me, 'But he doesn't rehearse *Crackerjack*, does he?' And to look unrehearsed, that's quite a compliment. Because it did look very much as if they just met up.

Despite the move to Friday, and the change of host, there was nothing markedly different about the start of the show. A series of captions listing the cast, followed by Leslie uttering the exact same words that Eamonn had used – 'Yes, it's *Crackerjack!*'

But there was one feature that firmly established itself this series – the Crowther and Glaze double-act. Up to now Peter Glaze had largely been used as one of Leslie's supporting players, and most of the sketches tended to be ensemble pieces. Now, for the first time, the 'Peter Glaze Lecture' was the comedy opener of the show. It made a lot of sense. Host Leslie could hardly introduce himself as the comic. Far better for him to hand over to Peter, wait a moment, then come on and start pestering him:

PETER: I'm going to talk to you about the history of the steam engine …
              about railways … about stations …
LESLIE: About me grandad …
PETER: About his grandad … Leslie, don't interrupt!

This is the blueprint for every lecture Peter Glaze ever gave. His way of blithely repeating the comic's entering remark before realising what he's just said. His double-takes. The exasperated 'doh!' (Peter's use of the exclamation may predate Homer Simpson, but James Finlayson had been 'doh-ing' decades earlier with Laurel and Hardy.) As Peter tries his utmost to educate us about James Watt and the steam engine, Leslie's interjections get him further and further off the subject:

PETER: He was sitting by his fire and the kettle started to boil. So what
              did he do?
LESLIE: He sent for Polly …
PETER: Why?
LESLIE: 'Cos Polly put the kettle on …
PETER: Why did Polly put the kettle on?
LESLIE: 'Cos she's nothing else to wear.

Peter Glaze's eyesight has already been mentioned. Offscreen he wore spectacles with thick lenses. However, on TV, lenses have a nasty habit of reflecting the studio lights, so his familiar round-framed specs didn't have any glass in them. Of course, to enable him to see anything at all, Peter needed to wear contact lenses under his lens-free specs. Leslie Crowther's eyesight was better, but far from perfect. He too wore glasses offscreen, but never bothered with contact lenses in front of the camera, even if things might sometimes have looked a little hazy.

Leslie was still very involved in the writing of the show, particularly the finales. His opening routine with Peter is most likely the work of another writer. I say 'most likely' because writers were not always named in the end credits, the scripts, or even the *Radio Times*. But the writer who is believed to have begun his *Crackerjack* stint at this time is Bob Block.

Bob's early success was as part of the regular writing team on *Life with the Lyons*, a BBC radio sitcom that ran more than a decade, featuring real-life American family Ben Lyon and Bebe Daniels with their children Barbara and Richard. Bebe was also one of the writers and Bob Block (very occasionally) was also one of the actors. After spending nearly another decade on *Crackerjack*, Bob went on to create and write the children's TV comedy favourites *Pardon My Genie*, *Robert's Robots* and *Rentaghost* (featuring former *Crackerjack* straight-man Michael Darbyshire amongst its cast).

Jillian Comber (in addition to her hostess duties) acted and sang in many of the sketches and spent much of her week in the rehearsal room:

> We were all such a happy show. There wasn't any narcissism. You're singing a bit of a number and then Peter Whitmore would say, 'We're going to cut that whole verse out.' He's possibly cut your entire number out. But it actually didn't seem to matter.
>
> One of the cleverest persons in the sketch used to be Peter Glaze. Because they'd have a joke with a ladder, and Peter knew five or six ways of hitting somebody's head with a ladder. Because he'd done the Crazy Gang for ten years. And so he knew everything. If you're going to put your foot in a pail, how do you do it? Is it because, when you open the door, *that* falls down and you turn around and put your foot in it? Or – is it because you come through the room, you walk across the room, you come back … He just knew every single way. Leslie knew what the sketch was going to be. But Peter put all the icing on the cake.
>
> I never heard Peter Glaze row with Leslie Crowther once. I've heard them sit and Leslie would say, 'Well, I don't think that'll work.' And then Peter would say, 'Well, it will do. I've done it.' 'Yeah, but it's not really very funny.'

There was one potential cause of friction, if Leslie had been the kind of person to rise to the bait, as he admits in *The Bonus of Laughter*:

> Peter Glaze's inability to learn a script, especially the 'double spot' between him and me which kicked off the show, made life very hard for both of us.

He had all the leads and I had all the funny answers, so it was important for him to get it right. I never said anything, just bottled up my anger, while feeling cold and resentful.

Pip Hinton remembers those opening routines being particularly popular with the kids in the audience:

They loved the couple – Leslie Crowther and Peter Glaze. Leslie of course was wonderful. And I think sometimes he had a bit of trouble with Peter Glaze going off the rails. Peter was bumbling – a bumbling bumbler. But Leslie was very good. He could interpret him. And it was a wonderful combination.

Pip also met Peter's wife, theatrical agent April Young, on many occasions:

Joyce Grenfell talked about 'stately as a galleon'. And she was *actually* stately as a galleon. It was so funny. She was very pukka. Absolutely lovely person. And she *adored* Peter. There was this little short guy, you know, tubby. And they absolutely adored one another. He went down one Sunday to see a cottage. He said, 'We want a cottage and we want a dog.' And he used to bring this dog to rehearsals. Behaved beautifully. And used to sit quietly during rehearsals.

As a young man, Peter Glaze's son Tony briefly worked in his step-mother's office:

Oh, she was a lovely person, April. She was a 'people person', she was one of those people. She was in the agency job because she enjoyed it. She loved the theatre and all the rest of it. But she was really empathetic, good with people. She was actually helping people to manage their careers and advise them. She wasn't just finding a job and taking the money. She was very, very good at what she did.

On Saturday 31st October 1964 Peter Glaze returned to the stage of London's Windmill Theatre, where his comedy career had first taken off, to attend its very last performance. He took the final curtain amongst a line-up of former Windmill comics that included Arthur English, Dick Emery, Bill Kerr, Richard Murdoch, Harry Secombe, Eric Barker and Alfred Marks.

Crackerjack continued weekly through to the end of 1964, apart from Christmas Day. But even then, not everyone had a week off. At midday, Leslie Crowther was hosting *Meet the Kids* from Hackney Hospital, with

Peter Glaze and the Bert Hayes Trio (a cut-down version of his Octet) which included bass player Ron Prentice:

> They were live Christmas Day. You had to get up at four in the morning and drive all the way out to the other side of London, to the hospital. Rehearse and go on the air live at twelve o'clock, and then drive home and hope they'd left some Christmas lunch for you.

Into 1965 – and the line-up of pop guests just got stronger and stronger. Freddie and the Dreamers, Gerry and the Pacemakers, Georgie Fame and the Blue Flames. Singer Pip Hinton met them all and more besides:

> Just across the road was an Italian restaurant. I had my first spaghetti bolognaise there. It was all the fashion that time, to have spaghetti bolognaise. And we all used to go there after the show. Of course Leslie couldn't because he was doing two shows – I don't know how he did it – two shows a night at the Victoria Palace. And I met some wonderful people – Sammy Davis – all the people that were rehearsing there at the same time, doing their own television shows at the BBC. Ah, that was wonderful! We were a very happy company.

For the pop acts *Crackerjack* and *Top of the Pops* were *the* shows to appear on. A sizeable TV audience of all ages that could help propel your new single up the charts. But, successful as *Crackerjack* was, it didn't stop the odd critic (in this case Bill Edmund of *The Stage*) having the occasional swipe:

> The sketches on BBC1's *Crackerjack* contained some of the weakest humour ever foisted on children, or men and women if it comes to that. Indeed, one small girl had brought her doll along in case it was needed and during the contests – which vied with *Beat the Clock* for the wooden spoon – I feel sure she must have sought comfort in it.

But this was all part and parcel of working in children's television, as Pip was only too aware:

> I remember going up in the lift with somebody – I think it was P. J. Kavanagh, the writer. He said to me very quietly, he said, 'You should get out of *Crackerjack*.' I said, 'Pardon?' He said, 'You should get out of *Crackerjack*.' 'Why?' 'Because you'll be known as a children's entertainer if you stay there any longer.'

At the end of the series, Pip did get out of *Crackerjack*. Not from fear of typecasting, but because of the imminent arrival of her second son, who was already giving the director a few logistical problems:

> When I got pregnant my husband said, 'What are they going to do now?' And I said, 'Well, I'm told they're going to do a lot of window-boxes. And I'll come on sideways.'

After bringing up her family, Pip Hinton returned to the stage in several musicals, plus a season with the Royal Shakespeare Company. Her presence was especially missed by Jillian Comber:

> In my book she was the best of the girl singers. She just had the right bubble. She could sing anything and was very, very professional. But also very generous in her working. This is what made it quite happy, because it wasn't, 'Oh God, it's my bit. It's your bit. Is the camera going to be on me?'

*

Series 11 of *Crackerjack* was even longer than the last. For the first time, but not the last, it ran for 26 weekly episodes. Now Peter Whitmore was in charge and, writing in the *Radio Times*, he detailed the minimal changes to this series, including news of the show's original producer Johnny Downes:

> Johnny has now left us to work in Australia and I am delighted to have the chance to continue his good work.
>
> On the musical side we welcome a newcomer to the programme, Valerie Walsh. Valerie, a vivacious redhead, has recently returned from New York where she was appearing in the Broadway production of *Oh What a Lovely War*.

For this series, Leslie's intro has rather more of a dramatic build-up: 'From the stage of the Television Theatre … Yes, it's *Crackerjack*!' Then it's straight into Valerie Walsh's opening number – *Put Your Shoes on, Valerie* (basically *Put Your Shoes on, Lucy* with some self-penned amendments):

> Put your shoes on Valerie, I have been so often told.
> I mustn't do a Sandie Shaw because I'm sure to catch a cold.
> Put your shoes on Valerie, you're appearing on the telly.
> Leslie Crowther's watching and I'm shaking like a jelly.

Apart from a long association with Joan Littlewood's Theatre Workshop, including the production of *Oh What a Lovely War* that transferred to Broadway, Valerie was also an experienced performer in West End musical theatre. Her *Crackerjack* opening number (a song-and-dance routine) usually came from a musical:

It was incredibly difficult finding songs, because all songs are love songs. So to sing a song for children and not make it at all sexy was really – you know – it took a bit of thinking. I remember singing to a snowman, with snow all round and winter coats, singing *Button Up your Overcoat.* So everything had to be totally non-sexy.

But I've got one funny memory. I had a big white poodle called Brandy and he was a real softie and he was lovely. And one week, I decided I would do *Tea for Two*, but with Brandy on the settee to the side of me, and sing the song to Brandy all the time. And he was very well behaved, and very loving. And we did the dress rehearsal – 'Tea for two and two for tea.' And halfway through the song – the middle eight, which was usually a sort of dance bit – I was with Brandy on the sofa, giving him a cup of tea out of the saucer, which he drank. And that was fine. And at the end of the song, I'd sing, 'Can't you see how happy … we … would … be.' Turned around, and blew just very gently into Brandy's nose, and he always kissed me if I blew on his nose. So I'd arranged that I would, at the very end, blow on his nose, and he kissed me as the song finished, and that was that and it was a lovely end.

Now, we did that in rehearsals, and we came to do the actual show which happened about an hour later. Anyway, we went all through the song with Brandy. I gave him cuddles and kisses, and all the while singing to him. I poured out his tea into the saucer. And he went down, took one lap of the saucer, and just disgustedly turned his back – because the prop man must have had an assistant, who got props all ready for the actual show, and in the teapot they hadn't put real tea. He just put a brown liquid, thinking that we didn't use it. And, whatever the brown liquid was, I mean Brandy just thought it was disgusting, turned his back on me, turned his back on the camera, and just sort of sulked. I had to sing the last half of the song, and I couldn't make him turn round and kiss me or anything. And, oh dear, what a pity it didn't work! And you couldn't go back, not without going through the whole show.

At that time the shows were still taped 'as live'. It was too technically complicated and expensive to retake an individual song or sketch. So, as with any stage show, mishaps just had to be dealt with and improvised around:

We did all the funny sketches and, of course, there was always space for things to go a bit wrong – running around the set and chasing each other up and down stairs and in and out of windows. All those sort of things. But nothing we couldn't cope with. No one broke a leg.

In *The BBC Book of Crackerjack* Leslie Crowther told of a hospital sketch when things went more than 'a bit wrong'. Leslie was the hospital patient and a burly actor was the hospital visitor who had come to cheer him up:

At one point this actor was supposed to describe a wrestling match and in his excitement demonstrate some of the holds on me. Well, he got a bit over-excited and threw me out of the bed. I landed head first on the concrete studio floor, got up, and didn't remember much about the rest of the sketch.

Valerie Walsh, like Ronnie Corbett before her, was able to combine *Crackerjack* with late-night cabaret at Danny La Rue's club:

I worked with Danny La Rue for ten years while I was doing musicals and things. Because at Danny's we didn't start the show till something like twelve-thirty, one o'clock. I never got home till half-past-two, three o'clock. Yes, I was doing Danny's in those years. But, you know, when you're young …

Valerie quickly found that starring in *Crackerjack* gave her far wider recognition than she'd had in the theatre:

My husband and I went to see the Rosetta stone – it was on display at the British Museum for the first time. And I was in the queue with my husband, waiting to see it, and there was a whole gang of schoolchildren came in. Because it was during the *Crackerjack* days. And the children all sort of mobbed around us, all wanting autographs.

Valerie was definitely of the opinion that it was Leslie Crowther, rather than producer Peter Whitmore, who was the driving force behind the whole show:

Leslie did all the driving, I think. Peter Whitmore I just remember as a jolly nice sort of army character, you can imagine him wanting to be the major in the army, that sort of feller. And I used to stand and spy on all the things Leslie and Peter did. It was wonderful, and it always stayed with me.

Leslie and Peter's opening spot in that first show sees them admiring the current *Radio Times* which has honoured the new series with their photo on the front cover:

PETER: It took the photographer all day to take that.
LESLIE: I know. Even then he missed the last bus home.
PETER: It was worth it. He's definitely caught my personality.
LESLIE: I wish he'd caught the last bus home!

Exactly halfway through the series came the usual *Christmas Crackerjack*, though *The Stage* wasn't impressed that the advertised 'Special Christmas Party' featured only a small select group of party-hatted children at tables laden with food and drink:

The children in the audience were there just to applaud and gaze with envy at the 'do' going on onstage. This was a great mistake – producer Peter Whitmore should have known that at a children's party there should be no children, so to speak, pressing their noses against the window gazing in. Besides, it spoilt the illusion.

Otherwise it was a jolly affair, with Leslie Crowther and Peter Glaze being very amusing, and especially with a sketch of a ring which dropped into the bowl of punch, the trifle and down Crowther's trousers.

Another familiar *Crackerjack* tradition made its debut this series. After the success of a speeded-up film sequence of Leslie in a previous series, he and Peter Whitmore decided to write and film some fast-motion silent movies, starring Leslie and Peter Glaze. As Jean Crowther recalls, this was one case of Leslie taking his work home with him:

We did one of those at our house at the coast. We did one in the back garden of our house in Twickenham. We did one in our piano teacher's house – the removal one, I think it was – charming man, taught our children piano. And, bless his heart, he allowed us to do one there. I mean, he must have been mad! I suppose the Beeb paid him, I don't know.

Two of these mini-movies ('The Playground' and 'Badminton') were so popular they were repeated at the end of the series. As Leslie wrote in *The BBC Book of Crackerjack*, filming in public locations tended to attract a lot of attention:

The sight of two raving idiots playing about on slides and swings in a children's playground was enough to interest the entire neighbourhood. We filmed all day in a London park, and had a bigger audience than the one we get in the Television Theatre! It's a good thing it was a silent film, otherwise you might have heard some of the rude comments on our performances!

Leslie also continued to write the musical finales with a vast range of historical settings and geographical locations. Every week a fresh challenge for both set designer and costume department. *The BBC Book of Crackerjack* listed a small selection of Jillian Comber's roles during this series:

She played the parts (amongst others) of a chimney sweep, Squire Trelawney (in *Treasure Island*), a royal lady-in-waiting, a Victorian parlourmaid, one of Leonardo da Vinci's art students, a Chinese girl Magnolia Blossom, a Swiss Mobile Ski Policewoman, Aramis of *The Three Musketeers*, and the first woman astronaut on the moon! So whatever disguises she finds herself in during the series, nothing will surprise her!

Responsible for many of the sets was Peter Kindred, who was both new to the BBC and new to *Crackerjack*:

It was about the first thing I ever did as a designer. A design assistant I think I was, made up to an acting designer. The two of us, me and Judy Steele, we took it alternately. Each episode needed a new set. I do remember doing a shop once, a complete shop. It had a gauze in front of it, so it looked like the outside of the shop. Then they changed the lighting and they were inside the shop, all dancing about.

I suppose we must have worked about a month in advance. Drawings had to be done and it had to be estimated and costed. And then sent off to a contractor to make. A script would be there. They'd all sit down and discuss it. And then you'd go away and come up with some ideas of how you think it should look. And then you started drawing it up. You'd always do a plan, there'd be a floor plan, showing where it was going to go, and where they're entering and coming out, where they're going to put the cameras and the lighting. And they might even lay it out in the rehearsal room, various props and chairs, and where the door was. And make a line on the floor where the set was. So they knew what they were going to do when they came to the theatre.

You'd choose all the props and everything. You'd go out and you'd choose all the furniture. All the pictures that go on the wall. All the bits and pieces that go to make up a complete set. If you needed anything like a stuffed elephant or whatever, you'd have to go out to a hiring company and get that sort of thing in. But a lot of stuff was from our own props department.

The 1972 *Crackerjack Annual* gives a good impression of the intense creative bustle on recording day – all the more intense because it was a late afternoon recording, rather than the usual evening recording of adult variety shows:

> Throughout the day, during rehearsals, scenery was being painted or moved, lights were being set in position, last-minute alterations to sets and costumes were often being made and the performers were trying to remember their lines – it was always a fight against time.
>
> Each item had a different setting, and these all had to be set, and then 'struck' (moved out of the way) in a very confined space. Very often the scenery flats or cloths were 'flown' – that is, they were attached by wires to pulleys high up in the roof of the studio. And they were lowered in at the press of a button, and lifted up out of the way at the end of each item. This has to be done very carefully to avoid knocking against the studio lights, which are also suspended from the roof.

Designer Peter Kindred would be working right up until the last minute:

> You'd watch the whole show being rehearsed on the screens in the control room. You'd watch it through to make sure everything was alright before the recording. We were looking at it and saying, 'Oh, I think we could improve it if we hung that drape differently, or moved that picture.' You're trying to create the best image you can. So we'd be there all day long, until the recording. And we'd probably stay on, because we got on with everybody so well, to make sure the recording was OK and go home afterwards.
>
> I remember it was a lot of fun. It was one of the first things I ever did after joining the BBC. Peter Glaze and Leslie Crowther were good fun to work with. And I got on well with Judy Steele – we enjoyed doing it together. So it was quite a jolly show to do.

As previously mentioned, when Eamonn Andrews left, so did *Double or Drop*. The game that replaced it required an additional hostess, and for this series actress Sheelagh McGrath was brought in:

> I was the *Jig-Jak* girl. *Jig-Jak* was a game where schoolchildren had to answer questions and each time they answered correctly I had to place a piece of the jigsaw puzzle on a large board, which eventually completed a picture of a famous TV show, such as a scene from *The Dick Van Dyke Show*.

One day I put a piece of the jigsaw in the wrong place. But the pieces were so big, and I couldn't see from where I was standing that it was incorrect. The audience fell about and Leslie said, 'Hmm, Sheelagh, I think that's the wrong piece!' I was so embarrassed but there was nothing left to do but laugh!

One of the *Jig-Jak* contestants was Phil Appleton, then a pupil at Haberdashers' Aske's School in Elstree. Earlier in the show he'd competed in an elimination game:

We had to put balloons in a box attached to our backs. I passed that test and went head-to-head against the winning girl from the other team. Whenever we answered a question correctly, a piece of jigsaw from a celebrity face was put up on a magnetic board. I won the contest by getting the most pieces, although I couldn't guess the face. I won a Merit microscope set and, of course, a *Crackerjack* pencil. In addition, I got to chat with the other winning contestant who was very pretty.

The guest spot of the show was filled by an ever-stronger line-up of pop acts. And hostess Sheelagh McGrath got to meet them all:

I remember holding Manfred Mann's spectacles at his request, while he played, which was a great honour! However, barefooted Sandie Shaw was a very temperamental lady and had a meltdown on one particular show. Stevie Winwood with the Spencer Davis Group was charismatic. Then we had The Ivy League on one week and I ended up partying with them after the show.

Once, on the way out of the stage door with some of the others, feeling the night air of Shepherds Bush on my face, I heard someone shout, 'Get their autographs!' So I signed away and as I walked off I heard someone say, 'Who's she?' Oh the ignominy of it all!

A particularly memorable guest – certainly to Jean Crowther – was Tom Jones, who caused producer Peter Whitmore and director Richard Evans a few headaches:

I remember with Tom Jones, Peter Whitmore was worried about all the gyrating of the hips. Though the mothers would like it, they were a bit worried about the children. And Tom's agent said, 'No, no, no, he's doing *Over the Sea to Skye*.' And he started doing it, and then suddenly – Dmm! Dmm! – and the hips started going!

Leslie's autobiography concludes the story:

Lulled into a false sense of security, the camera pulled back to reveal him in his full-frontal glory – whereupon he started to produce such pelvic thrusts and hip gyrations that they immediately cut to a puzzling shot of his left ear.

Shortly after the end of the series, Sheelagh McGrath got married – and Leslie, Peter and Jillian came to the wedding. Sheelagh continued to make a few TV appearances (including *Doctor Who* and *Emergency Ward Nine*, a play by Dennis Potter). She's now an author living in Australia.

Valerie Walsh went on to appear in West End comedy musical *Come Spy With Me* alongside her late-night cabaret chum Danny La Rue. In the early 1980s she was reunited with Leslie Crowther onstage, when she portrayed singers Florrie Forde and Vera Lynn in *Bud 'n' Ches* – a play about The Crazy Gang, with Bernie Winters as Bud Flanagan and Leslie Crowther as Chesney Allen.

*

Some catchphrases happen overnight. Some take a little longer. 'Yes, it's *Crackerjack*,' was a perfectly adequate way of getting things started, especially as it guaranteed a vociferous response from the audience, but it was never destined for TV immortality. However, at the start of series 12 in October 1966, Leslie Crowther had virtually nailed it:

It's Friday … It's Five O'Clock … Yes, it's *Crackerjack*!

Of course, he reckoned without the TV schedulers. After two weeks, *The News* was shifted from 5.55 pm to 5.50, and *Junior Points of View* was moved to before (rather than after) *Crackerjack*, giving it the new starting time of 5.05. Then, after the tenth show, *Junior Points of View* switched back to following *Crackerjack*, which now began at 4.55. It was enough to make Leslie Crowther swear, which (of course) a *Crackerjack* host would never do. Although, as Leslie told Terry Wogan on his TV chat show, there were exceptions:

On the technical run, before the live show, we used to get rid of all the traumas about doing material that had to be shaped, quite rightly, for children, by 'pepping up' the technical run with material that would not be acceptable for children, or anybody else. But this – I can't use the words, obviously, because … for reasons … well, I can't – but I actually went out and said something like: 'It's Fr****iday, it's Five to **** Five, and it's

Cracker****jack!' And Tom Sloan, the Director of Light Entertainment, was in the audience, and he said, 'Thank you very much. I've just brought fifty Girl Guides to watch the show.'

Jean Crowther can recall only one instance of Leslie being reprimanded for using bad language on air:

> Somebody rang the BBC and complained that Leslie Crowther had used a vulgar expression. He'd said, 'Oh pooh!' to Peter Glaze. I mean, when you think of nowadays, unbelievable! He was terribly amused by that. He came home and said he'd been hauled over the coals because he'd said, 'Oh pooh.'

Having got the show started, Leslie proceeds to introduce the show's new resident singer. Ever since Pearl Carr and Teddy Johnson, *Crackerjack* vocalists had epitomised the music of their era. And if you wanted someone that embodied the pop scene of the mid-to-late 1960s, then you couldn't have done better than Christine Holmes.

Very much in the Lulu and Sandie Shaw mould, Christine had started her pop career while still at school. She'd already released a number of singles when she became presenter on *Gadzooks! It's All Happening* – an early-evening pop show on BBC2, a channel that was little over a year old when the programme began. Of the many big-name pop acts that appeared on *Crackerjack*, Christine had met most of them previously on *Gadzooks!*

She also created the title role in West End musical *Charlie Girl*, playing a tomboy-turned-Cinderella character, opposite singer and actor Joe Brown and veteran stage and screen star Anna Neagle. When she joined *Crackerjack*, Christine Holmes was still just 17:

> The BBC came to see *Charlie Girl* and watched me in it, and then offered me the position. Mind you, I did nag the agent a lot. I was getting a bit bored with doing the same show every night. I think it was my persistence as a youngster, wanting to expand.

So, in addition to her nightly appearances in *Charlie Girl*, Christine came on board for the 26-week run of *Crackerjack*. Like Leslie, she was able to juggle both shows, apart from the recording day itself:

> I had to get permission from Harold Fielding, who was producer of *Charlie Girl*, to have my Thursday matinee off to record *Crackerjack*. What I gave back, for permission to have my matinee off and my understudy go on, I had

to agree to a complete run of the play. It was one way to save money for a deposit on an apartment, because I never had time to spend any money!

It was a tough bargain, because *Charlie Girl* was destined for a long run. But the repetitive nature of her evenings was offset by a TV show that offered new songs and new sketches every single week. Christine's opening number was generally taken from the pop charts, and the choice of number was pretty much left to her:

> The only time I did have a problem, well twice actually, once when I wanted to do a song from a musical comedy – and they said, if possible, don't do it from a musical comedy, because we have to pay much more in royalties. It was a very tight budget in those days.
>
> And the other time, I wanted to do *Puff the Magic Dragon*. We had a producer/director called Peter Whitmore, and he said, 'Oh, I don't think I can let you sing *Puff the Magic Dragon*. It's about smoking marijuana.' And of course I'd no idea. I was as green as the hills. I didn't know it was about that, I thought it was about this little cartoon character. So I never sang it.

Bert Hayes and his Octet were back, though halfway through the series they became Bert Hayes and his Orchestra. This perhaps was in recognition of the many chart-topping acts he provided live accompaniment for – enabling him to draft in the odd additional session musician when required. Christine recalls Bert Hayes with particular fondness:

> Bert was a very open musician. For somebody as young as I was then, for him to embrace any ideas that I might have … wonderful! He was my partner in crime. I'd throw an idea at him – a musical idea – and he would just expand it and he was a delight to work with. I used to love our band calls. I really enjoyed it.

Jillian Comber is also full of praise for Bert and Christine's creative partnership:

> She came on like another pop star. She always sang pop numbers – and sang them practically better than the person that recorded them. And you could see Bert Hayes, the admiration pouring out of him. It was the biggest love of his life, to be able to play and have Christine sing so well. You could see that Bert Hayes thought she was the greatest, you could really see it. And I really thought – ah, the star of our show is Christine Holmes. She had that lovely

95

way with her. She was so engaging, so charismatic. But it was her singing voice. It was her capabilities of what she could do with her voice.

Although Christine Holmes was already acting and singing onstage, she had a lot to learn about performing comedy sketches, particularly on TV. And much of it she learnt from Leslie Crowther:

He would always come into rehearsals with a news bulletin. It would be completely off-the-wall. Nothing to do with the scripts we had to work with at that time. And he'd say, 'Oh, did you hear the news today? So-and-so's done this.' And then, before you knew where you were, there'd be some kind of interweaving of stuff.

And subliminal stuff as well. Very good subliminal stuff, where there'd be a joke in there, and only the cast would know what was going on because it came out of Leslie's head. He had this magic ... like Peter Glaze was marvellous at slapstick ... but Leslie could do slapstick with clever comedy as well. He adlibbed too. He was naughty. You had to watch him. You had to be aware that he might throw something in.

I learnt camera technique very quickly through watching somebody like Leslie, for example, who would use the camera to do a reaction occasionally, and actually look at the camera. And that gets a laugh as well. Don't forget, the live audience could see what the camera was shooting. So you're learning that craft or practising it as you go along, doing it each week. And I did that in my singing, and I did it in the sketches. You're just absorbing what the process is, and learning as you're going.

One member of the studio audience also credits Leslie Crowther for triggering her fascination with cameras. Susanna White (who went on to direct Emma Thompson in *Nanny McPhee and the Big Bang* and Benedict Cumberbatch in BBC mini-series *Parade's End*) recalled the moment in a 2016 interview with Stefan Pape on movie website *HeyUGuys.com*:

I was a Brownie at the time, and we went to watch *Crackerjack* being recorded and I remember all of the other girls try and get up on stage and win prizes, but I saw a red light come on a camera and saw that it was a single shot on a presenter and I thought, 'Wow, that's how it happens.'

This massive lightbulb went on in my head and I went to the library and got a book out on how to make films. Then I begged my parents to buy me a Super 8 camera. I was eight years old and I started making films with my friend – we did bike chases at the local recreation ground.

Singer Christine Holmes was particularly aware of the contribution made in the rehearsal process by Peter Glaze:

> He was just a very sweet, very kind man. He brought to the table what Leslie Crowther didn't. Peter always kept to the visual of the slapstick. And he would often check with Leslie, and pull him up and say, 'No, you can't do that. That's going to take too long. Let's not do it that way.' And Leslie was, 'Oh, yeah, fine, right. Off you go. Do it.' Peter was a wonderful pro. He'd worked on stage so very long in his career. So to go to a stage like the Shepherds Bush Empire, and just have a camera or two or three in front of you and by the side of you, was no skin off his nose at all. Because basically he was performing to a live audience, which it *was*. And that was his craft.

The first musical sketch of the series was a celebration of England's World Cup victory a few months earlier. After that it was any time, any place, anywhere. Every week a different historical period, and the appropriate outfit for Christine:

> We had a very sweet costume lady and she would always say, 'Well, Henry the Eighth wouldn't have worn that.' Or, 'The lady-in-waiting would be like this.' She would do manual adjustments, on the day even, to get the authenticity right. She was quite pedantic about it being right on the spot.

It just shows how dedicated every department was to producing a finale that looked historically accurate – even though Leslie's Henry the Eighth was far more likely to burst into a rendition of *Green Door* than *Greensleeves*.

Christmas Crackerjack was always something special, and the 1966 version took a good-natured potshot at a number of current TV shows, including one that had yet to be broadcast but was already courting controversy, as hinted at by Leslie in his introduction:

> As you must have heard, on the 28th December the BBC is presenting an all-star cast in *Alice in Wonderland*. What you may not have heard is that *Crackerjack* has pipped them to the post with our version of *Alice Through the Looking Glass*. So now, especially suitable for everybody, we present *Alice Through the Goggle Box*.

Crackerjack previously presented *Cleopatra* before the movie had finished shooting. Now they'd managed to slip their *Alice* into the schedules just a few days before Jonathan Miller's darkly disturbing and not particularly child-friendly version.

Christine Holmes, as Alice, wanders through a derelict fairground where she discovers a broken television set. She switches it on and Leslie, her fairy godmother, appears:

> I am the fairy goggle box. I come here to enchant ye.
> I'm not the Man from Uncle – I'm the little girl from Auntie.

Alice's adventures take her via *The Magic Roundabout, The Beverly Hillbillies* and *Dixon of Dock Green* – with a midway intermission for a *Fairy Snow* commercial. But the undoubted highlight is a *Doctor Who* take-off. Less than two months previously, the first *Doctor Who* regeneration had taken place, when original Doctor William Hartnell made way for Patrick Troughton. *Crackerjack*'s version sees Peter Glaze as Hartnell and Leslie Crowther as Troughton performing to the Beach Boys' *Good Vibrations*, whose Theremin-type oscillator is a pretty close match to *Doctor Who*'s radiophonic tones, and a mighty challenge for Bert Hayes and his musicians:

PETER: I'm the old Doctor Who.
LESLIE: I'm the new Who. We're not in Who's Who.
PETER: I'm not. Are you Who?
LESLIE: Yoohoo! Now tell me, who knows the old Who from the new Who?
PETER: There can be few who –
LESLIE: – can't tell which Who is which –
PETER: – or who.

Earlier in the show (armed with mistletoe and hoping for a kiss from Christine Holmes) Leslie closes his eyes, puckers up, and calls for Chris. At which point *Blue Peter* presenter Christopher Trace makes his entrance. Ann Purser of *The Stage* noted a distinct lack of chemistry (and not just of the sexual kind) between the two men:

> Interesting to compare the prissy approach of Christopher Trace with the relaxed mateyness of Leslie Crowther. The BBC likes Christopher Trace to be thought of as an elder brother – mine wasn't like that thank heavens, but a lot of self-important school prefects were. The difference between Trace and Crowther seems to pinpoint the still-existing division in the BBC's attitude towards Education and Entertainment, and never the twa' etc etc.

Also on the guest list were Christopher's fellow presenters Valerie Singleton and John Noakes, plus Johnny Morris and Tony Hart (both veterans from the early days of *Playbox*), and current *Doctor Who* companions Anneke Wills and Michael Craze. As any self-respecting Whovian will tell you, the role of Third Sensorite (in a 1964 William Hartnell adventure filmed shortly after Eamonn Andrews' departure from *Crackerjack*) was played, astonishingly enough, by Peter Glaze. The actors playing the Sensorites wore rubber masks completely covering their heads – but the most sinister Sensorite of all (as well as the stoutest) is clearly distinguishable as Peter.

When TV ratings for the top five children's programmes of December 1966 (all BBC1 shows) were published, *Crackerjack* took third place with 4,550,000 and *Doctor Who* was fourth with 4,400,000.

Throughout the series there was a big pop act each week – sometimes even two, when Manfred Mann and Cat Stevens appeared on the same show. *Crackerjack* was not just widening its appeal amongst viewers, Jillian Comber also noticed a change in the studio audience:

> We used to have schools – they used to come in with lovely little tunics and ties. And then it used to fill up with the Shepherds Bush 'children', who were in hot pants and really came to see the pop groups. Because we had somebody who was in the Top Ten every single week. Announced by Leslie Crowther, they came on and did it, and then they went. And then all the, you know, hot-pants children – we used to try and keep the girls away from the boys, and the boys away from the girls. Yes, really, we did! They came to see Herman's Hermits. I remember Herman standing in a little blue suit. He was terrified as anything. But, I mean, the girls were very pushy at that time. *Very* pushy.

Jillian also recalls some of the actors who played minor supporting roles in the sketches. They were seldom big names. Well, not at the time, anyway:

> I can always remember standing with Ronnie Barker. He came and played a policeman in our sketch. And he stood there, and I was talking to him. And he said, 'God, if only I could just get a show like this. I *really* wish I could get a show like this. This is what you need in television. You need your own show.' And that was Ronnie Barker, before he teamed up with Ronnie Corbett or anybody. And Ronnie Barker and Leslie Crowther became exceptionally good friends.

The 200th edition of *Crackerjack* was broadcast on 20th January 1967, when Leslie told the *Radio Times*:

> I hate those sort of seaside shows run by a nauseating 'Uncle'. A newsreader on radio once said, 'It's time to hand you back to Uncle Leslie.' I could have throttled him. I'm just Leslie, thirty-three years old, doing a job of work, trying to entertain people of any age. And thanks to my work on *Crackerjack* I've enjoyed goodwill with adult audiences because their attitude seems to be, 'Any friend of my children is a friend of mine.'

In addition to *Crackerjack* Leslie was keen to cultivate his adult following. He performed late-night cabaret and, shortly after the end of the series, he took the starring role in his first situation comedy: *The Reluctant Romeo*. Following a *Comedy Playhouse* pilot the previous year, this six-part series chronicles the exploits of Thomas Jones, an ordinary man with a desk job. However 'Tom' Jones, like his literary forebear, is constantly pursued by a bevy of doting female admirers.

The critics hated it! Alice Frick of *The Stage* called it 'the worst *comedy* show I've ever had to review'. And if Leslie had hoped to distance himself from his *Crackerjack* image for a brief while, then he'd reckoned without Stanley Reynolds of *The Guardian* pulling him relentlessly back, describing it as:

> ... *Crackerjack* but unfortunately without the singing and dancing. What is left is the puns, ham-fisted slapstick and, of course, the basically asinine plot. Personally I don't see why *The Reluctant Romeo* wastes so much time with plot and attempting some sort of realism. It would have been more adventurous, and I trust more entertaining, if they had just done a grown-up version of those *Crackerjack* skits with the cast bursting into pop songs at the slightest nod from the plot.

More successful was Leslie's next career move which, like *Crackerjack*, involved both children and pop songs. The week before the start of the autumn 1967 series of *Crackerjack*, a new BBC radio station came into existence. Peopled by a good number of former 'pirate radio' DJs, Radio 1 began broadcasting on Saturday 30th September 1967. Many people know that the first DJ on air was Tony Blackburn. Far fewer are aware that the second show that day was *Junior Choice* presented by Leslie Crowther. Even more interesting is the next day, when Leslie is back with another edition from 9.00 to 10.00 am, followed by Ed Stewart (who later took over *Junior Choice*) for two hours, and then at midday *Family Favourites* with Michael Aspel. Yes, three *Crackerjack* hosts in a row.

Jean Crowther remembers those *Junior Choice* days with particular fondness:

> I liked it because, on the way back from *Junior Choice*, he used to go past the cemetery on the South Circular. And he would always stop, because there was a man who had a stand selling flowers outside the cemetery, and Leslie would *always* come back on Saturday mornings with huge bunches of flowers for me.

*

Throughout the next series of *Crackerjack*, Leslie spent each evening onstage in a frenetic Brian Rix farce. At a time when the *Radio Times* used to detail the theatrical engagements of artistes at the bottom of the programme listing, it's intriguing to speculate what Leslie's infant fans thought when they read, week after week, 'Leslie Crowther is in *Let Sleeping Wives Lie* at the Garrick Theatre.'

New to this series was the final quiz *Going To Town*, briefly described in the *Radio Times*:

> The youngsters will be racing from various parts of Britain to London – on an electronic map. For every correct answer, a competitor's route is lit up a little more.

There were more Leslie and Peter movies – with titles like 'Seaside' and 'Shed' – and more Peter Glaze lectures, scripted by Bob Block, including one on rodents:

PETER: Of course, mice are the best known of all rodents.
LESLIE: I bought one very nice mice at a reasonable price, but he got cold as ice, so he ran away twice.
PETER: Just a minute, it's *mouse*, not mice – when it's only one, the 'ice' becomes 'ouse'.
LESLIE: Oh, in that case I'd better say it right. I bought one very nouse mouse at a reasonable prouse, but he got cold as ouse, so he ran away twouse.

There was a rather learned piece in *The Stage* by Ann Purser, endeavouring to analyse the wide appeal of *Crackerjack*:

> A theory has lately been put forward to explain why the lower classes don't read books – because there aren't any books about lower-class children, who like reading about themselves and not about posh people.
>
> One of the secrets of *Crackerjack's* success is that it is unashamedly aimed at the lower social levels. Leslie Crowther and Peter Glaze work very well as a comic pair. Here is much evidence of the earthy touch, the commonness, the South London accent. Crowther's and Glaze's trousers fell off in absolutely predictable circumstances, but oh, how the children laughed and laughed.

Shortly before the final show of the series, it was announced that Leslie Crowther would be leaving *Crackerjack*. He explains the circumstances in his autobiography:

> After eight years or so I felt I was getting typecast as a children's entertainer. I knew it was time to make a clean break. Tom Sloan, then Head of Light Entertainment at the BBC, was furious when I told him of my decision and did his level best to talk me out of it. 'Do you know how much So-and-so is making doing children's television in America?' he said. I pointed out that the TV audience over here wasn't anything like it was in the States, and that anyway my mind was made up. He eventually relented and let me off the hook.

After the disappointing reception of Leslie's sitcom debut *The Reluctant Romeo*, it's interesting that his final *Crackerjack* sketch is a reworking of *Romeo and Juliet* with appropriate, if slightly dodgy, Shakespearean dialogue:

LESLIE: But soft! What light through yonder window breaks? It is the East and Juliet is the sun.

PETER: You are wrong, sir – Juliet is the daughter. And if your purpose here is to propose marriage, be warned – first you must ask her father.

LESLIE: But I do not wish to marry her father.

There's even a last-minute defiant use of strong language:

CHRISTINE: Oh woe!

JILLIAN: Oh no!

LESLIE: Oh pooh!

However, with a suitably anachronistic burst of Amen Corner's recent chart hit *Bend Me, Shape Me* and the slightly classier *Thou Swell, Thou Witty*, all ends happily.

Jean Crowther was aware Leslie had mixed feelings about leaving the show:

> He was reluctant to go, but he knew it was holding him back. He hadn't really gone into the theatre to become a children's entertainer.

Amongst the many who were sad to see Leslie go was *Daily Mail* TV critic Barry Norman:

> When the show finally returns it will lack Leslie Crowther, a splendid children's entertainer with the gift of befriending his audience on his own terms. They love him dearly because he never condescends to them. He is an adult and they are not and, both sides accepting these facts, they get on happily with the business of communicating with each other.

Throughout Leslie's later career he did little that couldn't be considered family entertainment. Most of his subsequent television work was for ITV, including the far more successful sitcom *My Good Woman* with Sylvia Syms, and culminating with gameshow *The Price is Right*. As Jean Crowther remembers, there was never a time in his career when he wasn't instantly recognised:

> It started with '*Crackerjack!*' being shouted when he was around. And then he did the Stork margarine commercial – could you tell the difference between Stork and butter? – so you'd get people shouting, 'I can tell the difference!' And then it was, 'Come on down!' There was always something being shouted wherever we went.

6
The Only Virgin
He'd Auditioned

Australia 1966 – 1968

I N 1965, PRODUCER Johnny Downes had left the BBC to work in
Australia. Leslie Crowther, who always acknowledged the debt he owed
Johnny for launching his TV career, had become a close family friend.
Nevertheless, on the day of departure, it came as quite a surprise when Leslie
turned up at the station at six in the morning to wish Johnny and his wife
bon voyage.

In October the following year, the Australian Broadcasting Commission
unveiled its exciting line-up of late-afternoon television programming. ABC
was a similar body to the BBC which, like its British counterpart, had started
life in the 1920s as a Company. But, whereas the BBC changed directly from
Company to Corporation, ABC went from Company to Commission and
only became a Corporation in 1983.

The ABC-TV schedule included a mix of home-grown comedy and
drama, such as the adventure series *Magic Boomerang*, together with a few
imports, like America's talking horse *Mr Ed* and Britain's itinerant Time
Lord *Doctor Who*. Every Friday at 5.30 pm there would be an episode of
Crackerjack. But not, as you might expect, a rescreening of old BBC
episodes. No, this would be a brand-new live Australian version.

Nan Musgrove of *The Australian Women's Weekly* was in the studio
audience of that first show:

Crackerjack is the gayest of the new ABC-TV shows specially produced for their new late-afternoon family programming. It is a fun show for teenagers, their parents, and young brothers and sisters. I was impressed when I saw *Crackerjack* being made. It had polish, smooth production, beautiful sets, an impressive cast.

Reg Livermore, who heads the permanent cast of four, is an accomplished actor, dancer and revue artist. As well as the four permanents, *Crackerjack* has guest stars – and what guest stars! I was sitting next to one young girl when the guest appeared one day. 'I'll die,' she moaned ecstatically. 'It's Normie.' Besides guests like Normie Rowe, *Crackerjack* has songs, comedy sketches, topical skits, competitions and prizes.

With its games, sketches and heartthrob pop stars, the Australian *Crackerjack* was practically identical in format to its British counterpart. And that was largely due to the fact that not only had Johnny Downes sold the format to ABC, but he was also on hand to make sure all the winning ingredients were successfully blended. Host Reg Livermore (like Leslie Crowther) was a fast-rising star, caught at just the right time:

I was beginning to make a name for myself in the theatre here – certainly I was becoming known for my versatility. Immediately prior to being offered the role as host of *Crackerjack* I was appearing in a popular topical revue: *A Cup of Tea, a Bex, and a Good Lie Down.* The style of that show encompassed musical numbers, sketch material, everything *Crackerjack* was to offer its viewers. And I guess I was judged to have a winning enough personality to play host.

I can't say I remember meeting Johnny Downes particularly. Obviously there was some such fellow at our first assembly, someone to acquaint us with the facts, how to approach the job, to gee us along, enthuse us. John Wynne-Jones became our executive producer, Tom Jeffrey was our director. Tom had already been involved at the ABC directing drama features.

As Reg recalls, the British and Australian versions of the show were strikingly similar, at times almost word-for-word:

I have a feeling some of the early scripts might have come from the BBC version. Later I wrote many of them. Particularly I enjoyed creating the extended sketches – the musical finale – that brought the show to an end each week. These were very much reflective of my theatrical disposition. As for general programme similarities I can only assume that our version must have been a dead ringer of the BBC version. Until we put our own stamp on the programme, which we did soon enough.

We had kids in the audience. I think they were groups from various schools round Sydney. They were enthusiastic, willing and quite excitable, especially when we featured a pop singer. And good sports when they played the games. Since it was live to air I never had any idea of how the programme started. Years later somebody from the ABC secured for me a copy of one of the taped shows. That was the first time I had seen the titles, heard the intro music, etc. Quite a surprise. A shock actually!

Another British tradition was the physical contrast between comedian and stooge – tall and short, thin and fat. But never before on *Crackerjack* had a short thin comic been paired with a tall fat stooge – namely 23-stone, six-foot-six Yorkshireman Michael Boddy. It was like someone had inflated Peter Glaze with a bicycle pump!

Other cast members were Judy Roberts and Sue Walker. Sue's recollections of Johnny Downes are clearer than Reg's, with very good reason:

Johnny Downes was in Sydney to get the show on, and was probably around for the best part of the first series. I remember he said he cast me because he thought I was the only virgin he'd auditioned. I didn't know what to make of that! I thought it was rather inappropriate and steered clear as much as possible.

We could all sing, dance and act. In Australia at that time most working actors had to have more than one string to their bow. The most employed actors at that time were working in radio, voice work. I was working in revue, as were Judy and Reg. I didn't know Michael Boddy at the start of *Crackerjack*, but he was a lovely man and a very valuable part of the team. I would say Reg was the 'star' – he couldn't help himself. He was – and is – a prodigious talent and I loved watching him work.

Reg Livermore (again like Leslie Crowther) doubled as principal comic and host. He steered the kids through the games, culminating in the jigsaw quiz *Jig-Jak*. And, as comic, he donned a tutu in a ballet spoof, became a suave James Bond, and dragged up with Michael Boddy as ugly sisters:

Michael Boddy was the perfect foil for me. We were extremely comfortable with what we were doing. I guess you'd have to say the show and the cast gave the impression of wholesomeness – as intended – but there was always a sense that some of the humour was specifically geared for the mums and dads who were watching with their kids at home, though we were careful not to go too far along that path. Over the hour it ran, the style and content moved from material that was specific for the kids watching at home, or in the studio, to something that was more encompassing by the time the adults had tuned in.

In August 1967, Nan Musgrove of *The Australian Women's Weekly* again turned her attentions to Reg Livermore and *Crackerjack*:

> Reg Livermore, who scored as compere of ABC-TV's teenage show *Crackerjack*, has hit the jackpot – he has gone adult, gone national, and taken the 7.15 pm Saturday night time-slot. *I'm Alright Now* is streamlined, glossy, well-dressed. It could be just what Saturday night TV is waiting for.

For Reg, this was an opportunity to be seized with both hands:

> The ABC offered me my own Saturday night variety show. That meant I couldn't continue with *Crackerjack*. I had enjoyed my time with it immensely, but even without *I'm Alright Now* coming into the picture, I think I was about ready to resume my place in the theatre where I really belonged.

Reg Livermore has continued to be busy in the theatre, having recently completed a lengthy run as Alfred Doolittle in *My Fair Lady* at Sydney, Brisbane and Melbourne – a production directed by Julie Andrews, the musical's original Eliza. In 1980 he brought his one-man cabaret to London, and received a scathing review from *Daily Express* critic William Spicer, a man apparently unaware of Reg's previous CV:

> He needs to find himself some creative new material (he writes his own) and drop the bump-and-grind burlesque which reminds me of nothing more than *Crackerjack* – without the sophistication!

For Reg, *Crackerjack* was a vital – if comparatively brief – stepping stone on the way up:

> For me it was about the camaraderie, being one of such a decent talented bunch, committed to turning out a quality product each week. And the reward of absolute enjoyment mirrored in the kids' faces. The kids were invariably great to play to and play with. Wonderful participants. They really wanted to be there.

*

Reg made his final *Crackerjack* appearance on April 7th 1967 and was replaced after Easter by new host James Smillie, a Glasgow-born presenter and singer, who had grown up in Australia. James had already worked with *Crackerjack* producer John Wynne-Jones:

> I did a television series with John, which was the first one that went national from Western Australia. It was called *Folk Cellar*, which I hosted and sang on. And then John left and went to Sydney. And, because he'd worked with me in Perth, I think he was instrumental in saying, 'Why don't you look at this bloke?' And at the time I was working in Melbourne and doing all sorts of things.

But, as the Australian press made abundantly clear, James was entering the show at a particularly difficult time:

> Few actors have had a tougher initiation to TV stardom than young Jim Smillie, new compere of Channel 2's children's show *Crackerjack*. It wouldn't have been so bad if *Crackerjack* had been riding the crest of a wave when Jim moved in. Then he'd have had a bit of latitude in which to regain control, in case of a tumble. But *Crackerjack* is sagging rather badly. This had little to do with Reg Livermore, who had a good following with those young viewers who did follow the show.
>
> After next Friday's show, the *Crackerjack* team go into recess for a month. And when they return, Jim has plenty of confidence that the problem will be licked. This is the first time Jim has worked with kids. Until he was signed up by the ABC, he had been a news reader and presentation announcer on Melbourne's Channel O. 'I've got it figured out, though,' he says. 'I've always liked the idea of entertaining children, and I think I can make out OK. The thing is you have to play up to adults, but with youngsters you can't be anything but yourself. I shall just try to be as natural as my script allows. There's no point in trying to emulate Reg. I've got to cut a completely new image.'
>
> Jim is settling down well with his *Crackerjack* team – tubby comic Michael Boddy and actresses Sue Walker and Jenene Watson. During their break they will get together with producer John Wynne-Jones and discuss possible changes in the *Crackerjack* format to try to attract higher ratings.

Jenene Watson had replaced Judy Roberts towards the end of Reg's series. Sue Walker remembers Jenene as: 'A tiny little thing with a huge voice – she fitted in really well.' Sue, herself, left the show shortly after James

Smillie's arrival – to join the cast of Reg Livermore's Saturday show *I'm Alright Now*. She later became Sue Gregson (this being the real surname of her husband, actor Michael Craig).

James Smillie was far from a carbon copy of Reg Livermore. Another newspaper piece paints a neat picture of the two *Crackerjack* hosts:

> Livermore and Smillie could not be more different. Livermore is 29, puck-like, with a versatile face and a rubbery elasticity in his movements, an alert mind and the ability to write his own scripts. Smillie at 22 is handsome in a stereotyped way, has a winning smile, a good baritone voice and a fondness for cricket and Australian rules football.

Journalist Harry Robinson – in an article headlined 'Crackerjim' – adds this observation:

> Jim Smillie looks older than Reg and more as though he's come from Marlboro country – but he's no less suitable.

James Smillie was taller and more dashing than Reg, but by no means as tall – and wide – as Michael Boddy. Michael was a tried and tested element of the show. And, as James recalls, so were the scripts:

> Mike Boddy and I sort of co-presented it and the scripts were written by a guy whose name was Bob Block. Because we used his scripts. They came to us with 'Leslie Crowther' on, and I would score out Leslie's name and put my own in. And basically the format was exactly the same as it was for the English version. And we used the same scripts. We did adapt some of them. And Michael, because he was a very clever writer, was quite adept at camouflaging them a little bit for the Australian market, but not really much. They were basically the same sketches and songs.

Apart from the odd sketch – like a Ned Kelly spoof, pitched slightly more obviously at the home crowd – the majority had the familiar historical settings that Australians could still relate to:

> Pirates, Dick Turpins, Tarzans, all sorts of crazy things. Whatever sketches Leslie was doing in those days, that's basically what we were doing. I was brought up on British history out in Australia when I was growing up. So back in those days people were pretty familiar with what was going on, whether Alfred was burning the cakes or Robin Hood or whatever, we were doing it.

Press listings of the time give us a flavour of the sketches, some of which have a more contemporary, or even futuristic, feel:

Crackerjack kicks off with Jim Smillie singing *Strike Up the Band*, followed by a sketch in which Jim, Michael Boddy, Jenene Watson and Gillian Hunter seem to be in danger of redundance from automation. A computer that has been bought to think up quiz questions gets a 'big head'. In another sketch Jim and Michael are taken in by a beautiful blonde who claims she is removing furniture for a neighbour and asks them to help. This they do, with disastrous results. The cast then turn back the clock to the days of the suffragettes demanding the right to vote, with Michael throwing his weight into chaining them to the iron fence of Parliament House.

At the end of the series, Michael Boddy decided to leave. 'I want to stick to writing – scripts, plays and books – in the future,' he told the press.

By the time *Crackerjack* returned for its proper run in October, it had lost every member of its original cast. As James Smillie remembers, it became a reduced ensemble. Not in number, but in mass:

There was a fellow called Barry Lovett who took over from Michael Boddy. And he was much smaller, more petite. More like Peter Glaze I guess. That style. Very different from Michael, but very good and very funny.

It was Barry Lovett's first television exposure, though he was an experienced theatre performer in everything from Shakespeare to Victorian melodrama. Jenene Watson also left early in the series, to be replaced by Penny Ramsey. A press photo of the new lineup was rather unkindly captioned:

The ABC's *Crackerjack* team: Jim Smillie, Barry Lovett, Penny Ramsey, Gillian Hunter – stars of a sugar-sweet series which neither offends nor excites viewers.

The revamped format made more of James Smillie's musical talents. He had a weekly Song Spot where he sang 'at least five songs each week'. The *Jig-Jak* quiz was still there, plus a regular star guest:

I do remember Jim Clark coming on, the racing-car driver. He brought the car on and I remember interviewing Jim. And it couldn't have been long after that, that he had that crash and died. But whoever was touring. Some of the visiting English artists who would be working at some of the major hotels or venues, and the Americans as well. They'd come on, they'd do their latest number, or a bit of a plug for whatever they were doing, and maybe I'd have a bit of a chat to them.

To coincide with the start of the series, ABC launched a special competition for viewers:

> To enter the national competition children must write a funny poem or limerick about the stars of the show. The five best entries will each win a record album, with *Crackerjack* dolls for consolation prizes.

The *Crackerjack* doll appears to be a uniquely Australian product. They were still giving out *Crackerjack* pencils to winners of *Jig-Jak*, but the *Crackerjack* doll was perhaps a less expensive runners-up prize. The little spiky-haired doll was possibly modelled on an early *Crackerjack* logo, that featured a jack-in-the-box bursting out of a cracker. Whatever it looked like, by the end of the year it had grown to Michael Boddy-like proportions, judging by the programme listing:

> *Crackerjack* has gone King-Size! ABC-TV's children's programme has developed the biggest *Crackerjack* doll ever. King *Crackerjack* is Jim Smillie's secret weapon for transforming evil people into modern citizens. Its potent force is directed at the diabolical Doctor Evil (Barry Lovett) and wicked Miss Gremlin (Gillian Hunter), two mad scientists who are planning to conquer the world with their disintegrator chair. Penny Ramsey innocently walks into their clutches seeking a love potion to win her dream lover, and becomes a guinea pig for the first experiment with the disintegrator chair. Jim and King *Crackerjack* arrive on the scene just in time to confront evil with good.

Crackerjack was currently going out at 5.40 pm, with the national news following at 6.30 pm prompt. For James Smillie and his team it wasn't always a simple matter to get the live show to run to time:

> You'd have the floor manager winding you up. Particularly when we had the quiz. 'For goodness sake, Jim, get through the questions so we can get into the final sketch.' And that was always the tricky thing. Sometimes we'd get almost to the end of the sketch, and all of a sudden you'd get the ABC News thing – which went 'Dum-dum-de-dum-dum-dum' – and we wouldn't be at the end of the show! So it would suddenly cut to the blinking news!

Crackerjack carried on into 1968 but, alas, no further than that. James Smillie had been with the show for about nine months:

> They pulled the plug on it, because they decided to take a children's television show called *Adventure Island*. And it was quite an expensive show to do. I had a two-year contract with ABC, so I subsequently went down to Melbourne for the final year of the contract and did *Adventure Island* for a year. It was a budget thing – and also they were spending a lot of money taking Reg over to a very high-production-value light-entertainment show. I think it was just a budget thing that eventually caused them to pull the plug.

And so ended Australia's brief flirtation with *Crackerjack*. Producer Johnny Downes' flirtation with Australia was even briefer – he was back working at the BBC well before James Smillie even joined the show.

James Smillie has had a busy career, starring in many stage plays and musicals as well as television dramas, in both Britain and Australia. Now living in Scotland, his *Crackerjack* days are half a world, and half a century, away. But, nonetheless, it is a period of his career that he remembers fondly:

> I spent a number of years in children's television in one way or t'other and it was probably some of the happiest times of my life. And you had that great freedom with *Crackerjack* – you could really go over the top. I just remember it with great joy.

7

I'll Make You Look Like Natalie Wood

1968 – 1970

I N EARLY JUNE 1968 *The Times* reported:

> Mr Michael Aspel is giving up his job as a BBC television news reader to present a new early evening weekly magazine programme, featuring people in the news, called *The Monday Show*. Mr Aspel will also take over from Mr Leslie Crowther as compere of the children's television programme *Crackerjack* when it returns in the autumn.

Both Eamonn and Leslie had been enormously important figures in the shaping of the show, and now Michael was to become only the third *Crackerjack* host in 13 years. Michael recalls the contrasting personalities of his predecessors:

> Eamonn was a very solid, very imposing man. He had a good sense of fun as well, but he wasn't an entertainer. That's the difference. Leslie Crowther *was* an entertainer. And then I followed him and, 'Here comes another non-entertainer.' Because I was a newsreader very shortly before that. But they spotted something wriggling to get out of me, I suppose.
>
> I wasn't burdened by too much gravitas. And I had been a radio actor for a couple of years. And newsreading, the serious bit, just got in the way. I

came to it just to stand in when Richard Baker was sick, and I did it for eight years, but that was never the intention. So I was really getting 'back on the road' as far as I was concerned.

Michael's acting experience would ensure his performance in the sketches lacked the self-consciousness of Eamonn Andrews. He wasn't a comedian, nor was he a children's entertainer. But, like Leslie Crowther, he was a family man:

I did have children of my own, so I knew how to entertain them. But it was a new world to me. And frightening, as many of the things I have done before, because it was so hugely popular. And children get very faithful to their presenters. When I first went on I just braced myself for this great wave of sound, 'Where's Leslie Crowther?' But, you know, the show was bigger than all of us.

When Christine Holmes joined the show, she had felt very much the baby of the team. Now, two years on, she was still the youngest member of the cast, but compared to Michael she was an old hand:

When we had Michael Aspel join us, he was terribly nervous. And I can remember Jillian and I really coddling him, you know, either side of him. And literally saying, 'No, it's going to be all right, don't worry.' I think in his head he was thinking of Leslie Crowther and 'Oh, how will I be like that?' But, of course, that's not the way you should think. You should always think, 'What can *I* bring? What are *my* talents.' And I thought he was fantastic at the games. He was very kind and he would be able to make little quips. And finally he did find his level. Which you do. You have to remember when you're in a cast, it's not just you performing, it's the whole family. The whole team.

While Michael Aspel was getting all the publicity and mounting expectation, another new member of the team managed to sidle into the job largely unnoticed – Rod McLennan:

The producer, Peter Whitmore, came to see *Sweet Charity* in which I played male lead opposite Juliet Prowse. And obviously he was looking for someone. Because they wanted two people to take the place of Leslie Crowther. And the decision was to bring two people in, so they got Michael Aspel and me.

It was perhaps comforting for Michael and Rod to remember that neither of them was replacing Leslie Crowther. In fact, they were each replacing *half* of Leslie Crowther. Combining the role of host and comedian was not something that just anyone could do, and it was a wise choice by Peter Whitmore to split the workload between two people, as was the case before Eamonn's departure.

Like Leslie Crowther, Rod McLennan had done summer season with the *Fol-de-Rols* seaside concert party. And, like Ronnie Corbett, Rod had played straight man to Danny La Rue in late-night cabaret. In fact, Rod had taken over directly from Ronnie at Danny's club two years earlier. And when he joined *Crackerjack* he was still performing in the musical *Sweet Charity* every night at the Prince of Wales Theatre and then going on to Danny's in the early hours of the morning.

While work had taken Johnny Downes to Australia, Rod McLennan had travelled in the opposite direction. And, in fact, his television career predated his stage success:

> I was, as it were, 'plucked from the street' in Melbourne, Australia, in 1958 as a latter-teenager. And given a 45-minute *live* children's programme to host. Television was pretty much in its infancy in Australia then. And they tried radio announcers. (PLUMMY VOICE) 'Hello, good evening, I'm here to make you all laugh a lot.' And that didn't work. Then they tried actors and they were too 'big'. So they thought, well, they'll have to just find 'people'. And I'd briefly appeared on a television minstrel show with my father, who had been in a very famous group in the 1920s and early 30s, called The Three Australian Boys. And a television producer in Melbourne saw me and said, 'Ah, come and talk to us and do an audition for this new show, which Peters Ice-cream is going to sponsor, called *Pete's Club*.' So I did.
>
> And I got the gig. And it was introducing, compering and doing the ads, and doing comedy sketches, and singing and dancing. All of which I learnt as I went along. And what I learnt is there was no point in worrying or having any fear. Because television was mostly live. And you just did it. And if you didn't have that attitude, you couldn't do it.

It was to be another marathon slog of 26 weeks when *Crackerjack* started its run in September 1968, with Christine Holmes still spending her evenings in *Charlie Girl* and Rod McLennan spending his in both *Sweet Charity* and late-night cabaret. Michael and Rod's endeavours to impose their own personalities on *Crackerjack* were possibly not helped by the children's comic *Playhour and TV Toyland* which, astonishingly, continued to run the weekly cartoon-strip adventures of 'Leslie and Peter' (even though on TV it was now *Rod* and Peter) right up until Christmas.

In addition to the changes of cast, there was also a change of location. *Crackerjack* was, yet again, moving house. The Shepherds Bush Empire had closed for another massive renovation, partly to equip it for the forthcoming launch of colour television. Their previous temporary home, the King's Theatre, Hammersmith, had since been demolished. So the BBC acquired the Golders Green Hippodrome for its audience variety shows. And it was the Hippodrome's stage that Michael Aspel strode onto, uttering the words:

It's Friday ... It's five to five ... and it's *Crackerjack*!

If the camera scripts are to be believed, Leslie Crowther had always concluded his intro with, 'Yes, it's *Crackerjack*!' – the very same words Eamonn had used from the beginning. So it's quite possible that Michael Aspel was the first person to utter that phrase *precisely* as we all remember it. In Rod McLennan's opinion, those opening words summed up the whole ethos of the show:

I mean, *Crackerjack* was the start of the weekend. 'It's Friday, it's five to five,' was a very important statement because the weekend starts ... here! People often seemed to skive off work a little early on Fridays anyway, and maybe watch *Crackerjack* to realise it *was* the start of the weekend, and then go down the pub. But it was a very important part of its structure, being 'It's Friday, it's five to five.' And, of course, only the BBC would start a programme at five minutes *to* something!

After Christine Holmes' opening number – *If I Had a Hammer* – Michael introduces Peter Glaze to newcomer Rod McLennan:

PETER: You've seen this programme before?
ROD: Yes, I was a great fan of yours when I was at school.
PETER: That's enough! Now on this programme we usually have quite a bit of slapstick ...

Pete then proceeds to give novice Rod a masterclass in slapstick, but naturally it's Pete who is forever at the receiving end. Ann Purser of *The Stage* enjoyed it:

Peter Glaze, without whom no *Crackerjack* would be complete, has newcomer Rod McLennan to initiate into the art of throwing custard pies and allowing your trousers to descend decently. Glaze has a promising pupil. McLennan has a funny, rubber face, instant self-confidence and the advantage of being an established singer before he arrived on the programme.

In the *1972 Crackerjack Annual* the costume department shared a few secrets about how they achieve the perfect trouser-drop:

> This is done by making the trousers extra large round the waist, with a piece that flaps over and is held with velcro material. One quick pull and the trousers promptly come undone and fall down, which is always good for a laugh. To make double sure, weights are sometimes put in the pockets.
>
> Another trick is to stitch a piece of elastic down the outside of one trouser leg, under the foot, up the inside of the leg, down the inside of the other leg, under the other foot and up the outside. If you think about it carefully you will see that if the elastic is stretched while it is being sewn on, it will automatically jerk the trousers down when the waist is released. I really don't recommend trying this out on your father's trousers, because he probably won't be very amused, but I can assure you that it does work!

For the messier slapstick routines, the costume department often had to provide an exact duplicate set of clothes, because there was not enough time between studio rehearsals and recording to get the first lot cleaned and dried.

As it had ever been, there was a physical contrast between straight man and funny man. Rod McLennan, like Leslie before him, was the tall slim comic, while Peter Glaze was the short fat stooge. Rod found it slightly illogical:

> I suppose he *was* the feed – although he looked funnier. With the two of us standing together, physically he should have been the funny man, 'cause he was little and portly and spoke very, very quickly. It was very old-fashioned. Even then. That programme wasn't a million years out of date, but it was *enough* out of date.

Currently, on Sunday evenings, BBC2 was showing quickfire American import *Rowan and Martin's Laugh-in.* Earlier in the year, ITV's Thursday teatime offering had been *Do Not Adjust Your Set* with writer/performers Eric Idle, Michael Palin and Terry Jones. *Monty Python's Flying Circus* was just a year away. Comedy had moved on, and perhaps *Crackerjack* was a little slow in catching up.

Rod and Peter's opening spot was always a pacey crosstalk routine that relied on both men being word perfect. During run-throughs Rod McLennan would sometimes give the sketch a novel twist:

We would get a bit of fun out of it – and help us to remember it – by pretending during rehearsals sometimes, it *wasn't* a children's show. And do it with a sort of 'nudge-nudge wink-wink' attitude. And it's incredible how you can actually change the whole feeling of a relatively naïve comedy sketch by just changing your attitude. But it helped to remember it – you just had to remember *not* to do it that way when you're recording!

And I'd learnt those tricks at Danny La Rue's. Because, when I first went to Danny La Rue's in 1966-67 all the comedy sketches had to go to the Lord Chamberlain's office to be vetted. To be censored if necessary. It was late-night stuff. And it wasn't written down as filth, but the words couldn't have meant anything else. I mean – a man walks up to Danny La Rue who's trying to mend his car in the street, and says, 'Would you like a screwdriver?' To which Danny replies, 'No thanks, I'm ten minutes late already.' And all this stuff went sailing through the Lord Chamberlain's office, because it wasn't dirty. And they didn't count *double entendre* – or they didn't know what it was. Who knows?

As for the show's new host, Ann Purser of *The Stage* believed that a change of style was no bad thing:

> It was the Crowther Show, and now he's gone there is obviously no desire to make this series the Aspel Show. Michael Aspel's function is to hold the show together, conduct the games and quiz, take part mildly in the fun, and add what he can from his own personality. In an absolutely relaxed and unpatronising way he puts the competing children wholly at ease, and it is no accident that the pair involved in the general knowledge quiz answered correctly nearly all the questions. Michael Aspel spread a kind of sunny relaxation over all, and the children blossomed out.

A new quiz format was tried out: this time it was *Jets Away*, but it was to be yet another one-series wonder. Although they rehearsed the whole show in the theatre on the day of recording, they obviously couldn't run through the games and quizzes with the same schoolchildren who would be playing them in the actual show. For some years, there had been an arrangement with a local stage school, who would supply children from the agency side of the school to play the games during the day, so the director could plan the camera shots and also test whether the games would actually work. Barbara Speake, principal of the Barbara Speake Stage School, explains:

> Well, at the time, June Collins, who was Phil Collins' mother, was my business partner and friend. She ran the agency, and what she didn't get for

the children wasn't worth getting. And the BBC would phone up and say they wanted some children, and then they'd try the games and things out on my pupils. Well, it was good publicity for us and the children enjoyed it.

One of many star pupils of the school was Sylvestra Le Touzel, whose mother was a pianist at the school for 22 years. In Autumn 1968 Sylvestra's TV career was launched with roles in both *Dixon of Dock Green* and *Doctor Who*. She followed this by an appearance in a Cinderella-themed *Christmas Crackerjack*, which also featured cameos by the Doctor's current companions Wendy Padbury and Frazer Hines.

(On Christmas Day itself, *The Black and White Minstrel Christmas Show* included a *Crackerjack* reunion between the show's compere Leslie Crowther and special guest Peter Glaze.)

Rod McLennan believes that Battersea-born Michael Aspel succeeded in his new environment because of the skills he'd learned along the way:

> Michael was very adaptable. He also had a photographic memory, probably better than mine, and didn't seem fazed by it at all. He taught himself two things, one that he didn't speak with a cockney accent. And then he became a BBC newsreader and, to do that, he had to become very calm.

After Leslie Crowther left, the show not only lost its host and comedian, it also lost half of its writing team. For this whole 26-week series every script was entirely the work of Bob Block. For the finale of the first show, Bob started where he had left off, with another piece of revamped Shakespeare – this time a *Taming of the Shrew* sequel entitled *Kick Me Kate*.

Early in the series Michael introduced a brand-new feature:

> And now we are going to meet a new addition to the programme. He is a white rabbit called Albert and from time to time you will be seeing some of his adventures. This week he has got some of his friends along into a recording studio and is conducting them in his own interpretation of *The Yellow Rose of Texas*.

This replaced Peter Whitmore's silent movies with Leslie Crowther and Peter Glaze. Instead, for this series, we were treated to the animated adventures of Albert the rabbit (who looked suspiciously like Bugs Bunny) and his friends (one of whom looked suspiciously like Speedy Gonzales). They were the work of stop-motion partnership Bob Bura and John Hardwick, who contributed short films to many BBC children's programmes and later worked on *Trumpton* and *Camberwick Green*. Their *Crackerjack* films used rubber Bendy Toys of animal characters (some from Warner Brothers cartoons) providing visuals to the zany comedy singles of Stan Freberg.

Apart from these novelty movies, there was little else to distinguish this series from those of the Crowther years. The pop stars were there in force – Status Quo, Mary Hopkin, The Who singing *Magic Bus*, comedy pop parodists The Barron Knights, even Tony Blackburn when he had a single to plug. There were fewer comedy guests, though there was an early appearance by Basil Brush. And Peter Glaze inevitably got the show going with one of his lectures, always with an introduction from Michael Aspel:

> We have had a letter from an ardent viewer, enquiring as to why no photograph of Peter Glaze has ever been shown on the programme. Well, we did have a photograph taken last week, but the photographer wouldn't develop it. He said he was afraid to be alone in the darkroom with it.

One of these intros had unexpected repercussions. Michael had received a number of letters from children wanting to know what happened to all the leftover prizes:

> And I used to write my own little bits here and there – not necessarily writing them, but coming up with them. And I opened one show by saying, 'People often ask what we do with the prizes that haven't been won. Well, I'm afraid we can't give them away, but if you send me some string and brown paper you can have Peter Glaze by return of post.' And I went into rehearsals the following week, and there was this immense pile of brown paper and string – a *huge* amount – with a handwritten notice from Peter Whitmore saying, 'Keep Your Bloody Mouth Shut!' The power of television – I was really impressed. And apologetic, of course.

Peter endeavoured to lecture uninterrupted each week, but seldom uttered more than a couple of sentences before Rod made an appearance:

PETER: I have decided to give a little lecture on the subject of feet. What is a foot?

ROD: About twelve inches.

PETER: Nowadays everybody travels by car. Now this is all wrong. After all, if your car broke down, you could always give it a push. But what can you do if your foot breaks down?

ROD: Give it a toe!

Bob Block's finales almost always had a historical setting, from Archimedes to Royalists and Roundheads, from Toulouse-Lautrec to Sherlock Holmes. A mid-series Victorian Melodrama was so popular it spawned a sequel – Sir Jasper's Revenge – a couple of months later.

The *1972 Crackerjack Annual* detailed the challenge those elaborate costumes posed for the backstage crew:

> Because the programme was always recorded in one go, with no breaks of any kind, there was often a frantic rush to get everyone into their new costumes and change the makeup in time, after the previous item in the programme. The performers would dash off the stage one by one – usually leaving Michael Aspel to hold the fort – and costume dressers and makeup assistants would all rush in at once to do all the changes.
>
> If it was Michael Aspel who was left to introduce the finale, then the script was so written that he didn't have to appear until a couple of minutes after the finale had started; but even so it was always touch and go. If you can imagine, say, Michael or Rod McLennan hopping around trying to put on a suit of armour or a Beau Brummell costume, while the makeup girls were trying to put on wigs or moustaches, you can see the sort of problems they had.

Bob's historical epics were always a rich combination of florid verbiage and perky pop numbers. Seldom were song lyrics modified, though one exception was an Alfred the Great sketch that incorporated *Yesterday's Dreams*, a Four Tops hit from a few months earlier. As Christine Holmes laments King Alfred's negligent burning of the cream cakes, she sings:

> Yesterday's creams, though gone and behind us,
> They're lonely reminders of flans that we made.

Christine Holmes had been a regular for three series, taking her from her late teens to her early twenties. At the end of this series her commitment to *Charlie Girl* was over and she left *Crackerjack* too. She finally had the opportunity to venture outside London and went travelling (which is still a passion of hers). She co-wrote and recorded *Devil Woman* which subsequently became a huge hit for Cliff Richard, before developing a cabaret act that included impressions of singers such as Cilla Black, Lulu, Sandie Shaw and Mary Hopkin.

*

The September 1969 series of *Crackerjack* welcomed singer Frances Barlow, originally from Williamstown near Pontypridd, Wales. Her dance training was with the Ballet Rambert and (like Michael Darbyshire) she had been a member of music hall ensemble The Players' Theatre. She had recently appeared in West End musical *The Boyfriend*, and had once been girlfriend to David Jason. Blonde and petite, she even looked up to Peter Glaze.

At the time Frances Barlow joined, *Crackerjack* had undergone a total makeover. Between series much thought had been given to the format of *Crackerjack* and this new run of 19 shows bore little resemblance to those of the Crowther era. The first big change was the opening number. Traditionally the host's welcoming remarks would lead straight into a solo number by the female vocalist. Now Frances' own song (a show tune, rather than something from the charts) was moved to a later spot in the show, and *Crackerjack* kicked off with a full-cast production number. This played to the strengths of the majority of the cast (less so to Peter Glaze and Michael Aspel) and the series began with *Back in the Old Routine*. One can only imagine what they made of *Quando, Quando, Quando* a couple of months later.

Another regular feature was introduced in dramatic voiceover by Rod McLennan:

ROD: *Crackerama* … Survey of the Nation … Your reporter –
          Michael Aspel.
MICHAEL: Good evening. Welcome to *Crackerama*, in which we plan to
          investigate a vital subject each week.

This *Panorama* spoof was not unlike the *Hornerama* segment of Kenneth Horne's radio show *Beyond our Ken* (which subsequently became *Trends* in *Round the Horne*). Taking a different topic every show, Michael would interview a succession of supposed experts. Here he questions outrageously attired pop musician The Thing (played by Rod) about fashion:

THING: Man, I really dig these clothes!
MICHAEL: You dig them, eh?
THING: I have to – my mother keeps burying them. Last week I
          thought I'd buy a kaftan – so I told the shopkeeper I'd like to
          see myself in something long and flowing.
MICHAEL: And what happened?
THING: He threw me in the river.

In a later show, Michael interviews a spoonerising professor (also Rod) about show business:

MICHAEL: What do you think of shows for the younger viewers?

PROF: I would recommend the programme called *Poo Bleeter*. Then there is *Vunior Joints of Piew*. And least but not last, there's *Jackercrack*. (AUDIENCE SHOUT *CRACKERJACK*!) I say, did you hear that? There beems to see an it of a becho!

Unlike Eamonn Andrews (who never needed to bother with sketch rehearsals, and whose presence was only required on the day of broadcast) Michael Aspel was fully involved in rehearsals throughout the week:

I remember rehearsing a great deal with them. And I was never more happy in my life, because I was doing stuff that I thoroughly enjoyed. And I imagined that I had some vague skill waiting to be developed, so that I would actually end up being as good an entertainer as they were, although remembering that my role was actually to be the host and *they* were the real entertainment. But it was great.

The cast worked out how the sketches would be performed, with the director suggesting the odd move and making sure no one was 'masked' (hidden from view behind someone else). 'It was technical direction, rather than comedy direction,' remembers Michael. During rehearsals he learnt a great deal from Peter Glaze:

Pete, as you know, worked with the Crazy Gang. He'd spent his whole life in that kind of entertainment, with the rough and tumble of that sort of stuff. And he was marvellous. He would tell you to wait, and not overlap and not interrupt. I hope I didn't need to be told too much of that, because your own instinct works. But I got very friendly with Pete. I liked him enormously.

He drove an old Bentley, and I followed him one day from the rehearsal rooms to the pub where we were going to have lunch. He was sitting in this car in front of me. And he had this huge dog. And Peter was so short, that they sat next to each other, the dog was in the passenger seat, and they were the same height. And their heads were the same shape. I remember driving behind them and they appeared to be two old men having a chat.

He had a little cottage in Kent, in a place called Fawkham, and he wanted to call this cottage Fawkham Hall. But his wife wouldn't allow it.

Peter Glaze's wife (and agent) was also Rod McLennan's agent, even before he joined *Crackerjack.* Rod remembers her as, 'Much bigger in every direction than her husband Peter. She was not intimidating, but she was a large woman.' Michael Aspel paints a similar picture:

> They looked rather like – I'm sorry to say – they looked like these McGill cartoons of the couple on a tandem. With the great big girl and the little bloke. She was tremendous fun and she kept him in control – snapped him down when he went too far. But being his agent, of course, she knew all his little peccadillos and was able to, as I say, control him. He was one of those guys the makeup girls were slightly wary of, you know. I don't want to put him down, but he was a cheeky bloke.

A comparatively tame story about Peter Glaze in the makeup room concerns a girl who was halfway through applying spots to his face to simulate German measles, when she realised she was giving him chicken pox instead. To avoid a bulging mailbag of complaints from eagle-eyed viewers, she had to wipe them all off and start again.

Michael also recalls a potentially hazardous visit to makeup by producer Peter Whitmore:

> He was a lovely man who didn't ostensibly have anything to do with showbiz at all. He was just relaxed and pleasant and could have done anything professional in the world, but not necessarily a children's television show. And he had a large red moustache, not that flamboyant, but big. He told me that he went into the makeup room at the end of recording once, and one of the girls sprang at him and tried to tear it off his face, thinking he was a member of the cast who'd just done a sketch.

Rod McLennan's own experience in makeup is equally memorable:

> I thought the girls, the makeup artists, were just fantastic, really talented. One day there were technical problems – it was going to be an hour or two – and the leading makeup artist said, 'Can I fool around with some makeup?' And I said, 'Yeah.' She said, 'I'll make you look like … Natalie Wood.' And I thought, 'Oh yeah? Okay.' So she put on the wig, the makeup. Twenty minutes. And I looked in the mirror. And I nearly crapped myself! It was scary. I had no idea you could do that. Our noses must have been a bit similar, I think. I mean I've always had a seriously retroussé nose. But she was just amazing!

The final quiz during this series was *Countdown* (no connection with the later Channel 4 letters and numbers game) devised by Daphne West. It was a series of quizzes and challenges that the competitors had to complete as quickly as possible, such as assembling a Russian doll or giving three boy's names beginning with B.

Between series, Michael had travelled the country filming questions for a special round of the quiz. He stood in front of a famous landmark, giving a series of four clues, getting progressively easier, with the camera giving progressively more helpful shots of the location:

> It was a game against the clock, the kids having to try and find out where I was and getting more or less points depending on how long it took. And if they got it in the first second, that was an awful lot of wasted filming. And one of the embarrassing bits for me – because I was *miles* from the camera on a very long lens – I would stand there alone, against Caernarvon Castle for example, shouting, 'Where am I?' And we had to do so many retakes because kindly tourists would explain to me where I was, and try to help me out with my obvious problem.

During his travels Michael also filmed quirky interviews at local schools, such as Westbury Leigh School in Wiltshire:

MICHAEL: What do you think people on Mars look like?
BOY: Oh, they'd have things sticking out from everywhere on their body. I think they've got horns, long noses, you know, three noses.
MICHAEL: Why three noses?
BOY: So they can breathe better. They'd live in stupid-looking homes and speak double-dutch.
GIRL: I think they'd be something like a kangaroo, only they'd have four arms and television aerials sticking out of their head.

A number of sketches for this series were contributed by Tony Hare, who we met earlier in this book when he was employed as a dresser for Leslie Crowther. He had worked in a variety of behind-the-scenes jobs while also submitting odd sketches and gags to comedy shows:

> I was doing the programme *Play School* as a floor assistant, and there were long breaks in that because you've got them all on the set and there were long rehearsal periods. And I used to sit behind one of the flats on the show, and

I used to scribble these things. And I remember that, on the other side, there was a props guy who would be doing the same thing. And of course he was John Sullivan, who became the creator of *Only Fools and Horses*.

Some time later I was working as a floor assistant on *International Cabaret* with Kenneth Williams, and I used to spend a lot of time in his dressing room chatting to him during breaks. And his writer was a guy called John Law who was the head of the script unit in Light Entertainment. And I was introduced to John, and we got talking and then he suddenly said, 'Your name's Tony Hare, isn't it?' And I said, 'Yes.' And he said, 'Are you the guy that's writing a lot of stuff?' 'Yeah, I have had a few things on.' 'Ever thought of doing it full time?' And I said, 'Oh yeah, I'd love to.' And he said, 'I'll see if I can arrange transfer for a year's attachment into the script unit.' And of course he did. And so then I was working on all sorts of things. And that's when I was asked, 'They're looking for a writer on *Crackerjack*, to help Bob Block out.'

In those days, Tony's particular strength lay in visual comedy, so he provided the middle sketch that had traditionally been of the slapstick variety:

The one I particularly remember was a fairground sketch where they went to a toffee stall, and I think there was candy floss involved as well. And I can remember Peter Whitmore the producer – because I worked with him a lot as a floor assistant – coming up to me and saying, 'Oh we're having such a problem with this. The things won't stick to their hands.' Because the idea was they got their hands stuck on the toffee slabs.

Although they worked on different segments of the show, Tony got on well with Bob Block:

Writers can vary quite a bit. You can get writers that are very quiet and unassuming. And then you get other writers who are telling jokes all the time, or are very funny people in their own right. Bob was very quiet, very shy, but he was a nice guy. And of course he wrote some great stuff for *Crackerjack*.

There was also a new look to the musical finale. The previous series had run the usual historical gamut, including a Victorian melodrama that had spawned a sequel. Now it was decided to make those Rodney Righteous escapades a weekly event, as Michael Aspel's introduction explains:

We now plan to show you further episodes in this saga, starring those two splendid Victorian sights, Sir Jasper Foulpest and Rodney Righteous – which is why we're tempted to call it The Two-Sights Saga.

The continuing storyline made things no easier for the set designer, as Peter Glaze's Sir Jasper pursued Rod McLennan's Rodney around the world, with episodes set in Russia, India, the circus and the seaside. And Michael Aspel would always make an appearance:

> One of the regular parts I had was a policeman, who always came on at the end. And it was always grotesque, that was the whole idea. I had an immense pair of blue boots, and I exaggerated every cliché about policemen. I had a notebook and wrote in it constantly – or rather was licking my pencil in anticipation of writing. And I had a letter from a policeman who said, 'In all my 24 years in the force, I never found it necessary to lick my pencil as often as you do. You're very lucky it wasn't indelible.' But it showed, once again, how many people watched the show.

(According to the *Crackerjack Annual*, viewing figures were currently around 7,500,000.) Michael's policeman signed off each instalment (and the show) in appropriate cliffhanger style:

> So ends another episode, with our thrilling serial going snap, crackle and pop. Will Rodney blame himself for his sister's playground tragedy – will he always remember that he saw what she saw when they saw the seesaw? Will I need to say that again? Will Sir Jasper wrestle with his conscience, and if so, for how many rounds? Tune in again next week, for another thrilling episode in the adventures of Rodney Righteous!

Anyone of a sensitive disposition may wish to skip a page or two, as Michael has a particularly vivid recollection of one Rodney Righteous instalment:

> You could have a section called 'dangers in the workplace' because Pete went on once and was actually sick on air. He'd had a rather dodgy piece of chicken one lunchtime before we recorded the show. Rod was Rodney Righteous and Pete was Jasper Foulpest and I was also on the set. And Rod just gave him a line and Pete, you could see him turning *green*. And he gave his line, being the pro that he was, then he turned and projectile vomited into the scenery. And then turned straight back and continued. It was all over in a matter of seconds but he made sure – you know, like they always say, pilots

who are crashing planes miss the towns – well he made sure he didn't hit anybody with his output.

Rod McLennan had observed this phenomenon offstage on more than one occasion:

> He was always slightly nervous. I've worked with people in theatre and they've forgotten their lines. And suddenly they're looking at you, and you can see that the light's on upstairs but nobody's home. It's that 'rabbit in the glare of the headlights' thing. Peter Glaze slightly had that look, nearly all the time.
>
> My feeling – I never really queried him at the time – he was probably given such a hard time when he worked at the Victoria Palace understudying the whole Crazy Gang, and they probably teased him mercilessly. Or maybe he was always a nervous performer, I don't know.
>
> But he was certainly more worried if ever we did the shows live. And just before we would start, I would make sure I was standing more than ten feet away from him, because … what was that horror film? … *The Exorcist*! I mean, he would bring up whatever he'd had in a major projectile manner. And it would last for three or four seconds and then he'd be perfectly normal again. Obviously something he was used to doing. First time I saw him do it, 'Oh good heavens!' But it didn't seem to matter.

Though Rodney Righteous was forever rooted in the Victorian era, elsewhere time and technology marched on. *Crackerjack* took a week off on 14th November 1969 to make way for James Burke presenting live coverage of the Apollo 12 launch – America's second manned mission to the moon. And when the show returned the following week it looked somehow different. Let's put it this way – from now on, if Peter Glaze turned green, everybody would know.

Colour broadcasting had begun on BBC2 in 1967 but, from 15th November 1969, much of BBC1 and ITV's output was now in colour. Designer Peter Kindred was privy to some very earnest discussions:

> I was there when they suddenly decided the BBC was going to go into colour. It was terribly concentrated. There were lots of meetings and discussions, and only being able to use certain bland colours, you know, soft pastel colours. I mean, it was rather overdramatised, because it didn't matter at all in the end. Doesn't matter what colours you use, it's all toned down. But at that stage they were always very nervous.

I suppose, when I did *Crackerjack* in the 60s, it must have been in black and white. I mean, we did all the sets in colour, obviously, it was for the audience. You didn't do a black-and-white set! Otherwise the audience would have said, 'Er, this is strange.' And, although they made a big fuss out of it, it was all pretty well the same when we went into colour.

For its colour debut *Crackerjack* returned to the newly refurbished Television Theatre in Shepherds Bush. Though it was business as usual for the performers, Rod McLennan remembers the behind-the-scenes bustle:

You had to have bright-coloured backdrops, and you couldn't vary different colours. It was very colour specific. It wasn't just a matter of pointing the camera and the colours came out. They had to do all sorts of weird things. I can remember Peter Whitmore, the producer, used to say something funny, 'Green-green-green-green-black-black-green-green-green-black-black-green-green-green-yellow-yellow-yellow-green.' It all made sense at the time. It was an extraordinary innovation and seemed much more difficult than necessary. And, interestingly enough, the quality of the picture decreased quite dramatically when it went to colour. And it's only relatively recently, with high definition, that it's got back to anything near what it had been 50 years ago in black and white.

There is a joke in the first colour *Crackerjack* that makes reference to the changes BBC1 had undergone to make this new technology possible. At one point in their opening routine, Rod points at Peter Glaze's face:

ROD: Just like the television, this face has 625 lines.

For that gag to work any earlier in the series, he'd have needed to reduce the number to 405. The finale of that same show is an especially colourful affair, with Rodney's travels taking him to Peking, described thus in Michael's intro:

... which even in the 19th century is a switched-on scene where everybody does his own Ming.

This is the cue for Rod, dressed as a Chinese coolie, to enter dragging a rickshaw on which is seated Peter in the guise of a Chinese mandarin. And if that isn't enough to make the 21st-century reader cringe ever so slightly, there is a sign reading, 'Mini-Rickshaws. For bookings ring Wun Too.'

The coming of colour to *Crackerjack* was also a pivotal moment for Jillian Comber, for very different reasons:

> We went into colour, and I think I did one colour show or two. And I went to Peter Whitmore and I said, 'Peter, before you have to get rid of me, I'm going. Because I've now reached …' I don't know what I was – 35 or something like that. 'I'm not young. And you *will* get rid of me. And I don't want to hear you say "I'm not going to renew your contract."' And he said, 'Well, I'd have kept you on for next year.' And I said, 'No, no.' Because he was only being nice. I just felt the time had come. My children were 15, older than that. And I was married again, my second marriage. And I'd not progressed into having big ambition. If I'd had big ambition I'd have never stayed in *Crackerjack*. But it was a wonderful job to do, and I loved every minute of it.

Even Jillian's children had divided loyalties when it came to *Crackerjack*. With ITV screening American sci-fi imports on Fridays, such as *Lost in Space* and *Land of the Giants*, they eventually reached a compromise and agreed to watch Mummy on TV every other week.

Jillian had been an integral part of the show for almost a decade. She was, and still is, the longest-serving female member of the *Crackerjack* team. And she very quickly became an all-singing all-dancing part of that team. With her old drama-school buddy Leslie Crowther she had helped form an enduring comedy quartet. And with Michael Aspel's greater involvement in the show, the quartet swelled to a quintet. *Crackerjack* would not be the same without her. But, at that time, she could never have predicted quite how different it would be.

Christmas Crackerjack had its fair share of guests – there were the *Blue Peter* presenters, of course. Comedy group The Scaffold were back for the second year running, as was Ed Stewart, now the host of *Junior Choice*. By February 1970 the global escapades of Rodney Righteous had come to an end but, as *The Stage* revealed in the week of that final show, Rod McLennan's own travels were far from over:

> Rod McLennan, who has been seen in cabaret, West End musicals and BBC-TV's *Crackerjack* since he came to England a few years ago, leaves for his native Australia this week, where he has a year's contract as host of his own TV show.

As far as Rod was concerned, it wasn't really that tough a decision:

> I went back to Australia in late February 1970. I walked away from the UK and I walked away from the BBC, and people were open-mouthed, probably quite correctly. But I *had* been given an offer I couldn't refuse, on television in Melbourne. I was doing a show that was paying five times as much as *Crackerjack* was. So what am I going to do? It was cutting my own throat to a degree, because I was never a company man. I probably wouldn't have enjoyed being at the BBC for the rest of my career. So I think I made the right decision. It was called *Showcase* – a very smart, upmarket talent show, but mostly for opera singers and classical musicians. And I presented it.

Following in Leslie Crowther's footsteps was never going to be easy. But Rod was slick, hardworking and knew a thing or two about comedy. Being cast as Rodney Righteous week after week might suggest a certain lack of versatility. But as long as the persona you present to your audience is likeable, does it really matter? And there was nothing faked about his enthusiasm for the job:

> The lovely thing about *Crackerjack*, it was just immensely enjoyable. I enjoyed very much working with the people I worked with. I didn't get to know them intimately or even socially really, but it just had a wonderful *wonderful* atmosphere. And it was a joy to come out of the Golders Green theatre after the show and stand there for maybe 20, 25 minutes, just signing autographs and chatting to the kids, who are so honest and so enthusiastic that it's bloody brilliant! You should never work with kids or animals – well, working with them can be a bit more difficult, but working *for* them is just a joy, an absolute joy.

Rod didn't permanently turn his back on the UK, which has since become his home. In 1972 he returned to the West End stage in *Applause*, a musical based on the movie *All About Eve* and starring Lauren Bacall.

The fashion choices of children's TV presenters over the decades could easily fill another book. But an interesting snapshot of the time is provided by this end-of-series memo from costume supervisor Sue Wheal to producer Peter Whitmore: 'I have also retained Michael Aspel's tan suit and peacock blue blazer for use on the next series.'

As it turned out, it wasn't just Michael Aspel's outfits that were being mothballed. It was *Crackerjack* itself.

8
What's That Horse Called?

1972

F IVE MONTHS AFTER the end of the previous series seems almost too early for the viewing public to be concerning itself with the next. But, in early July 1970, the *Daily Mirror* had this bombshell:

The BBC are dropping *Crackerjack*, longest-running children's programme on British TV. The show has returned every autumn for the past fifteen years. But not this autumn.

It's tough news not only to the show's millions of young fans, but also for comedian Peter Glaze, who has been a 'regular' for eleven years. 'I think the BBC had difficulty getting the old gang together again,' says Peter.

Peter, who spent the ten years before *Crackerjack* as 'spare man' to the Crazy Gang, is philosophic about it. 'It's obviously disappointing,' he says, 'but maybe one ought to make a change every ten years.'

In fact, there was very little of the 'old gang' left to reassemble. Jillian Comber had handed in her notice, Rod McLennan was in Australia, and Frances Barlow had only joined the previous year. That just left Michael Aspel, a veteran of two series, and Peter Glaze, an old gang of one. What was really needed was a new gang. But that wasn't going to happen any time soon.

The show didn't return in the autumn, nor did it return in autumn the following year. In September 1970 the traditional *Crackerjack* slot was filled by two programmes – half an hour of *The Basil Brush Show* with 'Mr Derek' Fowlds (produced by *Crackerjack* creator Johnny Downes and accompanied by the rather more affordable Bert Hayes Sextet) and a new programme of TV clip requests called *Ask Aspel* which, at least, provided regular weekly employment for one of the gang. Fast-forward a year, and the Friday teatime line-up of autumn1971 was very much 'TV on a budget' with the cartoon adventures of *Boss Cat* (as commercial-free BBC1 rechristened *Top Cat*) plus another run of *Ask Aspel.*

Ironically, the *Crackerjack Annual*, which up to now had been a sporadic affair, really flourished at a time when the actual show was off the air. Editions were produced in late 1969, 1970 and 1971. Michael Aspel's face adorns the first of this trilogy, but the following two (both produced after the show was reportedly axed) opt for less specific covers. So any child opening their *Crackerjack Annual 1972* on Christmas Day 1971, would still be reading about Rod McLennan and Peter Glaze, even though the pair of them, and indeed *Crackerjack* itself, hadn't been seen on screen for what was rapidly approaching two years. For your average youngster it was naught but a faded memory.

After a gap this long there were only two options – ditch the show forever or go for a radically revamped relaunch. And so, in early January 1972, not quite two years later (in fact, a mere 23 months) a brand new series with a brand new title hit the screens. It was time for … *Crackerjack 72.*

The title promised much. 1972 was a week old. People were only just starting to find their feet in a brand-new year, still concentrating their hardest not to write 1971 on letters and in chequebooks, and yet here was a programme with the confidence to deliver the spirit of 1972 before anyone really had a clue what that spirit would be. Forget the stuffy old dateless *Crackerjack.* Here was a *Crackerjack* so up-to-the-minute it was stamped with a 'use by' date.

It was a lot to live up to. And, notwithstanding everyone's best efforts and intentions, it remains possibly one of the least memorable series of all time – even by some of its participants.

Michael Aspel returned to front the show. He, like many others at the time, had no idea why it had been off our screens for so long:

> I was left in the dark the same as everybody else. I assumed it had run its time and they wanted no more. And I was very surprised when it came back. I'm sorry to say, inevitably it would be compared badly against its former glory. But it was a shadow of itself really.

The only other member of the team to return was Bob Block, who was the sole writer for the 13-week run. And, despite the promise of a totally new *Crackerjack*, he provided a script that couldn't have looked more like the *Crackerjacks* of years gone by. It even starts, as the previous series had, with a full-cast opening number – in this case, the Peggy Lee song *I Love Being Here With You* with appropriate new lyrics:

> We like TV just made for you, like Basil Brush and Boss Cat too,
> With Star Trek there and Doctor Who, we love being here with you.

The song concludes with everyone introducing themselves:

> I'm Stuart … I'm Elaine … I'm Heather … I'm Syd … I'm Eddie … I'm Mr Aspel.

The Syd and Eddie of this new ensemble were comedy musical double-act Syd Little and Eddie Large (whose actual names were Cyril Mead and Edward McGinnis). They were experienced stage performers but, as Eddie admits, television was something relatively new to them:

> We'd just won *Opportunity Knocks* and our manager at the time thought any telly was good, as *we* did actually, to be honest. And Hughie Green was pleased because he could announce that, because of him, we got *Crackerjack*. Like he used to do.
>
> So the producer of *Crackerjack*, he was a new producer called Brian Jones, he came to see us in a club in Leigh, in Lancashire. Well that was our domain, the clubs were our domain. We had a great club act. And we absolutely paralysed the place. And he wanted to have us on *Crackerjack*. Well, of course, that was a whole different medium to us. We'd never done sketches, we'd never entertained children. We were a sort of hardened club act. And, of course, we did it because we were going to be on telly for 13 weeks.

Syd Little agrees they were more than a little out of their comfort zone:

> We were grooming ourselves to be an adult show – not so much like Morecambe and Wise because they were in a league of their own – but sort of like an adult double act. We didn't ever visualise ourselves as children's entertainers. And then all of a sudden, in '72, this Brian Jones comes to see us at the Garrick Club in Leigh, a real rough working men's club, and says he's the new producer of *Crackerjack* and would we like to do it. And I said, 'Well, have a word with our manager.' And our manager Brian Hart was quite pushy, you know. 'You've got to do it. You've got to do it, lads!'

Brian S. Jones had directed the previous series of *Crackerjack* and now took over the reins as producer/director. He was a former variety performer himself, as Michael Aspel recalls:

> He used to do the warmup as well occasionally. And he always looked like one of those sailors on the seaside postcards, with the slightly red nose and the round face and the jolly manner. So he was ideal for it.

At the start of the series, Michael introduces Syd and Eddie to the audience:

EDDIE: It's nice to have such a friendly audience in the theatre. I'm delighted to see all of them.

SYD: (PATTING EDDIE'S WAIST) And they're delighted to see all of *you*!

There had yet to be a double-act in *Crackerjack* that didn't have some contrast in weight or height or both. That first exchange could just as easily have been written for Joe Baker and Jack Douglas, or Leslie Crowther and Peter Glaze. But, of course, Peter Glaze wasn't there, which came as a surprise to many, including Michael Aspel:

> It's very odd, isn't it? Considering you say '*Crackerjack*' and you think instantly of Peter Glaze. But they must have been thinking, 'We'll do an entirely new show.' Or almost entirely.

It's difficult to see how Peter would have fitted in alongside Eddie Large. The two of them were just too physically similar. And with Eddie's talent for mimicry, he would undoubtedly have been taking off Peter Glaze at every opportunity. You could say Little and Large were a double-act already, so had no need of a straight man. But they got one anyway.

Stuart Sherwin had experience as a pompous stooge in several Brian Rix farces, both on stage and TV. He had also appeared a number of times in *Dad's Army* as deputy to Bill Pertwee's Warden Hodges. His role in *Crackerjack* was as an actor-laddie type, instructing Syd and Eddie in the theatrical arts. His character's vanity is summed up in his opening lines:

STUART: Well, I must admit that people have been saying some very nice things about me. One viewer said I was second to none, well-groomed and handsome.

SYD: That's nothing – one viewer said I was none too well, second
         hand and gruesome.

Syd recalls Stuart with particular fondness:

> He was a real actor, a true actor. And he gave us some things that we still
> remember to this day. Like, when they cut, they'd say, 'Right. That'll do.' And
> he'd say, 'Yes, every one a Rembrandt!' He was really good. He was a real
> theatrical.

As the sketch proceeds, Stuart endeavours to instruct Syd and Eddie in
the art of slapstick but, of course, their bungled attempts mean that Stuart is
at the receiving end of every custard pie. If this sounds suspiciously like the
slapstick initiation Peter Glaze gave Rod McLennan two series ago, it's
because it is. He then demonstrates the 'disappearing water gag' with the aid
of a large funnel placed in the trouser waistband and a jug of water. And if
this sounds suspiciously like the *Christmas Crackerjack* routine that Ronnie
Corbett and Eddie Leslie did back in December 1958 … right again! One
might almost think that *Crackerjack 72* was, in fact, short for *Crackerjack
1872*.

In the previous series Michael Aspel had been one of the team, involved
in almost every part of the show and a frequent rehearsal attendee. Now,
with the quintet of regulars boosted to a sextet, and with Stuart, Syd and
Eddie taking care of the opening comedy routines, as Eddie recalls, there was
far less for Michael to do:

> We were rehearsing all week, trying our hardest to learn scripts. Michael just
> steams in on the day, or the day before. He's memorised everything in the
> script. Me and Syd are still struggling to say, 'Good evening.'

You may have observed in the previous two script extracts that writer
Bob Block gave Syd Little the punchline. It was certainly a departure from
your typical Little and Large routine, and Eddie had his reservations:

> He was clever in his way, Bob – and I wouldn't knock anybody on the show
> – but it didn't suit us. We weren't really a cross-patter act in those days. Mike
> and Bernie, and Eric and Ernie, and people like that. We just didn't do that.
> That's what made it different. There was no definite straight man and no
> definite comedian. I did it all and Syd, certainly for the first five, six or seven
> minutes, didn't say anything, which set the act up. So all of a sudden they

wanted the old-fashioned, 'Well, my boy, what have you been doing today?' 'Well, a funny thing happened to me actually on the way here.' 'Well, tell me about it.' That kind of old-fashioned double-act. So we were just out of our depth. We didn't have a clue.

I said to the producer, 'Can I write the opening on one of them.' He said, 'Yeah.' So I wrote it. It wasn't fantastic or anything. It was just as good as what Bob was doing. And he got very upset. He thought I was trying to take over his crown.

The final sketch employed full cast and orchestra – and even the musical director was different this series. In place of Bert Hayes was Norman Percival, another pianist, who had composed incidental music for *Steptoe and Son*, written musical arrangements for *The Kathy Kirby Show*, and been musical director on *The Dick Emery Show*. Working with Norman was another new experience for Syd Little:

> That was our first thing with a big band. I mean, all we had in the clubs was a bass, drums and piano, and that was it. And my guitar. Then you go in a studio like with Norman Percival and you've got this bloomin' great big band. You know, trumpets, sax, wow! It was unbelievable!

As always, the pop songs were cunningly crowbarred into the plot, much to the amusement of Eddie Large and his pals:

> We were in digs somewhere in the north-east with this group, and they said, 'We just love the way you go into these sketches that feature songs.' 'What's that horse called?' 'Oh, that's a horse with no name.' (SINGS) 'I've been through the desert on a horse …'

The first show of the series ends with two feuding Scottish clans. Neil McDougal (played by Eddie) is wooing Mollie McGregor:

NEIL: No doubt you are aware that I'm here to plight my troth.
MOLLIE: (COLDLY) Aye, Mr McDougal, and I must say you look a
             miserable plighter.

They plan a secret assignation with a secret signal – leading slickly into the Tony Orlando hit *Knock Three Times*. Mollie sings it pretty well. She ought to, because she's played by Elaine Paige, a relative unknown in her first TV series. Eddie could never have imagined the career that lay ahead of her:

Elaine was just part of the team. We didn't even know she was a singer. Just thought she was an actress who could sing. She was just supremely talented. We'd never seen her on anything, we weren't aware of the musicals. I think that came later anyway.

Syd Little found her modest and unassuming:

She was very quiet. I didn't get to know her that well. You saw the talent there. I mean, she'd come to rehearsals. Me and Eddie would be struggling with our scripts, and I'd be getting it wrong all the time. But Elaine, she was spot-on. She'd do it once and that was her, she was off and running. It was a doddle to her. She was a natural. And she did most of the singing, 'cause they'd spotted she was good.

Michael Aspel's memories of the series are hazy, and his memories of Elaine are hazier still:

Somebody told me once that Elaine said to them, 'Whenever I meet Michael, he never mentions *Crackerjack*.' I think she was a guest on one of the shows. She's such a friendly person.

Though it may have slipped Michael's mind, Elaine was, in fact, resident singer and actress on *Crackerjack* for the entire series. But back to the sketch. While Neil McDougal (Eddie) is wooing Mollie McGregor (Elaine), Willie McDougal (Syd Little, playing Eddie's dad) is wooing Mollie's mother Jean, though both are so nervous they can barely string a sentence together:

WILLIE: Well, I must say the weather's been very –
JEAN: Aye, and it'll probably continue. Would you care to join me in –
WILLIE: No, I went there on my holidays. Mind you, I always say –
JEAN: So do I! My my, isn't it a small –
WILLIE: Yes, I think it shrunk in the wash.

This is a pretty neat shoo-in to Nancy Sinatra and Lee Hazlewood's *Did You Ever?* – a song packed to bursting with half-sentences. The actress playing Jean was no stranger to children's TV, having previously occupied the Friday teatime slot in summer 1969, as reported in *The Stage*:

A series called *High Jinks* will take over from *Crackerjack* in the summer. There will be thirteen programmes of 45 minutes each and will of course be designed for children. Stan Parkinson is the producer and the series will feature Ray Alan, Tich and Quackers, George Chisholm and Derek Dene. Stan Parkinson says that he has a new girl lined up for this show for whom he predicts big things.

Tich was Ray's schoolboy dummy, and glove-puppet Quackers was originally operated by Tony Hart, crouched under a table with a duck-call in his mouth. Each show finished with a costumed sketch, such as Sherlock Holmes or Robin Hood, which couldn't be a better apprenticeship for *Crackerjack*. And the 'new girl' with 'big things' predicted for her was dancer and actress Heather Barbour.

It was perhaps a harsh *Crackerjack* initiation for 20-year-old Heather to be cast as Elaine Paige's mum. But, as Eddie recalls, things didn't exactly improve:

> I've never forgotten Heather because she was booked as what she called 'the juvenile lead'. She was always going to do the glamour stuff, the good-looking girl stuff.

Syd sets the scene:

> We always did sketches where you had to dress up. And I remember we did this Toytown thing. Eddie was like a real down-and-out fairy, he had holes in his tights and a tatty tutu and a wand. And he looked a right mess. Lipstick – it looked like his mother gone wrong. And Heather, she was tatty as well for some reason.

But Eddie could see she wasn't happy:

> We were ageing ballerinas. I'm there with my tutu, my little chubby red cheeks, blonde wig on. And we're waiting behind the scenery, waiting for the sketch to start. And she's crying away, she's bubbling away. And I went, 'What's wrong, Heather?' She went, 'I'm a juvenile lead. I shouldn't be dressed like this.' I said, 'Heather, I'm thirty-one, father of two. If anyone should be crying, it should be me!'

It wasn't the only sketch to cause an upset, as Eddie remembers:

> We did a sketch when Syd dropped his trousers and he had Union Jack underpants on. And we got a letter from this Colonel whatever-he-was. He slaughtered us! I'm not sure a lot of the mail reached us, if I'm being honest, because you'll always upset someone on TV.

As the series progressed, it started to take its toll. Syd and Eddie were learning a new script each week, doing material that didn't quite fit their style, and coming to terms with suddenly being pigeonholed as children's entertainers. But, for Syd Little, that was only the half of it:

> The trouble was the book was full with bookings for clubs. And it really was full every week. Six, seven nights a week. And they were all over the country – up north mostly – Newcastle, Manchester, Wakefield, Leeds. And a lot of the clubs wouldn't release us from the contract.
>
> So when we were rehearsing *Crackerjack* we had to get the 5.30 train from Manchester, about three or four days a week, to go down to London, rehearse at Goldhawk Road, the scout hut I think it was, and then come back home on the five o'clock train, get a quick something off your mum, a sandwich or your dinner, get a quick shave, cleaned up, and Eddie would pick me up and off we'd go to a club, not finish till about three in the morning, then up at five ... and this was for 13 weeks!
>
> It was a big mistake and we honestly didn't enjoy it. We just didn't have *time* to enjoy it. We learnt a big lesson and that was never do two jobs at once. Concentrate on one or the other. But we couldn't get out of it. It wasn't our fault, it was our manager's fault. We were tired. And we'd turn up at clubs and there'd be like kids in the audience – which we'd never had before, they were all adults. And mums with little milk baby bottles instead of a Guinness – and I'm sure I saw a few teats on the Guinness bottles!
>
> When we'd finished *Crackerjack*, after 13 weeks, it took us at least 18 months to get rid of the idea that we were kids' entertainers. 'Cause we weren't, we didn't *want* to be kids' entertainers. We were like the Gallagher brothers of *Crackerjack*, you know, we didn't fit in somehow. We were just two Mancunians, and we wanted an adult audience.

Eddie Large remembers a nightmare flight in thick fog in an attempt to honour an engagement:

> We were appearing at the Wakefield Theatre Club and I don't think they'd let us have the night off. We asked for the night off and they said, 'Oh no.' So we'd got this private plane. I always remember it because we'd done Laurel and Hardy and I had this moustache stuck to my top lip, and I was trying to get it off. This glue, I always remember the smell, and flying. And we were going to land at Leeds and Bradford airport, which isn't that far from Wakefield. And we couldn't do it. We had to go to Manchester and we weren't very popular at Wakefield that night.

They couldn't have afforded to turn down the clubs, even if they were able to. Doing *Crackerjack* was prestigious, but hardly lucrative. Eddie remembers it paying 'a pittance' – £175 per show, split between the two of them. In many ways Eddie was only too glad when the series was over:

> I always remember me and Syd on the train back, after the very last show. We'd both got the worst colds we'd ever had in our lives. Your defences had gone down, you know, working at this funny rate, flying here, flying there, rehearsing, doing this, doing that. Then as soon as we relaxed we had these terrible, terrible colds. But I remember Syd on the train back, looking at all the houses, saying, 'Look at them, they're watching telly. What are we doing? Going back to Manchester. We've got to work tonight in Yorkshire.'

For Syd Little, the bad memories of *Crackerjack* outweigh the good:

> On the whole it was quite traumatic for me. It was a workload I wouldn't want to do again. It taught us a big lesson. If you're doing something, concentrate on that one thing. Don't try and do too much. 'Cause you'll just burn out. We were miscast, I think. We weren't ready for it. But it was nice meeting the people and seeing where their careers have taken them.

Syd and Eddie returned to television before very long – working with writers and producers who had the time and money to develop shows that fitted their style and their kind of audience. Stuart Sherwin also had plenty more TV exposure as foil to Dick Emery, Terry Scott and Basil Fawlty. Later that year Heather Barbour had the chance to play the glamour girl at long last, in the Brian Rix bedroom farce *Don't Just Lie There, Say Something!* And as for the future career of Elaine Paige, in Syd Little's own words, 'Wow! She didn't do much, did she?!'

There is a 'black hole' in the *Crackerjack* television archives lasting almost ten years, from 1964 to 1974. None of the shows hosted by Leslie Crowther exist, nor anything from Rod McLennan's two series, and not one of Little and Large's 13 shows. The Syd and Eddie series may not have been vintage *Crackerjack*, but Leslie Crowther picked up many more scathing *Crackerjack* reviews than they ever did. If nothing else, they learnt from the experience. And the kids most certainly enjoyed Syd and Eddie, otherwise they wouldn't have turned up in such force to see their club act.

To finish on a more upbeat note, Eddie Large shared an anecdote that truly encapsulates the TV industry. The first show's gone out, and you're back at the BBC preparing for the next:

You wander in the wardrobe room, the makeup room. 'Right then girls, what did you think?' 'Oh, my husband thought those costumes in that Henry the Eighth sketch were great.' 'What about you?' 'Well, remember when you did that Frankenstein? My mother loved that makeup.'

They're not watching *you*! They're just watching their bits. You could never get a proper review of the show, because they weren't watching you. 'What about the jokes, did any of you laugh?' 'Oh, I wasn't really listening, I was watching for the costumes.'

9
Forbidden Fruits

1973 – 1974

I T HADN'T QUITE BEEN the spectacular relaunch that everyone had hoped for. *Crackerjack 72* never really got into orbit. It cruised at low altitude for 13 weeks then juddered to a gentle halt. There were no dizzying heights, but neither was there a crash landing. Would next year's model fare any better? Would there *be* a next year's model? Michael Aspel had his doubts:

> It wouldn't have surprised me if, at that time, they'd said, 'Thanks very much,' and just closed the door and forgot the whole thing. I was surprised that it kept going. It shows tremendous faith in the show, but they must have realised as time passed that the best had gone.

At that time it was far from clear whether *Crackerjack* was destined for yet another makeover, or for the scrapheap. Birmingham-born comedian Don Maclean was just starting to break into television, with a number of appearances at the local Pebble Mill studios:

> They were looking for a replacement for *Crackerjack*. And we did a show called *Boomerang*. It was me and Dilys Watling, and it was terrible. And Robin Nash was involved in that. And anyway Robin said, 'Well, that's no good. They didn't like the programme, but they did like you. And so, what we're going to do, we're going to resurrect *Crackerjack*.'

Boomerang was an unbroadcast pilot show produced in Birmingham by Robin Nash, who Michael Aspel knew very well:

He was the most flamboyant and extraordinary person I think I've ever met at the BBC. He brayed like a donkey when he spoke. He laughed at everything. And he was a strange mixture of being completely encouraging and completely detached. He never seemed to be quite looking at anybody. He just had this moustache and these great big teeth and these slightly glazed eyes. But very encouraging. And a well-known BBC character.

Also in the cast of *Boomerang* was Jacqueline Clarke:

They were going to dismiss *Crackerjack* and get a new children's series. That's how I was approached. But I was approached because Don Maclean saw an advert for Paxo stuffing. I was this girl that was closed in the back of a police van, and all she had to do was say, 'I didn't mean to do it!' Well, it was supposed to be Liverpudlian. Well, of course, I did Birmingham. Pure Birmingham. So obviously the casting people didn't know about accents, but I got the job and it was really quite a nice commercial. But Don Maclean saw that, and he said, 'Who's that Brummie girl? I'd like to see her.' Because he'd been approached by Robin Nash. He must have said to Robin, 'I want to see the girl from that commercial.'

So I went to see Robin at the BBC and got on very well straight away. I was working at the BBC anyway – I was doing the Dave Allens. So I was called in and we went up to Pebble Mill to do a new children's show. And I remember it was Dilys Watling, Barrie Gosney (who I eventually married) and Don Maclean. And we did these sketches and things and it was all very lovely and, you know, it was a pilot and we thought we might hear what it's going to be called. And then suddenly my agent rang and said, 'You'll never guess. They *are* doing a children's programme, but it's called *Crackerjack.*' And I said, 'What?! Okay.'

When weekday lunchtime magazine show *Pebble Mill at One* was launched in October 1972, the BBC was very keen that the show should have some comedy content. And that content was provided by Don Maclean:

They said, 'Every Friday, you're going to do a five-minute bit. We're going to say, "Over now to our raving reporter, Don Maclean." And you do something.' And some of the things were on film and some were in the studio. Now *Pebble Mill at One* went out at lunchtime. And there must have been kids coming home for their dinner. And *Ask Aspel* was on at the time. And the idea was – children wrote in to ask if they could see again something that they'd seen on television. And they started writing in to see things that I'd done. So Michael Aspel, who was presenting the programme, knew who

I was. And Michael had apparently said that he wouldn't do *Crackerjack* again after the last one. And the BBC were going to scrap *Crackerjack*. And then they said, 'Oh, we're thinking of using this Don Maclean.' And he apparently said, 'Well, if you're going to put Don Maclean in it, I'll do it as well.'

Michael Aspel was very happy with his new co-stars:

Don Maclean was as good as you will get. He helped put new blood into it and was really popular with the kids. And Jacquie Clarke did the lot and did it all beautifully. I mean, she's a natural. She's one of those lucky people who's attractive and funny at the same time. And that doesn't always work. But it did with her. She's one of the real top people the show ever had.

Jacqueline herself is far more modest about her talents, perhaps because she worked with one of the best ego-deflators in the business:

Ever since I was 30, I've been old ladies. Dave Allen used to say, 'Put a grey wig on her and she's an old lady in half a minute. But to be beautiful it took two-and-a-half hours in makeup.' So because I was used to doing a variety of stuff, and working with Basil Brush a lot, and having to be various characters, I think I was just the 'in thing' at the time at the BBC, because I could do all this sort of stuff.

Crackerjack couldn't be credited with discovering Jacqueline Clarke. She was currently playing all the women in Dave Allen's sketches and was a regular on *The Basil Brush Show* (also produced by Robin Nash). But this was the first time that *Crackerjack* had engaged the services of a female comedian. That's not to say that the likes of Pip Hinton and Christine Holmes couldn't get laughs, but they were singers who also did comedy – whereas Jacqueline Clarke was a comedian who could also sing. It was an important step forward for *Crackerjack* in an era when the question 'Can women be funny?' was still a matter of serious debate.

Jacqueline was interviewed by *The Sun* in 1974 about being female and funny. Her views seem very old-fashioned now, and were doubtless heavily influenced by society's expectations of women in comedy at that time:

Being rude or blue just doesn't work for a woman. And if she's grotesque or peculiar I don't think she's funny any more. She doesn't have to be sexy, but she should have a vulnerable quality and be attractive. Then there's another problem. Show me anyone who can really write comedy material just for a woman.

That last point said it all. Many writers couldn't (or didn't want to) write for women. But that was because the vast majority of comedy writers were male. Fortunately, during Jacqueline's time on *Crackerjack*, she was given a wide range of roles and ample opportunity to demonstrate her comic talents. But it's worth remembering that, over the whole history of *Crackerjack*, not a single writer, director or producer was female.

With Michael Aspel back as host, and Don and Jacquie on board, all that was needed was a straight man for Don. Of course, using the tried and trusted *Crackerjack* formula of physical contrast – as the comic was (once again) tall and thin, ideally the stooge needed to be short and fat. As Don Maclean recalls, Robin Nash had the very man:

> And Robin said, 'Do you know Peter Glaze?' Well, I'd done two pantomimes with Peter Glaze playing Dame. 'And would you be happy working with Peter Glaze?' I said, 'Yes.' He harked back to the fact that *Crackerjack* had been great, and had gone downhill since Crowther left.

So, after a break of one series, Peter Glaze resumed his role as feed to new boy Don Maclean. Describing Peter as 'the man whose face was made for custard pies,' *The Sun* ran a piece early in the series, in which they asked Peter if he'd ever yearned to be a serious actor:

> I've always wanted to be a comic, and the part I play in the show – a little man who's a bit stupid – is just the way I am anyway. Being small doesn't worry me, because so many of the best comedians were little men.

Crackerjack 73 (and this was the last time the year would receive joint billing) started its cautiously commissioned run of a mere 12 shows in February 1973. There must have been a slight feeling of 'one last chance' amongst all concerned. Don's *Radio Times* interview at the start of the series suggested he was determined to grab the show by the scruff of the neck, and either seize victory or go down with all guns blazing. But some of his remarks must have rung alarm bells with protective parents, and perhaps raised the pulse rate of the pubescent:

> Comic Don Maclean's formula for making children laugh is to treat them as adults, enticing them with what he calls Forbidden Fruits. 'If you aim comedy at children you can't talk down to them because they feel insulted,' he says. 'So I try to keep the standard high, avoiding slapstick.'

In *Crackerjack* he beguiles the young with a variety of sketches about X films, censorship and other adult preoccupations. 'Children are very aware of these things from what they hear and see on television. They constantly surprise me,' he says.

To the relief of the many (and the disappointment of the few) there was scant evidence of a raunchier, racier *Crackerjack*. This exchange, in a Peter Glaze lecture on fishing technique, is about as smutty as it gets:

PETE: Trail it along the bottom and you get a bite.
DON: On your bottom!
PETE: Don't be rude.
DON: He'd have to have a big mouth to …
PETE: Stop it!

Those with keen hearing may have detected the odd burst of strong language on *Crackerjack*, though it certainly didn't emanate from Don Maclean's side of the camera:

In the main the kids were fine. Groups of brownies or cubs were very good. But you could get kids that were too old. We had one group and they were 13, 14-year-olds. They were a rough load of kids. And they worked out that the microphones above their heads were the audience participation mikes. So, while the show was on, they were shouting four-letter words into these mikes. You couldn't go over it all again – so the sound men had a hell of job blocking it all out.

The Don and Pete chemistry was there pretty much from the start, helped on its way by a good strong script. But to Don the opening routine was uncharted territory:

I'd never done a double act as such before. I'd done various things with Peter. In one pantomime we were in, we did a balloon ballet when he was the Dame and I was Rudolph Nureyev. So we *had* worked together, but I can't say we'd done a double act. Bob Hedley used to write the double. And it didn't take very long to get it right, because basically Peter Glaze was very much a Captain Mainwaring personality. He was pomposity. And what you did, you pricked Peter's pomposity. And that was the joke really.
   Occasionally Peter would forget where he was – and we never did anything twice. If you got it wrong – tough! It was 'as live'. I used to help him out, used to bring him back, and sometimes he used to have a right go at me

afterwards. 'I was alright! I knew where I was!' He wasn't the easiest man in the world to work with.

Crackerjack's long-term writer Bob Block was hard at work on a couple of children's sitcoms for Thames Television. *Pardon My Genie* was currently running on Mondays and, later in the year, the first series of *Robert's Robots* would begin. Although missing from this series, he did contribute to the next. But most of the script for this series came from newcomer Bob Hedley, who had written for Dave Allen, Jimmy Tarbuck and Frankie Howerd amongst many others.

Don Maclean quickly came to admire the show's new Bob:

Bob Hedley was an encyclopaedic gagman. He literally knew every gag that had ever been done. Ever! Anywhere! And they were all up there in his head, you know. And he latched on to me somehow. He used to write to a certain extent the way he knew I was going to say it – after a little while – it didn't take him long. And it was almost like I was getting bespoke material.

Tony Hare, who along with Bob Block would rejoin the writing team next series, got to know Bob Hedley well:

Well, Bob was a Geordie, you see. And he used to do the warmups at the beginning of the shows. And he had been a comic in the old days, like a 'first on' comic, he was never a star. And I always remember him standing with his elbow on the mike stand, holding the mike in the other hand. A real typical comic's pose.

Bob and I used to stand and watch the show from the side, which was the ramp that went up on the side of the orchestra room, where the camera tracked up and down. And I remember us standing there, and the sketches would be going on, and Bob would say, muttering under his breath, 'Laugh, you little bastards!' Because the trouble is, the kids were more interested in the technical side, and they were watching all the cameras moving about and all the monitors up there. And it was only the obvious stuff that they really laughed at.

And also, when there was a joke, particularly in his duologue at the beginning, Bob used to go, 'Ha-ha-ha-ha!' Sort of a deliberate laugh to try to get the kids going.

One feature that always got big laughs was the silent movie, perhaps because the kids could just concentrate on the monitor screens without any of the distractions of moving cameras and other paraphernalia. They had last been seen in the Crowther era, but this series they were back. And many were directed by Alan Bell (who, as Alan J. W. Bell, was later to have a long association with *The Last of the Summer Wine*):

> I was taken off *Morecambe and Wise* for being a naughty boy, for being too bossy. And one of the punishments was to be put on *Basil Brush* and *Crackerjack*.

Don Maclean, who had already written and starred in a number of short comedy films at Pebble Mill, scripted some of the *Crackerjack* silents, including this scouting escapade entitled *Hello Campers*:

> Peter enters dressed as an old-fashioned boy scout, covered in badges. Don joins him pulling a trolley with a gas stove on it – he has an enormous rucksack, shovel, pick, etc on his back. Peter tells Don to do the washing-up while he cooks the soup. The two pots get mixed up. Peter serves neckerchief and sock soup – reacts. Don hangs out cabbage leaves and carrots on the line.

Silent movie accompaniment was improvised at the piano by Bert Hayes who (like Peter Glaze) had returned to his *Crackerjack* residency after a one-series break.

As well as having to establish himself as half of a newly formed double-act, Don Maclean was also getting to grips with character acting in the sketches – another new experience for him:

> Jacquie Clarke was great at all sorts of different characters. And she used to say, 'Oh, you want to do so-and-so.' Or, 'You want to do that.' And she was ever so good. By the time she left I was okay at working out my own characters. But she was really, really helpful to me. She was fabulous. A great comic.

During those rehearsals, Jacqueline noticed the contrasting acting styles of Don and Pete:

> Peter Glaze, being the sort of robust figurine in everything he did, he was always 'over the top' if you like. In other words – panto style. And there are two ways of doing comedy. There's very broad panto stuff, which is very funny. Or there's the much more clever 'acting' side that brings out comedy from reaction. From the way you say something and, you know, just generally acting it rather than trying to pretend to be somebody.

I don't think I can ever remember saying to Don, 'Oh, I wouldn't do it that way.' I think it's just, when you work with someone for a bit, and you say, 'Well, if you just wait and do something on *that* line perhaps. Or we could do …' And you work something together. We would have the time to sit and discuss how we'd react to each other.

Various episodes of the series were directed by Michael Goodwin, Bill Wilson and Robin Nash himself. But, as Jacqueline recalls, that direction was much more about camera angles than interpreting the script:

Robin was lovely, but he would employ you because he just knew you would find a way of doing it. Or he might just say, 'Perhaps you should try that again.' But he wouldn't direct. So I never found that *Crackerjack* was directed. It was expected that the people employed would get on with the job.

She also learnt that Peter Glaze's 'panto style' of acting could have its hazards:

Actually, Peter was a good egg. He *was* a good egg. But I just found him, as he is on the telly so he seemed as a person. And I found that slightly irritating if I'm honest. I remember he once hit me, only by accident, in some Tyrolean sketch or something. We were doing some dances, and of course he was way over the top, and threw out his arms and went straight at my eye. And it really hurt and I had to stop and we had to go back and re-rehearse it. So it really upset me. And he didn't say much. 'Ohhh, making a fuss!' or something. And the next day brought in a huge bunch – I think they were tulips – a huge bunch of flowers. And then threw them at me and said, 'There you are, I'm sorry!' And I thought, 'Yes, that just about sums you up!'

There are many tales of Peter Glaze's generosity, particularly when apologising after a row, but this is one uncharacteristic instance when the apology was less than heartfelt.

Less uncharacteristic is the tale Don Maclean tells of a job offer that Peter received following that same *Crackerjack* Tyrolean sketch:

There's a wonderful story. April Glaze was not just his wife but his manager. And Peter came in and said, 'Oh, I've got to have a day off this week. I've been offered an advert in Scotland. It's for a beer. They saw me do something in lederhosen on *Crackerjack* and they said, "Oh, this is the man we want."' So he went up, and the next day he came back and we said, 'How did you get on?' 'Oh, it was fantastic,' he said, 'They dressed me up, and I'd got the shorts on and the little hat with the feather in it, and there was this – phoar! – beautiful girl, big knockers …' So he told us the story.

Now, April Glaze, being a conscientious agent, had rung up the people who booked Peter Glaze, and said, 'I'm just checking to see if you were happy with Mr Glaze.' 'Oh,' he said, 'he was absolutely perfect. He looked marvellous! Very, very funny! Exactly what we wanted,' he said. 'Mind you, he's a randy little bugger, isn't he?' To which April replied, 'They *do* tell me!'

Many a sitcom has featured the high-flying agent or long-suffering wife. Few have realised the comic potential of combining the roles.

This series of *Crackerjack* saw yet another final game – a general-knowledge quiz called *Target Time* – but otherwise everything was much the same, with Bob Hedley's final sketch incorporating pop songs in the time-honoured tradition. One finale has a Gypsy setting:

JACQUIE: Don't tell me you live in a pigsty!
DON: Oi've lived so long with pigs, oi've got Danish stamped all over me.
JACQUIE: Does the squire charge you rent?
DON: He charges the *pigs* rent! And I've a witness to prove it.

At this point Don brings on a pig and sings Slade's *Cum on Feel the Noize*, subtly adjusting the lyrics to: 'Come on, feel his nose.'

Slade themselves were guests during the series, as were Thin Lizzy (whose lead singer Phil Lynott later married Leslie Crowther's daughter Caroline), The Electric Light Orchestra and The Sweet. Jacqueline Clarke also remembers a more unlikely guest star:

Frankie Howerd came on one of them, you know. Yes, he was very odd. I can't remember what he did. He was quite dour. It was something you didn't expect him to be in. Something to do with a pool. God knows what it was all about! He was standing on the edge. 'Ooohhh yesss!' Doing all the usual. That *is* something I remember. Now why? Because I suppose it was someone called Frankie Howerd, standing there doing a children's thing. It was all rather bizarre in a way.

Michael Aspel's memories of Frankie are unsurprisingly vivid:

When we finished the series, Frankie Howerd graced us with his presence. He said he'd been asked by the Director General – or 'Thing' – whatever he called him. And I was simply to be hurled into this custard pie, which was an indoor swimming pool filled with crazy foam. And they hadn't, as it transpired, put a cushioned base in it. And there was this short set of steps, off which I was to be pushed by a crowd of children as part of the celebration.

'Are you going to have a slice? asked Frankie. 'I certainly am.' 'Right then – you can have the lot!' I could hear footsteps behind me, and I was shoved sharply in the small of the back and went hurtling – head first actually – into this foam and smacked up against the studio floor. And I could breathe under there, so I was able to lie there thinking about it for a minute. And then I got up. My nose was bleeding slightly and my arm hurt.

I went to the *Today* programme, which I used to do bits for on Radio 4 for the weekend, and somebody said, 'Your fingers are looking a bit strange.' I looked, and they were all different colours and swollen like a blue bunch of sausages. And I went to the hospital near Broadcasting House and they X-rayed it and said, 'Yes, it's broken.' In fact it led to a slight freezing of relations between me and the BBC, because they told me I did it deliberately. And there was no question of any compensation at all. In the end, I think, after some months, they gave me £100, which didn't cover anything of the things that I'd had to put off as a result of this injury.

The *Daily Express* headlined the story 'Crackersnap' and told how Michael had been pushed into a ten-foot custard pie, while *The Times* went with 'Sticky End to Show' and added an extra two feet to the pie's diameter. Whatever its dimensions, it was a ruddy big pie and an ill-conceived stunt. While Michael was recovering from his injuries, he recorded a number of appearances on the ITV show *Jokers Wild* (a gag-telling panel game chaired by Barry Cryer):

I did half a dozen with the broken wrist and the other half without it. And I grew a moustache while the wrist was broken. And they put the shows out in a different order. So the viewers saw me one week with a broken wrist and a moustache, and the next week *without* a broken wrist and *no* moustache, and the week after that again with moustache and plaster. They must have thought I was very accident-prone, breaking it every other week.

And so the series came to an end, with both a bang *and* a whimper. But what of Don Maclean's pre-series enticements of X-rated Forbidden Fruits? Were they no more than empty promises? Well, any boy who had matured beyond the 'girls are soppy' stage, and a good number of dads as well, could not have failed to notice the sultry glamour-puss who assisted Michael with the games. Suzette St Clair may have been Sussex-born, but she owed her

Double or Drop tours the variety theatres in 1954 – the year before *Crackerjack* began

Jack Douglas (top) and Joe
Baker, *Crackerjack* 1955-57
(David Bryceson)

Joe Baker Senior (aka 'Mr Grumble'),
Crackerjack 1955-57

Michael Darbyshire (*Crackerjack* 1957-58), Eamonn Andrews and Ronnie Corbett

Eddie Leslie, Ronnie Corbett's second stooge, *Crackerjack* 1958-59

Raymond Rollett, Ronnie's third stooge, *Crackerjack* 1959-60 (Chris Boxall)

Pearl Carr and Teddy Johnson, *Crackerjack* 1958-60

Leslie Crowther, *Crackerjack* 1960-68

Peter Glaze, *Crackerjack* 1960-79
(Jon Anton)

Leslie and Peter comic strip in *Playhour and TV Toyland* 1968

1. One evening, Leslie and Peter were looking at the television when they saw a programme about the last of the big steam railway engines. "What a thrill it would be to ride on a steam engine!" said Leslie. "I'd love to."

2. The next day, Leslie was reading the newspaper when Peter pointed to an advertisement. "Look, Leslie!" he gasped. "It says there's an engine for sale, for only one-pound-ten! And it's at our railway station *now*!"

Vivienne Martin, *Crackerjack* 1960-61
(Photo by Peter Simpkin)

Pip Hinton, *Crackerjack* 1961-65

Valerie Walsh, *Crackerjack* 1965-66
(Photo by Ben Jones)

Christine Holmes, *Crackerjack* 1966-69
(Christine Holmes)

Crackerjack Australia 1966: Michael Boddy, Sue Walker, Reg Livermore, Jenene Watson
(Photos on this page courtesy of Reg Livermore and John Pearson)

Judy Roberts and Reg Livermore

Michael and Reg

Sue Walker seducing Reg as James Bond (Courtesy of Reg Livermore/John Pearson)

Ex-British hostess Vikki Hammond with
new Australian host James Smillie

1967 Australian *Crackerjack* team – James Smillie,
Barry Lovett, Penny Ramsey, Gillian Hunter
(Bottom two photos courtesy of James Smillie)

Rod McLennan, Jillian Comber, Michael Aspel, Frances Barlow, Peter Glaze in 1969

Rock Steady record sleeve with Syd Little and
Eddie Large, *Crackerjack* 1972

Peter Glaze looks up to Don Maclean,
Crackerjack 1973-76 (Don Maclean)

Jacqueline Clarke, *Crackerjack* 1973-74
(Photo by George Wilkes)

Don Maclean as Gitarzan
(Don Maclean)

Michael Aspel, Don Maclean,
Jacqueline Clarke and Peter Glaze

Christine Ozanne, *Crackerjack* LP 1974
(Christine Ozanne/Simon Dell)

BBC audience ticket for *Crackerjack* 1976 (Jan Hunt)

Jan Hunt, *Crackerjack* 1974-79, as the
Queen in pre-credits quickie (Jan Hunt)

Jan with Ed Stewart, *Crackerjack* 1974-79
(Jan Hunt)

Jan as Sarah Jane Smith in *Hallo My Dalek*, with Don and a BBC towel (Jan Hunt)

More nudity in *Cleopatra*, with Jan, Ed, Peter and Don (Jan Hunt)

Musical director Bert Hayes, *Crackerjack* 1957-79, with Jan as a crone (Jan Hunt)

Jan, Peter, Don and Ed in *The Earlier Life of Groucho Marx* (Jan Hunt)

Don, Jan, Peter and Ed wear their own clothes for a change! (Jan Hunt)
(All photos from Jan Hunt's collection were taken by Maureen Flenley)

Peter, director Alan Bell, and Don rehearse a *Crackerjack* silent at Pinewood (Alan Bell)

Alan Bell directs Henry Cooper in a celebrity 'cowcatcher' with Ed (Alan Bell)

Crackerjack

JAN HUNT — ED STEWART — BERNIE CLIFTON — PETER GLAZE

BBC audience ticket for *Crackerjack* 1978 (Peter Raggett)

Bernie Clifton, *Crackerjack* 1977-79, and Peter Glaze,
filming at Romney, Hythe and Dymchurch railway
(Alan Bell)

Jan Michelle, *Crackerjack* 1980

Janette Tough (front) with Sally Ann Triplett, Stu Francis, Leigh Miles and Ian Tough in 1981
(Leigh Miles)

Sara Hollamby, Stu Francis and Julie Dorne Brown in 1983 (Sara Hollamby)

Shepherds Bush Empire, home of *Crackerjack* from 1955 to 1984,
pictured in its early days and (inset) as the BBC Television Theatre

distinctive looks to her Egyptian father and Estonian mother. Wearing a bejewelled headdress, she had also gyrated in the *Top of the Pops* opening credits. And it was that show's producer who had approached Alan Bell, who was then assistant producer on *Crackerjack*:

> So Johnnie Stewart came up to me and said, 'I've got a friend. Would you mind thinking of her for a hostess on *Crackerjack*?' And I said, 'All right.' And he said, 'Oh, she's a lovely girl. Don't worry about her, she'll be good.' Well, it's nothing really – it's about three minutes in a forty-minute show. By the way, the girl was terrible. She didn't know what she was doing, she was walking in front of the camera.
>
> But the following year, I was in the bar at the BBC. And this girl turns up, and she's got a carrier bag in her hand, and she says, 'Have I got publicity for you?! You won't believe this!' And she opened the bag.

What Suzette St Clair produced from the bag was the latest copy of *Mayfair* magazine. Suzette was the cover girl, wearing platform shoes, stockings, a fur coat and not a lot else. The cover boasted, 'Bared: the Girls You Fancy on TV' – including 'The Bird from *Burke Special*', 'The Blonde from *Clockwork Orange*' and 'The Hostess from *Crackerjack*'.

Inside, over half-a-dozen pages, the fur coat and pretty much everything else came off. The interview that accompanied the photo shoot detailed her life and career, but naturally gave *Crackerjack* pride of place:

> Facing three or four hundred shrieking children might not seem the ideal way to spend an afternoon but 24-year-old Suzette St Clair would be unlikely to agree. As hostess of television's perennially popular children's programme *Crackerjack* she had 'enormous fun. It was an invaluable experience.' *Mayfair*'s readers thought so too. Wrote a reader from Bath: 'Who is that exotic-looking dolly who appears on *Crackerjack*? Couldn't she be persuaded to reveal her splendid attributes a little more fully?' Yes, she could and splendid indeed is 5 feet 7 inch Suzette's 37 – 25 – 37.

'Stunned' would be an understated description of the reaction of those around Suzette in the BBC bar, as she gleefully flourished this top-shelf magazine with the *Crackerjack* girl on the front. Alan Bell was mystified:

> I mean, how stupid can the girl get? But she was so proud of this ... 'indiscretion' you might say. Needless to say she was out of the show next year.

Michael Aspel shared Alan's astonishment:

> She really thought she was doing us a favour. We just stared aghast at her lack of perspicacity. She really was sincerely pleased at what she'd done. I mean, for her personal career perhaps it was wonderful, but it didn't do a lot for the image of *Crackerjack*.

Thankfully, the national press never went big on this potentially explosive story, and Suzette subsequently appeared in plenty more TV shows and movies (some clothed, some not) including *Come Play With Me*, which became the longest-running British movie in cinema history.

Don and Pete also spent the latter part of the year in front of the cameras, though (mercifully) fully dressed, as *The Stage* reported in late October 1973:

> Don Maclean and Peter Glaze have recently formed their own company and are now in the process of making a series of five-minute comedy films for showing in *Crackerjack*.
>
> They have already made 15 of these films and they hope to have completed 26 by the end of the year. 'The success of the silent films which Peter and I made together in the last *Crackerjack* series decided us to make this move,' says Don. 'A number of them are already scheduled to be broadcast on German television in December. Interest has been shown from all over the world – even the People's Republic of China – and of course they will be shown each week in the new *Crackerjack*.'

In the previous series, the shooting of the silents had been incorporated into the rehearsal week. This new arrangement was basically a brainwave of producer Robin Nash and, as before, direction was in the capable hands of Alan Bell:

> Robin really liked the films. I could do a seven- or eight-minute film in a day, which is a lot for a film, because you're getting the props in and the actors in the right place, but I could move them along. And I was a film editor as well. So it was my sort of genre.
>
> Robin said to me on the second series, 'Why don't you make the films privately and we'll buy them from you.' And I said, 'Well, is that legal in the BBC?' And he says, 'Oh yes, if it's going to be an ultimate saving.' And of course there *was* a saving, because you didn't have all the red tape. It was just a matter of going out and doing them. And it proved to be quite good, except a company we aligned ourselves with had financial difficulties. And it ended

up with me going to the high court and suing a German company that tried to buy the films.

The thing that warmed my heart, and I'm boasting here, is that I overheard Peter Glaze saying to somebody in the caravan, 'It's alright now. We've got someone working with us who knows what he's doing.' And I thought, 'Thank you Peter, you will be my hero forever.'

Don Maclean received the odd writer's credit, as did Leslie Crowther and producer Peter Whitmore for a couple of revamped remakes of their original mid-60s movies. But the main writer, and sole writer of many, was a reclusive character called Mort Kingsley. Biographical material on Mort is in very short supply, though Alan Bell knows him better than most. In fact, almost as well as he knows himself:

> The thing about me writing the short films – or rather, should I say Mort writing the short films? – was that you had to be economic in what you could do. There was no point saying a car crashes into another. Where are you going to get two cars? So what I would do is I would just walk around a good set. When we had an office at Shepperton Studios – the BBC didn't have an office, *I* had an office there – I'd walk round the set and say, 'Oh, we could film a bit there and a bit there and a bit there.' Because they filmed *Oliver!* there, but they left the set standing.

Those splendid Victorian streets formed a classy backdrop to the *Roadsweepers* episode, which at one point involves Don Maclean outside a church tower, holding a bell rope. Don is jerked skywards as the heavy bell plummets to the ground, then it's the bell's turn to rise while Don plummets, and so on and so on. Hearing the continued tolling of the bell, a baffled policeman checks his watch. It all sounds very dangerous to film, but that's because it was. As was another of Don's scenes in the same movie:

> We did a thing with a dog, an Alsatian. That was in *The Roadsweepers*. And the idea was, Peter had got this Alsatian on a lead. And I went over and lifted the Alsatian's ear and whispered into it and pointed, and then the next thing you saw was the dog going down the road at a hell of a rate, dragging Peter with him, and then Peter crashed into this barrow full of fruit.
>
> So I lifted the dog's ear, and whispered in his ear, and put the ear back. And Alan said, 'That was alright. One more for luck.' So, by now, the dog knows what's going to happen. So I lift the dog's ear, and the dog goes 'Rrroarrr!' and sticks his teeth right through my nose! I'm stood there, all this blood dripping down my nose.

I'd have a go at anything. I mean I was mad. They wouldn't let me do it nowadays, because they'd never get me insured. But I did some ridiculous things.

Every week Don and Pete were bungling odd-job men – circus hands, window cleaners, gardeners, barbers – and every instalment would finish with them retreating (in fast motion) into the distance, leaving a trail of havoc behind them. Peter Glaze, as previously mentioned, wore round-framed lens-less glasses on TV. However, any stunt that involved custard or foam hitting him in the face required him to wear his ordinary glasses, which were a totally different shape and had thick lenses. Otherwise it would be obvious that his glasses had no glass in them. On a few occasions you can actually see his glasses change from shot to shot.

Peter was never going to be up to the physical recklessness of Don, but the partnership worked superbly because of Peter's mastery of visual comedy, as Alan Bell fully appreciated:

> Peter had been brought up with the Crazy Gang. And if you told him to pick up a bottle and look at it and let it fall out of your hand, he wouldn't just take it up and drop it, it would be a flurry of hands. And everything he did was superbly mimed. Had he been in America, he'd be a multi-millionaire, owning studios, because he just had the gift of performing.

Jacqueline Clarke makes a few appearances (usually as old ladies), as well as *Crackerjack* writer Bob Hedley, who can be fleetingly spotted as the exasperated owner of a demolished crockery stall in a *Roadsweepers* sequel. The relationship between Don and Pete in these movies is a little different from their usual *Crackerjack* routines. Rather than comic and stooge, they are a pair of incompetents. So therefore a stooge was still required. And their regular stooge – often a policeman, frequently losing his trousers, perpetually thrown into a river – was Evan Ross. Large, portly and bald, Evan was actually a trained opera singer who had taken up TV extra work, and was often seen in a back row of Captain Mainwaring's platoon in *Dad's Army* where he never uttered a single line. As a silent-movie stooge, he never spoke on *Crackerjack* either. He just took whatever was thrown at him, and wherever he was thrown, with surprisingly good grace.

When the movies were shown in *Crackerjack* they were accompanied, at a suitably tinny piano, by Bert Hayes. When 12 of the films were later released on DVD, Alan Bell went to some expense to have his *Summer Wine* colleague Ronnie Hazlehurst score them for small orchestra. One of Ronnie's trademarks was that you could often sing the title of the show to the theme tune – be it *The Last of the Summer Wine* or *The Fall and Rise of Reginald Perrin*. In this case it's hard not to hear his jaunty theme without the words 'Don and Pete' ringing in your head. But far more than that, every gesture (however large, however small) is reflected in the music. When window cleaner Don lands in the bath with a naked Evan Ross and starts shammying his bald head, we hear *I'm Going to Wash that Man Right out of my Hair*. As he moves down to Evan's chest, so the music shifts down a key. When Don and Pete are hairdressers we hear *The Barber of Seville*. When they turn their attentions to a Japanese customer we get *Barber of Seville* oriental style. Ronnie's twin inspirations were Leroy Shield (who scored many of the Laurel and Hardy movies) and Scott Bradley (composer for Tom and Jerry). For many of today's generation of composers and arrangers, Ronnie himself is something of a role model.

But the true battle-scarred hero of the *Crackerjack* silents is unquestionably Don Maclean, who picked up further injuries while filming the Leslie and Peter remake *Removal Men*:

> We're moving stuff out into a van, and at one point I come out of the front door and I've got this set of library steps on wheels. And the thought is – why should I carry these when I could scoot down the path? So I stand on the top of the library steps, and they've got these nylon ropes and they're pulling me – bear in mind that everything's speeded up – they're pulling me down the path. And as we got to the gate, one wheel hit the gatepost. I literally cleared the whole of the pavement, and was catapulted into the middle of the road. So I stood up and there's blood everywhere. And my eyebrow's cut, my hand's in a terrible state, my knee's rapidly swelling.
>
> And somebody comes out and says, 'He's got to go to hospital, Alan. He's got to be stitched up.' 'Bloody hell!' he said, 'We're going to lose two hours' filming now!' So off I went to the hospital, came back all bandaged up. And I was doing *The Black and White Minstrels* on stage in the West End of London, and I've got my eye out here, and my hand bandaged – and I was limping because the week before he'd got me to slide down the roof of a circus Big Top, grab a rope and swing and land in the pool. But he hadn't measured the length of the rope properly. So when I actually swung, instead of clearing the ground, I hit the ground, and I'd got a bloody great swollen ankle. Yes, he did me quite a lot of damage did Alan, one way and another.

*

By the start of 1974 Don was fully fit and ready to face another 13 weeks of – not *Crackerjack 74* – but just plain unadulterated *Crackerjack*. Rather like the second Rod McLennan series, this one really hit its stride from the word go. There was now a three-man writing team. Bob Hedley continued to script the opening double. Tony Hare (who hadn't worked on the show since that second Rod series) and Bob co-wrote the middle sketch. And *Crackerjack* veteran Bob Block was back to take care of the finale.

Bob Hedley's opening crosstalk routine now had a regular and successful formula, thanks to a memorable entrance he wrote for Don Maclean:

> Bob used to come up with certain lines that worked and then became catchphrases. I don't think he sat down to write a catchphrase. Peter used to start and then I'd interrupt him, and he'd turn round and say, 'Maclean!' And then Bob had written a line, 'Yes, I had a bath this morning.' So that became a catchphrase.

This, coupled with Peter's automatic repeating of Don's opening line before he realises what he's said or who made him say it, became the template for Peter's lectures for years to come. It was all there in the very first show of the series:

PETE:	It was Shakespeare who said, 'If music be the food of love …'
DON:	(ENTERS WITH VIOLIN) Get your fish fingers off the piano!
PETE:	Get your fish … (SEES DON) Maclean!
DON:	Yes, I had a bath this morning.
PETE:	You a violinist? Waste of time you buying a violin!
DON:	This violin is an old 'un. I gave Yehudi me new 'un.

Bob even got a little extra mileage from that Yehudi pun. Later in the show there's a Robin Hood sketch, with Don as Robin and Peter as Friar Tuck:

PETE:	I have heard the wealthy merchants have hidden a gold and silver shipment in the forest.
DON:	Hi ho, Silver!
PETE:	Not that kind of silver, you fool. And the sheriff is pulling strings to obtain it for himself.
DON:	Well, you can't pull strings without Notting 'em. (TO AUDIENCE) It's an old gag, but I gave Yehudi me new 'un.

Of course, if the advance publicity was to be believed, every series of *Crackerjack* was going to be infinitely better than the previous one. With the regular inclusion of the silent movies, and a strong writing team, perhaps this time around when Robin Nash boasted to the *Daily Mirror* of the show's 'new look' it was more than empty bluster:

> Producer Robin Nash tells me it'll all be much livelier and more fun. Out goes the general knowledge quiz. In comes a new studio game.

After all this time, they still hadn't found the winning formula for that final game. One series it would be a quiz, the next a more physical challenge, and so it would continue for some time to come. What never really changed were the elimination games earlier in the show, used to select the contestants for the final showdown. Soon after Michael Aspel had joined the show, the BBC published a *Crackerjack Book of Games*. These were cheap and cheerful versions of the already shoestring-budget TV games, including: carrying paper cups on feet, marbles into jars with fish slices, lassoing matchboxes, bouncing table-tennis balls into egg boxes, eating marshmallows blind-folded, and (of course) sitting on balloons.

Michael's suave manner and throwaway delivery helped calm any nerves the young contestants may have had. Sometimes, as Don Maclean recalls, he'd toss in the odd remark that would go way over the children's heads:

> He asked this lad his name and he said, 'Eamonn.' Michael just looked into the camera and said, 'He used to do this show, you know.' It's not that funny, but it tickled us. We all laughed at it because the kids didn't know what he was talking about.

Another of Michael's unscripted links subtly pokes fun at some lazy sexual stereotyping:

> Okay, listen girls, this is what you've got to do. It's an idea we had to perpetuate the myth that ladies love mucking around with plates and cups and saucers and things.

Marina Lambrou was an 11-year-old pupil of Southgate School in North London when she appeared on the show. But, however the host may strive to put you at your ease, a TV studio is full of distractions:

> We wore flippers on our feet and had to waddle across the stage and pick up something and walk back. But when the game was being explained, I looked up and there was a TV monitor. And I was *so* focused on the TV monitor. I

moved my leg to the left – and so did the leg on the screen. 'Oh, that's my leg!' And the next thing I know is, 'Okay, ready to go.' And I hadn't listened to the instructions! So I kind of lagged behind everybody.

It was Michael Aspel's conscious decision to adopt a seemingly effortless manner with the children:

> I wanted it to be fun rather than intense competition, so I used to try to ease it along by cracking a few jokes, and be careful not to be favouring one rather than the other. But I knew that at the end of it all, apart from the prizes they won, was the ultimate – the *Crackerjack* pencil. The number of times I used to be approached in the BBC Club by producers of quite important programmes just saying casually, 'Oh, could you get me one of those for my daughter?' And I used to say, 'Certainly not!' They'd get really quite cross, but that's the way it was. And that was the great thing about it. The more we refused to spread it around, the more precious it became. And more coveted.

As ever, Michael makes a last-minute appearance in the musical finale. But first he has to introduce it, lending his cultured tones to a load of highly bizarre old rubbish:

> Doctor Frank Furter was a silly old sausage with a chip on his shoulder, who created all kinds of monsters and was even on squeaking terms with the old vampire. For our finale we present – Frank Furter's Dying Circus.

This is Bob Block's first sketch of the series, in which Peter Glaze plays the doctor and Jacqueline Clarke is the monster he has created. It's a typically unglamorous role, and Peter is given an excessively contrived intro to some subtly butchered song lyrics. You can almost hear the squeak of Bob Block's crowbar:

> PETE: Due to a slight mistake in her chemical formula, I'm afraid her real nose grew upside down, which means that when she sneezes, she blows her hat off. Therefore I have given her another nose made of papier-mâché – and a box of spares in case she feels like a change.
>
> JACQUIE IS MADE UP TO LOOK VERY WEIRD, AND SHE WEARS A FALSE NOSE – SHE SITS UP AND SMILES, SHOWING SEVERAL TEETH MISSING.

JACQUIE: Paper noses! Paper noses!

Oh, how real those noses seem to be.

But they're only imitation,

Like the big red conk that you gave me.

The following week, Jacqueline had the rather more alluring role of Juliet, opposite Don Maclean's Romeo. Bob Block had written a similar sketch for Leslie Crowther's final show six years earlier. Those with long memories would recognise many of the jokes. However, pop had moved on, and it was a stroke of genius to set the dramatic action to Elton John's *Goodbye Yellow Brick Road.*

The whole sequence is intricately plotted to fit in with the lyrics, involving some spectacular stunt work for Don:

DON MAKES A DRAMATIC LEAP FROM THE LOW BALUSTRADE TO THE BALCONY FLOOR – WE HEAR A LOUD SPLINTERING NOISE AS HE GOES RIGHT DOWN THROUGH BALCONY FLOOR AND DISAPPEARS. JACQUIE REMAINS WHERE SHE IS, WAITING IMPATIENTLY WITH ARMS HELD OUT AND EYES CLOSED.

JACQUIE: When are you gonna come down? When are you going to land?

Don came through all this unscathed. But the build-up to that final stratospheric succession of 'ooohs' didn't entirely go to plan, as he told Bernie Clifton and his aghast studio audience on BBC Radio Sheffield in 2016:

Peter Glaze was incredibly short-sighted. He used to wear these big stiff contact lenses *and* glasses when we did the show. He was double-glazed! And we were doing Romeo and Juliet. I was playing Romeo and Peter was playing Tybalt. And we had this swordfight with these terrible, really old, rusty rapiers. So we're doing the swordfight and, at the same time, singing *Goodbye Yellow Brick Road.* So, all of a sudden, our swords clash and the button from the end of the rapier comes off the end of Peter's sword. So now he's got a jagged end. But he's blind, he can't see this. So we carry on with the swordfight and it comes to the part where I drop my sword and run up the ivy growing on the side of this building, to get to Juliet who's on the balcony. And at this point, Peter is going to shove this sword up my bum, because we've got to the bit where it goes, 'Oooh-oooh-oooh!' But, of course, he doesn't know that the button's come off the end of the rapier. So he sticks it up …

And I had to be treated afterwards. I had to go and lay on this bed with me knickers down and have iodine poured all over me bum!

A disaster of a different kind affected the fifth show of the series, as the *Daily Mirror* reported:

The children's programme *Crackerjack* will be scrapped on Friday because of a pay dispute. The dispute is over a long-standing claim by TV electricians for more money at meal times. The electricians have now decided to stage 'walk-outs' on selected programmes.

This wouldn't be the last *Crackerjack* to be affected by industrial action. The scheduled show was replaced by a compilation of highlights from previous programmes, shrinking the series from 13 shows to 12.

Whenever the serious press gave *Crackerjack* a mention, it was inevitably accompanied by a barely concealed sneer. During the series, Katharine Whitehorn wrote a piece for *The Observer* about studio audiences at television recordings. This included a visit to *Crackerjack*, where she exposed a blatant example of TV fakery:

Crackerjack, the programme where children go to clap and clapped out jokes go to die, has only just enough grownups to control the children, whose eager smiling faces are shown on the screen – but at the time those shots are taken, they have simply been asked to applaud to an empty stage. They look considerably more blank while the show's actually going on. 'Well, some of the younger kids like it,' said a 13-year-old kindly.

While Robin Nash continued to produce the series, the direction was in the hands of two Bills – Bill Wilson and Bill Ersser – both of whom Michael Aspel had previously encountered as floor managers at Alexandra Palace in his newsreading days. Messrs Wilson and Ersser took it in turns, directing alternate episodes throughout the series. Don Maclean quickly noticed their contrasting styles of direction:

Bill Wilson was smashing. He was a very down-to-earth man and he laughed a lot. And as a comic, particularly when you're trying stuff out, you want people to laugh at what you're doing. And Bill Wilson was very encouraging. He used to say, 'Why don't you do this? Why don't you try that?'
Bill Ersser just used to lean over a camera script. Never said anything. 'Bill, how shall we do this?' [AFTER A LONG PAUSE] 'Why would I know? You do it. And I'll film it. That's what I'm here for.'

After the potentially scandalous behaviour of the previous *Crackerjack* hostess, this time Robin Nash opted for an over-qualified actress, rather than an under-dressed model, and approached Lesley North:

> My husband Roy North was working with Basil Brush, and the wonderful Robin Nash was the producer. He asked me if I'd be interested in hostessing *Crackerjack*. I wasn't that keen, but he said I could do some of the sketches, so that was that.
>
> I particularly remember a caveman sketch – Jacquie and I were in skimpy animal skins, as was the way then. And I think there was a lot of being whacked with polystyrene clubs. I also remember Michael Aspel singing *Tiger Feet* wearing giant tiger feet. It was all very enjoyable, and a happy company as I recall.

Michael Aspel shares Lesley's recollection of his avant-garde performance of Mud's chart-topper:

> I remember it very clearly, and how much I loved doing it, and how funny I thought it looked.

The caveman sketch wasn't a new scenario. It had been done back in Eamonn's day by Leslie, Peter, Pip and Jillian. And in Bob Block's decade of writing for the show he must have plundered every period in history with greater frequency than Doctor Who. For his final sketch of the series he revisited King Alfred and those overcooked cakes. Five years earlier Christine Holmes had sung of *Yesterday's Creams*. This time round the Neil Sedaka hit *A Little Lovin'* becomes *A Little Oven*. And naturally there is *Burn Baby Burn* (the pre-*Disco Inferno* Hudson Ford song).

King Alfred was Bob Block's *Crackerjack* swansong. Within two years Bob had created and written *Rentaghost*, whose cast included former *Crackerjack* stooge Michael Darbyshire. The show ran for nine series, finishing just a month before the final episode of *Crackerjack*.

*

In August 1974, five months after the series had ended, the *Crackerjack* cast reunited to record an LP record of songs and sketches. Ever since Don Maclean had joined the show, there had been a gentle jostling between newbie Don and old-timer Peter for top billing, with the *Radio Times* swapping the order of Don and Peter each week. Previous to the recording session, both agents wrote to the BBC agreeing that if Don Maclean's photo was on the left on the *front* of the sleeve, Peter Glaze's name must be on the left on the *back*. And that both names should be 'in the same sized type'.

But what of the third member of this comedy trio? A BBC internal memo, a few days before the scheduled recording, had this bombshell to drop:

> Jacquie Clarke has asked to be released from her commitment to take part in the recording session for the *Crackerjack* gramophone record on Sunday 11th August 1974.

In fact it was due to circumstances rather beyond Jacqueline's control:

> Oh, there was quite a hoo-hah over that! They were going to do this recording and I had already got another new comedy series. And my agent had already accepted the job on my behalf. It was six episodes and it was a very nice cast. And then this cropped up. I mean, what could I do? My agent asked me to ring and speak to the BBC and say, 'I'm already under contract and I don't think I can do it. I can't do your LP because I'm already signed up.' So it was a very difficult time.

The comedy series (also for the BBC) was *Second Time Around* by Richard Waring, starring Michael Craig and Patricia Brake. Sundays were a very popular day for recording sitcoms, as any theatre actor working in London could rehearse throughout the week, perform onstage every evening, then devote their entire day off to camera rehearsals and recording.

A compromise was reached whereby Jacqueline would record some of the songs on the following day. But because the LP was being recorded in the concert hall at BBC Broadcasting House with a studio audience, a replacement needed to be found. Christine Ozanne shared the same agent as Jacqueline Clarke. She had already used her diminutive stature to great success in a variety of comic roles, from a cleaner in *Carry On Nurse*, to a duchess in Ronnie Barker's original TV version of *The Phantom Raspberry Blower of Old London Town*. Knowing she could also sing, her agent asked if she was free for the weekend, and she had two days to familiarise herself with script and music.

Christine Ozanne played vastly contrasting roles in three of the sketches – Jim Hawkins in *Treasure Island*, Flora Macdonald in *Bonnie Prince Charlie*, and a flapper in *The Twenties*. All the sketches incorporated songs, which Christine rehearsed beforehand with Don, Peter and the Bert Hayes Orchestra:

The music call went pretty well. I'm a good sight-reader and the songs were familiar or easy enough to pick up. Except for one. *Anything Goes* is very well-known, but I had great difficulty with that bit of rhythm on 'silly gigolos'. It wasn't correctly sung, but I trust that only someone who really knows the song would wince.

If it was a challenging day for Christine, she soon became aware that a more seasoned member of the cast was also feeling the stress:

> Looking back I remember that Peter Glaze was nervous and 'hyper' all day. My thinking at the time was that he seemed to be out of his element, working at this pressure. Calm and collected he was not, although he had performed in goodness knows how many shows by this time.
>
> Robin Nash was quite the opposite, as I recall, and came over as relaxed and charming. He always reminded me, physically, of Lee Marvin but with the nature of a pussycat.

It sometimes happens that a sketch that works fine on television needs some subtle adjustment for it to succeed in an audio-only version. In *Treasure Island*, Don is Long John Silver and Peter is Captain Smollet:

> PETE: Now look here, you're supposed to be Long John Silver. He only had one leg.
>
> DON: Don't be ridiculous! You don't think I'm havin' me leg off for a record, do ee?

The sketch culminates with them digging up Blackbeard's buried treasure, which turns out to be nothing more than 16 silver fillings. But the sketch needed a stronger finish and, in the final rehearsal, Christine and the team were still no closer to finding one:

> They were struggling for a tag line. I suggested, 'Silver fillings? Foiled again!' which highly amused Peter, who insisted it was brilliant!

There are plenty of Don and Pete duologues on the disc, one of them featuring another of Don's regular catchphrases:

> They don't call them milk bottles in Venice. They call them oggle-cockles. When you put them outside the back door for the milkman to collect, as they sink they go oggle-cockle, oggle-cockle, oggle-cockle.

Peter Glaze also recites *Esau Buck* – a tongue-twisting monologue dating back to turn-of-the-century America – which he performs flawlessly:

> But when he saw the saw, he saw he couldn't saw with the saw, so he looked around for another saw, but that was the only saw he saw, so Esau saw he couldn't saw, you see?

Jacqueline Clarke was back the next day, recording (without an audience) a couple of solo songs and two duets with Don – a Tarzan rock-and-roll number called *Gitarzan* and *Money Money* from *Cabaret*. This song is neatly incorporated into *The Twenties* sketch and, although Christine sings the other two numbers, *Wam Bam* and *Anything Goes*, it is Jacqueline's voice that is heard on *Money Money*. Performing this song on *Crackerjack* and then on the LP was a particular highlight of Jacqueline's time with the show:

> My fondest memory is doing *Money Money*. Because I think it was very stylishly done. And Don Maclean was such fun and used to have so much energy to create and want to do things properly and in the right way.

After *The Twenties* routine, the LP is rapidly running out of grooves:

DON: Well, that's it, Pete. It's the end of the record. You'd better get off now, because you're getting a bit close to that hole in the middle.

PETE: Never mind about the hole in the middle. I know exactly what I'm ab-ahhhhhhh! (LOUD SPLASH!) Oggle-cockle, oggle-cockle, oggle-cockle …

Although it was recorded on stage in front of a live audience, they are nothing like as vociferous as a typical *Crackerjack* crowd, as Christine Ozanne noticed:

> Listening to the LP now, I am slightly surprised that the audience reactions were not very evident during the sketches. Were they a bit puzzling for the youngsters? There seemed to be silences where the writers would have expected laughs. I secretly wonder if this was the reason Don's characters all had rather manic laughs after each line. 'If no one else is laughing, I'll fill in the gaps!'

Jacqueline Clarke's sitcom *Second Time Around* made an extremely rapid return, and a second series was broadcast in early 1975, meaning she was unavailable for the next series of *Crackerjack*. Jacqueline left the show with mixed feelings:

> *Crackerjack* wasn't my most joyous employment, really. I liked it to begin with and then, because there was so much more happening in my life, I just thought 'hmmmm'. And I don't think I'm a great lady for children really. I'd rather have adult humour to play to than children, which probably sounds awful, but that's how I really feel.
>
> But I've never known anything I've done at the BBC to be anything but fun. Because, when you're doing entertainment, that's what it's all about, isn't it? My only sadness was, because I was so busy doing other things, I probably didn't give my whole 100 per cent to it, which I couldn't do because I was *tired.* I used to fall asleep at lunchtime. But my fond memory is thinking of the TV Theatre, and of Mike Aspel and Don Maclean and Peter. And just being part of a very nice team.

Jacqueline continued with a busy and varied career on stage and screen. In 1976 she starred in sketch show *Battle of the Sexes*, alongside former Australian *Crackerjack* host James Smillie, with former *Crackerjack* producer Peter Whitmore in charge. When I interviewed her for this book, we were in her dressing room at London's Gielgud Theatre, where she was nearing the end of a long run in *The Curious Incident of the Dog in the Night-Time.*

But it wasn't just Jacqueline Clarke and Bob Block who were saying farewell to *Crackerjack*. In late October 1974 *The Stage* revealed:

> Michael Aspel has announced that he is leaving the BBC's *Crackerjack* because his other commitments prevent him from giving the time he would wish to the programme. He recently joined Capital Radio in London to run a daily radio programme.
>
> Although several names have been discussed, the BBC cannot yet confirm who will be taking his place.

Following his departure from *Crackerjack*, Michael's career frequently mirrored that of Eamonn Andrews. He had his own ITV chat show and panel games, before succeeding Eamonn as presenter of *This Is Your Life.* But he looks back on *Crackerjack* with great affection:

> It's still in people's minds. I do less and less talking to people at lunchtimes. But if ever I mention *Crackerjack* there's always a selection of increasingly croaky voices shouting '*Crackerjack!*' from the back. Never fails. Never.

For me it was just going into an entirely new world. And the volume of the kids' screaming. And suddenly confirming that I was entering something that was really very special, much loved and valuable, and I'd better not muck it up. And finding that I was allowed to find my way, as well as being pointed in the right direction.

I mean, every company on tour with a play, they have little quarrels and go off each other. That never happened with anybody. It was entirely fun and good natured and a real family. Only less temperamental than a family. As far as the group of people I worked with, they were my pals and my family and I loved every moment of it.

10
What Brings You to These Parts?

1975 – 1976

JACQUELINE CLARKE WAS NEVER going to be an easy act to replace. She was the show's first 'funny lady' at a time when there were comparatively few around – which was far more to do with a lack of demand from TV producers than any lack of supply. Although recruiting Jacqueline could be seen as an imaginative decision by producer Robin Nash, he was hardly taking any risks with one of the most familiar female faces in TV sketch comedy.

From its very start *Crackerjack* had taken pride in its flair for seeking out promising performers with little or no TV exposure. Jan Hunt was just that. She'd been in the business since the age of 11. She'd swelled the ranks of scruffy schoolgirls in *St Trinian's*, she'd sung in a double act at London's Windmill Theatre, and had recently played the spoons in the role of Ellie May in *Show Boat* at the Adelphi Theatre. But so far television stardom had eluded Jan. Until:

> Suddenly I got this call from my agent saying, 'Oh Jan, I've got you an audition for *Crackerjack*.' And I went, 'Wow! That's fantastic!' So I went along to the audition and saw Robin Nash, who was the overall producer, and I had to sing a bit and dance a bit and – I can't remember what else I did – I don't think I read any scripts or anything. And he said, 'We're seeing quite a few people, but we're making a shortlist, and if you get to that stage we will

recall you.' So I went away with my tail between my legs and I thought, 'Well, you've done your bit, forget about it.'

Then I got a call saying, 'We'd love you to come back for a recall.' So my hopes built up again. I went back in and had a lovely conversation with Robin Nash. And then he said, 'Oh, Jan, I'd like you to meet the rest of the team.' And I felt a bit like – I don't know what to say without being rude – like a prize bull or something. I sat there and first of all Don Maclean came in and I was introduced. And they were, you know, giving me the 'once over'. Then Peter Glaze came in and he did the same thing, 'Oh, lovely to meet you, blah blah blah.' And I thought, 'I *think* this is a good sign.' And then Robin Nash said, 'Jan, we would love you to become part of the *Crackerjack* team.'

I thought my agent was great, getting me an audition. I thought, 'Oh, I've got a good agent here.' But it was two years later that I learned it was Jacquie Clarke, my predecessor, who had put my name forward. And I felt so bad that I'd never had the opportunity to say thank you. But I contacted her and I said, 'Gosh, I just can't thank you enough.'

Both Jacqueline and Jan had a passion for music hall, and both had worked at the Players' Theatre. And Jacqueline Clarke had also seen Jan on stage:

I went to see *Showboat* at the Adelphi. And I saw this very, very bubbly sort of girl. And also met up with her at the Players'. And her name was Jan Hunt. And we were talking and I was saying, 'Oh, I'm going to leave.' And she said, 'Are you?' And I said, 'Yes, I am.' And she said, 'Oh, I've never had a chance to get onto telly.' And I was doing a lot. So I went to Robin one day, and I said, 'Robin, have you cast yet?' And he said, 'Why?' So I said, 'Well, I just know someone who's absolutely right and would fit the bill. She's great and you'll love her. But it *is* a friend of mine. Her name is Jan Hunt.' He said, 'Well … might do.' So anyway, yes, Jan got the job.

For many years, in her early career, Jan Hunt had been one of the Lionel Blair dancers, and it was while working in Scotland that she unexpectedly got the opportunity to break into comedy:

I used to stand in the wings and watch all the sketches and the comics, because I just loved all that. And Rikki Fulton used to work sketches with his wife. And I just watched thinking, 'I'd love to do what she does.' And it was like *42nd Street* syndrome. One night Rikki came in, and his wife was ill. She wasn't able to do the show. And I thought – am I going to be brave enough to say, 'I know what she does. I know the part.' And I did. I said, 'I know what Rikki's wife does. I know I can do it.' And I did it.

And Alec Finlay, he was a very popular Scots comic, he said, 'I think you've got the potential to be a feed for a comic. Would you be interested in that?' And I said, 'It's something I would love to do.' And I started doing sketches with them, and learned about comedy and comedy timing and feeding and characterisation. And for three years I worked as comedy feed to Alec Finlay and Johnny Victory and Rikki Fulton and Jimmy Logan. That's where I did all my training.

After Robin Nash offered Jan the position of *Crackerjack* girl, things moved quickly. Extremely quickly:

And I went, 'Oh, I'm so excited – that's wonderful!' I said, 'Will you be contacting my agent?' And he said, 'No, you leave here now. And you go straight to wardrobe, because you're going straight into the *Crackerjack* pantomime.' So I never even got home after it. I went straight through to wardrobe – I was so nervous – and got my costume. And it was *Aladdin*. And within a couple of days I was given the script, and that was it.

Christmas Crackerjack had once been a regular tradition but, because more recent series had run early in the New Year, there hadn't been a *Christmas Crackerjack* since 1969. And, although there had been a pantomime element to some of those Christmas editions, there had never before been a proper *Crackerjack* pantomime.

Aladdin was a lavish affair. Running for a full hour on Christmas Eve 1974, it was scripted by *Crackerjack*'s two regular writers, Bob Hedley and Tony Hare. The new comedy trio was quickly established, with Jan Hunt as Aladdin, Don Maclean as brother Wishee Washee, and Peter Glaze as mother Widow Twankey, launching into *You've Got to Give the Public What they Want*.

And here we return to Forbidden Fruits, X films and censorship. Somehow, in the midst of this wholesome panto song, they succeed in slipping in a sly reference to the most controversial and sexually explicit movie of 1973:

JAN: In cinemas, the good and bad are slowly being reversed.
DON: With X films making headlines, we can soon expect the worst.
PETE: *Last Tango* doesn't bother me, I didn't see the first!
ALL: You've got to give the public what they want.

Peter Glaze makes a convincing dame, not through elaborate makeup and high-pitched voice, but subtle gestures and mannerisms. But at one point he stretches credibility so far that Don momentarily breaks the illusion:

PETE: After all, what's Raquel Welch got that I haven't?

DON: (LOOKING HIM UP AND DOWN) Oh, come on Pete, be sensible!

As usual, the music is composed and arranged by Bert Hayes, who Don Maclean remembers as a model of creative efficiency:

He wrote quite a bit of original music for the pantomimes. He wrote some dance for Flick Colby and Pan's People. I think it was the *Dance of the Jewels*. That was beautiful music. And he just knocked that out in a morning.

Pan's People (plus the odd risqué gag) may have been pitched at the adults, but the villainous Abanazer is *Play School* favourite Derek Griffiths, who Don instantly recognises. 'I've seen him before, through the round window.' There's also a preponderance of policemen, with Deryck Guyler (Constable 'Corky' Turnbull from *Sykes*) as Sergeant Ying Tong in command of a bunch of non-speaking clumsy coppers, comprising several *Z Cars* regulars, including James Ellis and Nicholas Smith. (Nicholas was then appearing both as PC Yates in *Z Cars* and as Mr Rumbold in *Are You Being Served?*) There's even a cameo from Jack Warner, rapidly approaching 80 and still pounding the beat in *Dixon of Dock Green*.

Richard Wattis (another *Sykes* regular) also makes an appearance, along with singer Dana and The Goodies. And when Peter Glaze falls through the floor (during an Alan Bell filmed slapstick routine) he lands in a bath containing Les Dennis, naked apart from a beret, doing an impression of Frank Spencer.

There's even a fleeting appearance of the Tardis. In fact, the whole show has the feeling of a *Doctor Who* regeneration episode. Former host Michael Aspel appears as judge in a courtroom scene, and former female lead Jacqueline Clarke turns up in silver makeup as the Genie. The Slave of the Lamp, stripped to the waist and similarly coated silver on every visible body part, is Ed Stewart, *Crackerjack*'s other incomer along with Jan Hunt:

Of course Ed Stewart joined the same time that I did. And Jacquie was in it, so it was a nice handover. Ed was far more nervous than I, because I'd been used to learning scripts and all that sort of thing. And although Ed did a lot of dialogue obviously in his radio shows, a lot of his was 'off the cuff'. So suddenly having a script landed in front of him …

Leslie Crowther was the first host of radio request show *Junior Choice*, but when Ed 'Stewpot' Stewart took over about six months later he swiftly made the show his own, right from his opening greeting – a cheery falsetto 'Morning!' Ed was one of many pirate radio DJs who had achieved respectability by joining Radio 1 at its inception.

As Aladdin rubs the lamp, Ed materialises with a gruff 'Hello Darling' (another *Junior Choice* catchphrase) and swiftly demonstrates his magic prowess:

> Signed, sealed and delivered, one consignment of precious jewels to Aladdin. Anything else you'd like? Saturday morning request? Wombles? Donny Osmond?

Donny Osmond (alongside sister Marie) was on the first *Crackerjack* of the series proper, just over a week later. The following month The Osmonds appeared, while younger brother Jimmy had guested on the last show of the previous series.

The *Daily Mirror* gave the panto an extraordinarily scathing review:

> *Aladdin* was another example of the bad rubbish we have to suffer. Peter Glaze and Don Maclean with their corny jokes were bad enough, but they weren't content with this. The pantomime version is never the original story, but this was so far from *Aladdin* it turned into an all-time fiasco.

Okay, the show was never going to win any awards, but ironically this review *did*. Its writer, 13-year-old Jackie Harris of Beckenham, Kent, was crowned Britain's Champion Child TV Critic and received an all-expenses-paid trip to the Monte Carlo Television Festival. A cynic would say that if she'd written a good review she might never have won!

The 1975 series was produced, as before, by Robin Nash. This time, as Don Maclean recalls, one director was responsible for the whole of the run:

> Phil Bishop, he was an enthusiast. I didn't think he was that good, but he was an enthusiast. I did like Phil Bishop. He had the idea for the highwayman sketches, which I thought was quite good. And he also directed some of the silent films.

The highwayman sketches were short pre-credits quickies all filmed in advance of the series. The device of a short gag (on film or in the studio) preceding the opening titles had made its first appearance a series or two ago, and would continue in some form or another for many series to come. All these quickies involved a coach and horses and a mounted highwayman. Not cheap but (as costume, props and location never changed) enough quickies for the whole series could easily be shot in a day. The writers referred to these opening gags as 'cowcatchers' – something to immediately grab the attention of viewers – much like the cowcatcher on the front of an old American locomotive was the first thing to hit any straying livestock.

Each week novice highwayman Ed Stewart is instructed by Don Maclean. In one sketch, Don teaches Ed how to use spurs on a docile horse. Don mounts his steed and slips on his mask as the coach, carrying Peter and Jan, approaches. He digs in his spurs and the horse gallops furiously straight past the coach, with Don yelling, 'What time's the next staaaaage?' Ed replies, 'I don't know! But what I do know is it's Friday, it's five o'clock …'

The previous series had been written by Bob Block, Bob Hedley and Tony Hare. Bob Block had now moved on, leaving the other Bob and Tony as writers for the series. Don Maclean saw this as an improvement:

> I don't think Bob Block had anything to give to the show at that time. He was, sort of, stuck in his ways. He knew what he thought was funny and that was what he was going to do. He liked slapstick and I don't think, in the early 70s, that kids wanted slapstick. They *would* listen to the spoken word. They liked visuals, but that's different from hitting people in the head, and physical violence almost.

Bob Hedley and Tony Hare were the first writing partnership *Crackerjack* ever had. A winning combination, according to Don:

> The way I think it worked – Bob wrote the double, Bob and Tony collaborated on the middle sketch, and then Tony did the lion's share of the finale – because he was into his charts and his pop music.
>
> They wrote well individually and they wrote well together. And there was never any rivalry between them. And I know that Bob Hedley used to think, 'What's Tony Hare going to come up with next?' But he always used to like what Tony came up with. And then, if Tony hadn't got a tag, then Bob would probably come up with a tag. And they, sort of, helped one another out.

Tony Hare's strength was in visual humour, whereas Bob Hedley was a joke machine. They were very different people, but nevertheless their writing partnership flourished, as Tony Hare recalls:

> Bob was quite a bit older than me. I was 32 then, and Bob, I reckon, must have been in his 50s. He was a great gag merchant and I think I learned a lot about writing jokes from him. And we nicked jokes from old stuff. There's a few 'thanks for the memory' jokes in the pantos and sketches.

Tony Hare later wrote for Don Maclean on the radio series *Maclean Up Britain* and *Keep It Maclean*, and Tony's way of looking at things particularly appealed to Don:

> Tony Hare has got a mind ... I'd hate to have that mind. I don't know how he sleeps! He'd come at everything from the side, Tony Hare. He just used to come up with some bizarre things. Sometimes he'd write a sketch, and it'd be a great sketch, but there'd be no tag on it. He wouldn't finish it. But it didn't matter because we'd always think of something to finish it. He wasn't great on tags. I used to say to him, 'Tony, why don't you write the tag first and work backwards?' But he'd got a fantastic mind.

A good example of collaborative writing is the musical finale *Annie Get Your Goon*. (Tony's enthusiasm for The Goons and other absurdist humour is frequently evident in his *Crackerjack* sketches.) Jan Hunt is Annie Oakley and Don Maclean is her incredibly conceited rival Frank. Tony wrote the majority of the sketch, but he remembers Bob Hedley being responsible for the following gag:

DON: I should be a star on Broadway.
JAN: Yer darn tootin'!
DON: I should be a star (COCKNEY) dahn Tootin' Broadway.

Ed Stewart makes his customary cameo appearance in the closing moments as Buffalo Bill:

PETE: Why Buffalo Bill, what brings you to these parts?
DON: (TO CAMERA) We daren't give him any other parts.

This was the gentlest of digs at Ed Stewart's acting shortcomings which, in his autobiography *Out of the Stewpot*, Ed freely admits to:

Crackerjack was a children's show that had everything – corny jokes, star guests and the all-singing finale, in which Eamonn Andrews mimed the words and I usually forgot them!

Jan Hunt had first-hand experience of these occasional memory lapses:

Ed wasn't good at remembering lines. So, if Ed had quite a bit of dialogue, I would position myself next to him, or Don would. And when it was time for Ed to speak, we used to give him a little gentle nudge. But he was great with the children. He was very popular, had a good following.

Ed had no dramatic pretensions. Whereas Michael Aspel *could* act, but often pretended he couldn't. And Eamonn couldn't even pretend. But Ed (whether he forgot his lines, or forgot to learn them in the first place) always gave it a go. And the kids loved him for it.

Jan Hunt had much stage experience to draw upon, but live TV (or TV that was recorded as non-stop as possible) was still very new to her:

The big fear I had, when I first joined … It wasn't live, of course, so I knew we could do retakes. But I never wanted to. And I thought, 'Oh, I hope I never make a mistake, and have to stop, and cause the cameras to stop and reroll and everything.' And I got really worried about it. And a couple of times maybe I'd made a little hiccup, or I'd paraphrased a line or something. And I'd let it go, I'd carry on. And at the end of the programme, then it was in the can. And I would say to Peter Glaze, 'I'm going to worry about this until it comes out now, on Friday. Because I messed up, basically.'

And he said, 'Jan, I'll give you a little tip.' He said, 'It's not live television. So if you think you've made a boo-boo that you are going to worry about until it's transmitted, just go – poo bum willy wee-wee! And of course they'll have to stop. Whereas, if you don't say anything, they'll keep rolling. So just go – poo bum wee-wee belly! They'll stop for you. They *have* to!' So that was a good tip. I just hope I didn't get a name for being somebody who used foul language!

Over the series, Jan portrayed any number of historical characters, always authentically costumed, even if their behaviour was not quite as you'd expect:

They said, 'We need to make Queen Victoria a bit different.' And I used to be quite acrobatic. So I said, 'How about, when she does the number, I can turn cartwheels across the floor?' Which they let me do. And then I also said, 'I play the spoons,' which actually, funnily enough, I did at the Players'

Theatre. And so at the end of the number I had Queen Victoria playing the spoons. But they allowed you to bring your ideas to the table. And Tony Hare was always very happy at the initial readthrough. He said, 'If you've got any ideas, then please bring them to the table. We can always chuck them out again if we don't agree with them!' So we were able to inject *ourselves* into what we were doing. It was such a happy time, it really was.

Doctor Who had always been a popular target for *Crackerjack*. And now there was a new Doctor to poke fun at. In the sketch *Hallo My Dalek* (a pun on Charlie Drake's catchphrase), Don Maclean is Tom Baker and Jan is a 'stage school' Sarah Jane – both of them very clever impersonations. The sketch features a large futuristic TV screen, and the costume department was instructed to avoid the colour blue, in case it interfered with the CSO (colour separation overlay) visual effect. During the sketch Sarah Jane repeatedly steps on the Doctor's overlong scarf, almost strangling him. 'Now you know why my eyes bulge!' As usual, one of the Doctor's pieces of equipment is playing up:

DON: It's a mere lassification of the humperdinkular residule in the cross-section under the gander-shank.

JAN: The important thing is – can it be repaired?

DON: Not only that, it can also be mended. After all, I'm an electronic genius, aren't I? If it wasn't for me there'd be no *Crackerball* later.

Crackerball was the show's brand-new final game and was about as hi-tech as *Crackerjack* ever got. It was nothing more than the most rudimentary of computer football games, with a couple of paddles hitting a square representation of a ball. But it lasted for a whole two series, which was a distinct improvement on many previous games. New hostess, blonde actress Suzanne Moore – who had actually appeared in *Doctor Who*, as well as bit-parts in *Softly Softly*, *Black Beauty* and the X-rated *Percy's Progress* – was there to pick a card from a sack each time a goal was scored, entitling a child in hospital to a prize.

Another musical finale was a compressed version of *Pygmalion*, titled *My Fur Lady*. Jan (as Eliza Do-Nothink) has succeeded in convincing Ed Stewart's Count Popofski that she is of noble birth, and Don's Professor Wiggins is keen for her to give a further demonstration of her newly acquired linguistic skills:

DON:	Why not tell the Count more about the hurricanes in Hampstead, Hereford and Hertfordshire?
JAN:	(BACK INTO ROUGH COCKNEY) Wot? Go frew all that rubbish again? Not *Crackerjack* likely!
KIDS:	Crackerjack!

This is possibly the only example of the show's title being substituted for an expletive. You may think the writers occasionally tried to slip something a little dodgy into the show, and you may possibly be right. By the last show of the series, Bob Hedley and Tony Hare were in an exceptionally mischievous mood:

> Bob and I wrote a sketch together set in the twenties by the river. Don and Pete were dressed in white flannels, striped blazers and boaters vying for the attentions of Jan. For a bit of a laugh we titled the sketch: *Cruising Down the River* or *The Right Care of Punts*. I do remember that some of the production team thought it amusing and others not so. Whether any were downright offended I can't recall. Needless to say, only the first half of the title was displayed on the caption at the beginning of the sketch!

*

For the second year running there was a *Crackerjack* pantomime, on Christmas Eve 1975, as a prelude to a new series of 13 shows starting in January 1976. This time Bob Hedley and Tony Hare turned their attentions to *Robinson Crusoe*. The guest list was even more star-studded than the last, with Windsor Davies and Don Estelle from *It Ain't Half Hot Mum* and John Inman from *Are You Being Served?* The linking narration was provided by King Neptune, alias John Laurie from *Dad's Army*.

Jan takes the title role, Peter again drags up as Mrs Crusoe ('looking uncannily like Dandy Nichols', said *The Stage*), and Don is Robinson's brother Billy. The script somehow succeeds in being both bang up to date and as old as the hills. In this scene, which references a movie not due to be released until Boxing Day, they are sailing along in a dinghy when they spot a shark:

DON:	It's from that new film *Jaws*.
PETE:	What's *Jaws*?
DON:	Not for me, I'm driving. When I nod my head – hit it!

(PETE BANGS DON ON HEAD WITH MALLET)

DON:	Fool! You're supposed to hit the one with the big mouth full of teeth.
PETE:	I did!

The previous year Ed Stewart had been stripped to the waist and daubed in silver body-paint to play the Slave of the Lamp. This time the level of nudity is the same, but the paint is a shade darker:

ED:	You can call me Friday, man.
JAN:	Why? What's happening then?
ED:	Oh – a smart cat, huh? That's my name, man. Friday.
JAN:	Oh, Man Friday!

As iffy as this seems, it's worth remembering that *The Black and White Minstrel Show* was still running on BBC1, and that Don Maclean (like Leslie Crowther before him) would be hosting the 1976 series, shortly after the next run of *Crackerjack*.

The writers were excellent at capturing the vocal quirks of performers such as John Inman and Windsor Davies, but nonetheless the actors would tinker a little with the lines to fit their own style of delivery. Don Maclean remembers rehearsing the final scene with Windsor, Jan Hunt and Ed Stewart:

And right at the end, Windsor Davies puts his hand on Jan's shoulder, and says, 'Robinson, my boy, I am terribly sorry that I have misadjudicated you.' And everybody fell about laughing. And Ed went up to him and whispered in his ear, 'It's mis*judged* – it's mis*judged*.' And Windsor never got over that. He said, 'I cannot believe it!' Ed was ever such a nice bloke, but he was just a bit thick, really.

As so often happened when *Crackerjack* changed its line-up, the second series with Jan and Ed was even stronger than the first. Though it didn't get off to a particularly good start. The middle sketch in the first show was *Two Weeks at Fort Night*. As Jan explained on radio documentary series *Trumpton Riots Again*, the setting was an American fort under attack from Indians:

I was the real granny, with a clay pipe in my mouth. And they started throwing boots and guns and goodness-knows-what over the scenery. And the heel of one of the boots caught me on my cheekbone. And the producer couldn't understand why they covered me in blood to make it look like I had been caught in the crossfire, and why they hadn't got blood on any of the other performers.

John Adams was the production manager at the time, working on the studio floor:

> Blood was pouring out and Jan, being Jan, never stopped. And we carried on filming. And at the end of it, I suddenly saw all this blood coming out of her cut, ran over, and of course we had to get her off to hospital. She never stopped. She carried on working.

From there on, fortunately, things improved. There weren't too many changes to this series, apart from a small but significant tweak to the stars' pecking order. Ever since Don Maclean had joined the show, there had been a strict alternation between Don's and Peter's names every week. Now the order became fixed and, if Peter wasn't totally happy about it, at least he went along with it. But, to Don, it made a lot of sense:

> Pete was very 'old school' and it mattered to people in those days. I don't think it particularly mattered to me. But if you look at that series, you will see the credits go up and it says, 'Starring Don Maclean – with Peter Glaze and Jan Hunt.' And I think that was something that was done by the BBC. They were desperate to keep me. Not that I was going anywhere at that time.

Peter Glaze must have thought he'd been with the show long enough to be considered the star. But when has the straight man ever been billed above the comic? He probably had a private grumble about it, but grudgingly accepted it.

Direction this series was in the hands of assistant producer Brian Penders, who came from a theatrical background, as had Jan Hunt:

> I remember the first time Brian directed me and, because he had the theatre technique, he knew that you've got to be larger than life onstage. And he said to me, 'Jan, you're now on television. You've got to start reducing. You're still going to come across, but you've got to start taking it down.' Because if you do an expression on stage, you know, you go to number ten. On television you only have to go to number two, otherwise it looks too big and too unnatural.
>
> You've got to find the right balance between playing to a live audience and also the thousands that were down that little lens. Making it big enough for the studio, but not so big that you looked gauche. And he did say to me

in the first couple of programmes, 'All too big. Just bring it down a bit. You've still got the energy coming from within, so we're not going to lose anything.' But that was a good lesson learned.

Brian was also one of Don Maclean's favourite directors:

> Alan Bell and Brian Penders would be my dream team to be honest. Brian Penders was the best in the studio and was always, always coming up with ideas. For instance we did a Tarzan sketch – I was Tarzan and Jan was Jane. And we said, 'Okay, we're going to do it in Birmingham.' So Brian Penders says, 'Why don't we have a phone? And every time you answer it, instead of saying hello, you go (DOING TARZAN CALL) ohh-oh-ohhh-ohh!' So we're rehearsing, and the phone rings and I go ohh-oh-ohhh-ohh! And then I look at the phone and I say, 'What do you mean – who is it? It's me, Tarz.' And he thought that was so funny. But he was so inventive all the while. And he'd always got a smile on his face.

Writing duties were slightly altered this series. Bob Hedley continued to do the opening double on his own, while the middle sketch was written by Bob and *Crackerjack* newcomer Peter Robinson, whose previous TV credentials included material for Kenneth Williams and Frankie Howerd, plus several episodes of the Wendy Craig sitcom *And Mother Makes Three*. The musical finale was now the sole domain of Tony Hare:

> I think my age helped with this, because Bob Hedley – bless his heart – being older than me, he was not *au fait* with what was in the charts. And I was a great fan of pop music in those days. So I did know a lot about the songs and the people that were doing them. I used to look at the charts every week, and I'd say, 'That's going to go up.' And I used to think of a way I could get a song into the sketch. I used to write the sketch about two weeks ahead of the actual recording. And I remember on several finales I actually had the Number One in the show.
>
> Most of the pop groups were fans of *Crackerjack*, believe it or not. And, of course, they loved the fact that their songs were being done in the show. And I can remember being in the makeup room and one of the guys from Showaddywaddy, who was being made up at the time, said, 'Oh, we saw that sketch a couple of weeks ago. That was really funny. I loved the way they got our song in.' And the makeup girl said, 'Well, here's the guy that wrote it.' I said to one of the guys, 'Oh my God, it didn't worry you that Peter Glaze ruined your number?' And they said, 'No, no, it was really funny.' And I said, 'I'd like to think it helped get you up the charts a bit.'

For Jan Hunt the musical finales were the highlight of the show:

> That was our favourite time, because we were very 'with it'. We were up with all the chart songs and everything. And we all loved going into the band room on a Tuesday, to hear Bert Hayes' arrangements for all those great numbers. Because they were full-scale presentations really.

Don Maclean agrees that Bert Hayes was a key ingredient to the success of those pop numbers:

> He'd got a ten-piece band including himself. And the respect that every musician had ... They just couldn't wait to work for Bert Hayes. He was absolutely marvellous. I mean, you'd walk in some days and you'd got Kenny Baker on trumpet, he'd have Ronnie Verrell on drums, who was an amazing drummer, and Don Lusher on trombone. And there was a guy, a Chinese guy, who played the most brilliant guitar. And there was another bloke who played trumpet, and he used to play with one hand, 'cos he'd got a fag in his other hand. I've never seen anything like it! But they were a marvellous band.

The third show of the series is arguably everybody's finest hour – with the Tarzan sketch in the middle, and a studio-shot cowcatcher opening featuring Jan Hunt as Margaret Thatcher, addressing her shadow cabinet:

DON: And what of the future, Mrs Thatcher?
JAN: Well, I can promise you a *wonderful* programme. After all, it is –
DON: Friday.
PETE: Five o'clock.
ED: It's Crackerjack!

The musical finale was *The Fat Tum of the Opera*. This was ten years before Andrew Lloyd Webber penned his own musical version of the tale. So any link between Peter Glaze's crazed composer (who nicks other people's material and passes it off as his own) and anyone else is purely in your own imagination. In a nod to the horror-movie original, Jan's waitress (the Phantom's muse) is called Doris Karloff. Don's tube-train guard, who took a wrong turn and ended up in the Phantom's subterranean lair, is Feller Yugosi. And Ed's London bus driver is Loo Chainey ('I *thought* he was looking a little flushed!').

As always, Tony Hare incorporates a few current hits into the sketch, including one chart-topper that was just too good to resist:

I remember going into the rehearsals one week, and I said, 'I've got this idea of doing a send-up of *The Phantom of the Opera*.' And Brian Penders said, 'Oh yeah?' And I said, 'I want to do *Bohemian Rhapsody* in it.' And he went, 'Oh Christ, you're joking!' It was number one already. And, of course, nobody thought it would be possible to do it. And it was the longest song they ever did in a finale.

And there were quite a lot of tantrums during rehearsals of that. And Bert Hayes, who was the musical director who'd arranged it, was going, 'They're *never* going to get this right!' And they rehearsed and rehearsed and rehearsed it. I think they worked a lot longer on that one song than they'd ever done on any of the other songs, because there were three other songs in that sketch as well. But, anyway, it worked. I have a feeling they did it twice – they didn't quite get it right the first time. And they did it pretty well. Even Glaze was alright – you know, he was screaming away in the song. And I remember Don saying to me, 'Don't you ever do that to us again!' But it fitted perfectly. I used a line to get into the song – it was so crowbarred in – but at least it worked really well.

Peter Glaze's phantom, seated at the organ, has just burst into a rendition of *Oh, I Do Like to be Beside the Seaside* – which, naturally, he claims as one of his own compositions:

JAN: (TO DON) He can't help it if he's a bit Bohemian in his attitude.
PETE: Bohemian! That's it! You've inspired me again. I shall write an
         opera – *Bohemian Rhapsody* – and you will sing it like a Queen.

And off they go! *Bohemian Rhapsody* is not the easiest of songs to recreate live – even by Queen. *Crackerjack* should be commended for even attempting it. But, in fact, it is far more than an attempt. The opening section is taken totally seriously, and sung in harmony by Don and Jan. The musical break is performed by Bert Hayes and his Orchestra and mimed with a manic lack of accuracy by Peter who, at one point, stands on the organ stool and plays the keyboard with his foot. During most of the final section, Peter bids for escape, and is continually dragged back by the other two. Jan hits an unbelievably high 'Galileo' while Don responds in his gruffest bass. For the final bash of the gong, Don wields an outsize mallet and strikes Peter on the belly. Don then faces the camera and says, 'Well, it's a lovely little number, but it'll never make the top twenty.'

Pop songs in *Crackerjack* sketches are easy to sneer at, if you're the kind of person who looks back into the TV archives only to sneer. But credit where it's due. It's a classy performance with classy production values. Sometimes it's played straight, and sometimes for laughs. And it never claimed to improve on the original.

Jan Hunt was particularly aggrieved when this clip subsequently resurfaced on one of TV's sneeriest shows:

> Somebody brought it up on *Room 101* and it got ditched as one of the worst numbers on children's television. It was terribly unfair, because I thought we did a pretty good job on that. I thought that was very unfairly judged. And even Peter Glaze held his own in that.

Don Maclean took care to give a distinct voice to each of his characters, which were often based on favourite comedians. A Scotsman might have the laid-back drawl of Chic Murray. An American would be given the high-energy delivery of Phil Silvers' Sergeant Bilko. His tube-train guard was inspired by *Steptoe and Son*'s Harry H. Corbett. But for Tony Hare's next sketch, Don gave a deliberate impersonation of one of America's all-time great movie comedians – Groucho Marx.

Tony had always approached comedy in visual terms. His ability to write gags had come later, and had particularly developed during his writing partnership with Bob Hedley. But his verbal comedy often had a touch of the absurd. Hardly surprising as he was a huge fan of radio's *Goon Show*. In turn, Spike Milligan had drawn inspiration from the anarchy (both physical and linguistic) of the Marx Brothers' movies.

Tony's visual humour is evident in the weekly list of challenges he would set the *Crackerjack* props department. For this particular sketch he required:

> 1 cigar (18" long) to resemble pendulum in grandfather clock and to be removed.
> 1 grandfather clock with stick-on Groucho Marx moustache, eyebrows and glasses, and a hole big enough to hold the cigar on face.

In the sketch – *The Earlier Life of Groucho Marx* – Don Maclean plays Groucho, while Jan and Peter (also with glasses, and with heavy greasepaint moustaches and eyebrows) play Groucho's parents. Don does much slick wise-cracking straight to camera throughout and – perhaps uniquely for a *Crackerjack* sketch – blatantly admits how clumsily the songs have been forced into the script. As here, when Groucho's parents tell him they've invited a famous film director to call round:

JAN: Mr Blanca. He's of Italian extraction.

DON: (TO CAMERA) His father used to be a dentist in Rome. (TO THEM) He's not by any chance *the* famous Paloma Blanca?

PETE: He's the one!

DON: (TO CAMERA) You wanna bet there's a song comin' up in a minute?

Groucho's mother is called Onya Marx, which gives rise to the sketch's (literally) running joke:

JAN: One day I'm going to strangle that boy as sure as my name's Onya Marx.

DON: Get set, go!

        JAN AND PETE RUSH OUT OF DOOR – THEN RE-ENTER.

JAN: We fell for it again. Mamma mia!

DON: (TO CAMERA) Want to bet there's another song coming up?

Towards the end, Ed Stewart enters in curly wig and top hat as Groucho's mute brother Harpo, whose only form of communication is via a bulb horn on the end of a walking cane:

DON: Who did you see on the way home?

        (ED HONKS)

DON: Really? You mean the one with a body shaped like an hourglass? (DOES GESTURES)

        (ED HONKS)

DON: Too bad he's a feller!

        (ED HONKS)

PETE: What's he say?

DON: He said, 'Let's get into the last song quick!'

Even though Ed hadn't been entrusted with any dialogue, it was vitally important that he knew his part thoroughly. Don Maclean was there when director Brian Penders decided to ring Ed up:

Ed Stewart, he was a lovely bloke, but he just wasn't very bright. And me and Penders, we sent him up terrible. It was a Saturday afternoon and we were rehearsing, and Ed didn't used to come in until the Monday, 'cos he hadn't got much to do. And we were doing the Marx Brothers. And he was Harpo, who of course didn't speak and just used to blow this horn. So Penders said, 'Come on, let's have a laugh.' And he got on the phone, and I was on the extension. And he rings Ed up and says, 'Ed, we've changed the script. Can you go and get it?' 'Well, alright then.' So he goes and gets the script. And Penders says, 'Now, Ed. If you look on page whatever-it-is, when Don says so-and-so, and you go – beep-beep. We wondered if you could go – beep-beep-be-beep-beep.' And Ed said, 'Alright, I could do that.' And Penders said, 'Well, could you let us hear it please?' He had him on for about ten minutes doing this. It was terrible! And Ed never ever knew.

Using current pop songs, especially in a children's show, could sometimes be problematic, as Tony Hare explains:

The thing was we weren't really allowed to change lyrics. There was the odd word you could change to suit the moment, but we weren't allowed to change the lyrics.

The final song of the sketch is 10cc's *Art for Art's Sake*. One of those permissible one-word alterations was: 'Money for *Dad*'s Sake.' But the line, 'Gimme your love, gimme it all,' continues with the more graphic and less teatime-friendly, 'Gimme in the kitchen, gimme in the hall.' How they solve this problem is pure inspiration. Don, as Groucho, sings the first line. Then Ed, as Harpo, is given the second line which he performs as a series of honks. What better way to deal with horny lyrics?

In a later show, Bob Hedley's opener is a Peter Glaze lecture about the forthcoming Summer Olympics:

PETE: Hello there. Today I'd like to talk to you about this year's
        Olympic Games and Britain's chances of success. Now, how are
        we going to get those gold medals?
DON: (ENTERS IN RUNNING VEST AND SHORTS) Pinch them off
        the Russians.
PETE: Pinch them … (SEES DON) Maclean!
DON: Yes, I did two lengths of the Olympic bath this morning.

The middle sketch in that same show hit a problem at the initial readthrough. Jan Hunt had seen this happen before:

Dear Peter was a lovable chap, but sometimes he was his own worst enemy. Because he'd look at the script and be a bit upset that maybe Don had got more lines than him.

Don Maclean was also familiar with Peter's artistic temperament:

We used to have a readthrough on the Wednesday morning of the new script. We used to do the show on Tuesday, and on Wednesday we were back with the new scripts. And Peter did the readthrough, and at the end he threw his script on the floor and he said, 'If we had any decent writers, I might get a few funny lines!' And Tony went, 'Right! That's it! I've had enough! I'm leaving! You can stick your show up your arse!' And he walked out.

Peter was very rude to the writers I think, because I always thought the writers did a good job. The stupid thing was that he was a good straight man. But why he wanted to get laughs I don't know. And he always got a laugh when he came on because, no matter what you dressed him in, he looked funny. And he would always get a laugh on his first entrance.

In this particular case, Tony Hare wasn't at the receiving end of Peter's wrath. It was a French Resistance sketch, written jointly by Bob Hedley and Peter Robinson, in which Don Maclean played the good guy:

In the script I was a secret agent. I'd been parachuted into occupied France. I came to Jan's house and she was the girl from the Resistance. She was going to hide me. It was well before *'Allo 'Allo!* And Peter was this German officer who was going to capture me. And he read this script and he threw it on the floor and said, 'I'm sick and tired. There's no funny lines in there for me.' And I said, 'I'm sick and tired too, Pete. I tell you what – *you* be the parachutist and *I'll* be the German officer. And the director, Brian Penders, said 'No, you can't do that.' And I said, 'Yes, we can.'

So they swap roles and Don becomes the villain of the piece:

DON: My name is Oberleutnant Hans Niessen – and no jokes about 'bumps a daisy!'

JAN: Why are you doing the goose step with only one leg?

DON: Because I'm only half German.

Later on Peter turns up as the British secret agent:

PETE: Algy, Algy calling base, base.

JAN: Why do you say it twice?

PETE: I'm a double agent.

So that's the way they performed it. And it was a success, at least as far as Don was concerned:

Anyway, we did the sketch. And on the night I got all the laughs and he didn't get any! It was the kids' perception as well. Whichever way we played it, the kids would think, 'Oh, here's Don, he's going to be funny. And there's Pete, he's going to be the put-upon buffoon.' And in the end he shot me!

During the series, the odd bit-part in the musical finales (even briefer than Ed Stewart's appearances) was played by new hostess Jillianne Foot, who had little else to do but hand out the *Crackerjack* pencils. She subsequently acted opposite several TV comics, including Dick Emery, Benny Hill and Kenny Everett, and was at one time tipped as Anthea Redfern's replacement on *The Generation Game*. She later dashed around the stage in a theatre tour of Ray Cooney's farce *Run for your Wife* playing one of the bigamous lead character's two wives. The other wife was played by Jan Hunt:

I played the dippy wife and she played the sexy one. Yes Jillianne Foot, lovely girl. She was 'eye candy' really on *Crackerjack*. Whereas I wasn't. I'd always got a red nose or a grey-haired wig or something. But Jillianne certainly was eye candy. And very warm and very lovely. I knew Jillianne because she'd done quite a few pantomimes. And she had a son who was more or less the same age as my son. And we used to share digs together.

With the exception of Jillian Comber, *Crackerjack* hostesses tended to come and go, few lasting beyond one or two series, and most of them going on to far greater things. Jillianne Foot was just such a one-series wonder. But she wasn't the only person not to be returning in the New Year. Don Maclean met with Bill Cotton (then the Head of BBC Light Entertainment) and took one of the toughest decisions of his life. Even to this day he's not convinced it was the right one:

When I did decide to go, it was the most stupid thing I ever did. Why my friends and everybody didn't lock me in a padded room and say, 'Stay there until you've changed your mind,' I shall never know. But my agent and I had this meeting with Bill Cotton. And Bill Cotton said, 'Look, we had terrible trouble replacing Leslie Crowther. And *Crackerjack* wasn't right until five years later when you came along. And obviously we want to keep you.' We weren't arguing about money at that time. He said, 'Look, you do 13 weeks on *Crackerjack* at the moment. I'll give you 26 weeks! You can do *Crackerjack* the first 26 weeks of the year. And then you've got *The Black and White Minstrels*, which is another eight weeks.'

Anyway, I had this chat with my agent. And I've got to be honest – Peter Glaze was getting on my nerves more than usual by that time. And I said to my agent, 'Will you say to him, "Don would like to carry on with *The Black and White Minstrels* but he doesn't want to do *Crackerjack* any more."' And Bill Cotton's retort was, 'If he doesn't do *Crackerjack*, he doesn't work for the BBC ever again.' And that was it. And I was so stupid. I think if I'd done it for another three years, I would have been so established at the BBC that they would have had to have found something else for me to do. But I was in such a bloody hurry. I was in such a rush to be a superstar. And I don't think ambition did me any good. It didn't make me happy. I've been a lot happier since I've been less ambitious.

Since *Crackerjack*, Don Maclean has never stopped working as a comedian. He has both hosted and guested on many TV gameshows, and became a familiar voice over the airwaves presenting *Good Morning Sunday* on Radio 2. When asked for a favourite memory of *Crackerjack*, Don succinctly summed up the bizarre nature of both the show and its audience:

We did a sketch one week and we were building Hadrian's Wall. Peter Glaze was Hadrian, and I was the Irish labourer in charge of building it. Brickus Cementus I was called – Tony Hare at his best! And there's a big gap in this wall, and we've got a chicken coop at one end. And there's a chicken in this coop, and it's laying the bricks. And I go, 'Come on, Gertie! Let's have another brick, Gertie!' And there's all this clucking and somebody throwing a load of feathers in the air. And this brick slides down the ramp and I put it in the space in the wall. Presumably we're singing something at the same time.

So the show went out on the Friday, and on the Saturday I was back home in Birmingham. And I was walking down the road and this kid's coming towards me. And, as he got to me, he never said, 'Oh, you're Don Maclean,' or anything. He just looked at me and said, 'That hen never laid that brick, it was polystyrene!' And walked off. And it was one of the funniest things that ever happened to me!

11
Gone to Thames with Eric and Ernie

1977 – 1979

O N Thursday 6th January 1977 *The Stage* ran a piece about a rapidly rising star:

Bernie Clifton, Chesterfield's own comedy boy, recently made a very successful return to the Aquarius night spot (where, incidentally, he was resident compere three years ago!).

Future plans for this 'crooked spire' comedian include a BBC TV spectacular with Ronnie Corbett (which he's at present recording) and, later in the new year, a 13-week run as resident host on BBC TV's popular *Crackerjack* saga.

And, indeed, later in the new year (one day later, to be precise!) the new series of *Crackerjack*, with new boy Bernie Clifton as resident comic, hit the screens running. Not only running, but running early. A month earlier Edward Barnes, the assistant head of Children's Programmes, had written to *Crackerjack* producer Robin Nash:

The early evening news has been scheduled to start at 5.40. This has caused a rearrangement of all the start times of programmes in the Children's block, which means that *Crackerjack*'s new billed time will be 4.55. I am sorry about this, as it rather messes up your 'It's Friday, it's 5 o'clock, it's *Crackerjack* ...' routine, but I am afraid it's unavoidable.

There are those who remember *Crackerjack*'s starting time as five o'clock and those who remember it as five-to-five. Older viewers will swear it began at five-to-five, and so will not-so-old viewers. And they're both right. It changed from 5.00 to 4.55 while Leslie Crowther was hosting, and remained at that time throughout the Rod McLennan years. When Don Maclean joined, it moved back to 5.00 and stayed that way for four series. But for the *next* four series it was to have the regular starting time of 4.55.

Light Entertainment producer Michael Hurll will take his proper place in the *Crackerjack* story a little later on. He had produced a wide range of variety shows with stars such as Cilla Black, Cliff Richard, and former *Crackerjack* funny-man Ronnie Corbett. Michael was rapidly becoming a major figure in the department and (although Robin Nash was still producing *Crackerjack* at this time) Michael's intervention helped shape the show over the coming years. Tony Hare had worked with him in the past, first as floor assistant then as writer:

> We knew Don Maclean was leaving at the end of that series. And I was sitting with Michael Hurll in the stalls during rehearsals, and Michael said, 'It's going to be a hard job finding somebody to replace Don.' And I said, 'Well, I know of a guy. He's very funny. He's great with props – Bernie Clifton.' He was appearing in Jersey at the time. And I'd worked with Bernie a lot in the past – I wrote bits for him. Michael Hurll came back at the end of the week and said, 'Thanks ever so much, Tony, for that. He's terrific. I've booked him!' And he turned out to be a very good replacement for Don.

Like many a *Crackerjack* comic before him, Bernie Clifton had plenty of stage experience but very little TV exposure:

> I'd had one skirmish with national television two years earlier with the Lulu show, but it wasn't right for me. And then, a year later, it was made clear that Don Maclean was leaving. And Michael Hurll came to Jersey to see me, and said, 'We want you to take over.' I didn't think twice. Nowadays it would be a stigma to be part of a children's show. Back in the day, when I was doing *Crackerjack*, I was doing late-night cabaret as well at the weekends. I'd go in for a band call on Saturday to do a one a.m. cabaret spot to a room full of drunks. And the band, the musicians, would say, 'Oh, we love that *Crackerjack*! Every Friday, we're there at five-to-five and we watch it. That sketch you did about Wellington and Napoleon – we were on the floor!' And I never thought twice about it. There was no real division. People like The

Krankies were doing late nights, and Keith Harris. We were all doing the children's-stroke-family shows, but we were carrying on a career of adult entertainment.

It was after an appearance, very early in his career, on the BBC's long-running music hall series *The Good Old Days* that Bernie received some invaluable advice:

I did my very first TV show – *The Good Old Days* – at Leeds, and Les Dawson was topping the bill. And I loved mucking about when I was on stage but, of course, on *The Good Old Days* I did what people did at the time. And afterwards, Les took me to one side and – well, he gave me a bit of a bollocking really – and he said, 'Yeah, you're alright.' He must have seen something in me. He said, 'You're okay, but you're just doing what a hundred other comics are doing. What is it that you really like doing? What's your style?' And I went, 'Well, I just love visual comedy. I love props.' And he said, 'Well, why don't you go out and be a prop comic? Be a visual comic. Just plough a furrow and stick to it, and be an individual.' And I thought, 'Do you know, he's right!'

And the following morning, in October 1971, I was in Chesterfield town centre and one of the shops had been closed and it was open to Oxfam. And it had a big banner, 'Everything ten bob, 50 pence.' And in the window was a full-size lion-skin hearthrug. And I took this out, and I'm walking round Chesterfield with it as if it was a dog. 'Heel, heel!' And I went for it! Because I'd got Les's sort of 'blessing' if you like. And he was such a star. I was motivated by the fact I would have to answer to him the next time I saw him.

Then I was in Jersey doing summer season two years later, and I flew out to Shepperton, when Shepperton Studios were closing, and I bid for – and got – a big rubber shark about 15 foot long, and I brought it back on the plane that evening. And then I was at a Halloween party and begged for the black cat that was up a tree, and I had a cat on my shoulder. And I was on a roll.

And, in terms of *Crackerjack*, I was halfway there. With comedy that was silly and innocent, and could be appreciated by children as well as their parents. And during the late 70s, I would meet Les doing a *Seaside Special* and I would have a dwarf dressed as a Mountie and an inflatable horse. And Les saw me at rehearsals, and he said, 'I didn't put you wrong, did I, with those props?'

Surprisingly, Bernie's best known visual prop came quite a while later:

Someone saw a man in a carnival, on the back of a chicken, and he went, 'Do you know, that would work for you.' And I thought, 'Yeah, sounds a bit of fun. A bit visual.' Anyway, I sent a sketch off to Peter Pullen, who was the ace props maker at the time. He did Rod Hull's emu, all Keith Harris's dummies, the Honey Monster, he did all that. And some time later he said, 'I've finished it. Do you want to come and try it on?' So I went down to Coventry – he had a workshop in the city centre. So I jumped on it. I ran out into the street in the rush hour. And the whole city ground to a halt. Because nobody had seen anything like it.

Like Rod Hull's emu, the trick with Bernie Clifton's ostrich was to make it seem like part of his body was another creature, dragging him around helplessly behind it or, in this case, on top of it. Bernie's legs were those of the ungainly and impulsive ostrich, while the rest of him (including the dummy legs flapping about astride the bird) clung onto this avian anarchist for dear life. And it was the ostrich that helped Bernie make an instant impact on the show:

> I know the ostrich appeared on *Crackerjack*. It would have been an earlier model, and I don't know how effective it was. But I'm sure, for a fact, that would have been its first TV appearance.

That debut was in Bernie's very first show, in a Canadian-set sketch entitled *The Great Gold Robbery* or *I Should Have Put the Yukon*. Requirements from the props department included:

> Moose's head (hollow, to fit over head and to fall off wall on cue).
> Stuffed toy dog on wheels with zip – hollow to hold coins.
> Golden ostrich egg (about 15 inches).

There were no work opportunities for *Crackerjack* hostesses in the foreseeable future, because no games of any kind were being played. For the first time in the show's history, the two elimination rounds and the final competition were all sit-down quizzes. Michael Brereton was commissioned to provide a set of general-knowledge questions for the final and, for the two earlier quizzes, the questions were based on the sketch the children had just been watching. Naturally, in that first show, a few of the questions were ostrich-related:

What was the name of Bernie's ostrich? (OSWALD)

When Jan saw the egg, she asked if she'd be charged with – what? (POACHING)

What was Pete going to call his chain of restaurants? (KENTUCKY FRIED OSTRICH)

The new quiz format suited Ed Stewart, as he told radio documentary *Trumpton Riots Again* in 1997:

> I've always loved quizzes, and that was an integral part of it. In fact, there was a programme on the telly at the beginning of the year. And they got a kid who was in *Crackerjack* at the time, and they showed him the old film of the game. And one of his questions was, 'Sir Francis Drake died on one of his three voyages around the world. Was it the first, the second or the third?' And this little kid full of lovely little golden curls said, 'The second.' And when he came back and saw that clip on the telly, he just couldn't believe he'd been so thick. And everybody laughed at him, and I was very unkind to him at the time. And I looked at that clip and thought, 'My God, wasn't I horrible to that poor boy?'

At times in the past, *Crackerjack* could have been accused of attempting to replace like with like. Writer Tony Hare doesn't believe this was the case with Don Maclean and Bernie Clifton:

> Bernie had a totally different approach to Don. Because Don was very fast, and Bernie wasn't quite so fast. He was lugubrious, I always felt. But of course he was great with the props. And he had all these ideas.

Jan Hunt agrees:

> He actually fitted in very well. He was, as he is today, a naturally funny man, a great props man. More laid back than Don, a more gentle performer than Don. Where Don is eyes and teeth and sock-it-to-them, Bernie is a lot gentler, but still funny in his own way. I think both myself and Ed slotted in well when we joined. And Bernie did too. So I think it was quite lucky really. And he got on with Peter immediately.

For an out-and-out solo act to become one half of a double act isn't necessarily easy. But Bernie Clifton had few problems establishing that screen chemistry with Peter:

I think I was very easy-going. And Peter was a strong character. So I was very much the new boy. But it didn't take me long to assert myself. If I say it myself, I'd got a few things going for me. The props and the visuals and the creative juices that I'd got. Though I was following a tough act with Don.

And I remember Robin Nash giving me a heads-up and telling me about my projection against Peter. Because Peter was very forceful and it was Robin that said to me, early days, 'Make sure that you're not swallowed up.' And that was a good pointer. Because what did I know about camera work and TV sketches?

In comedy you *do* need a counterpoint. You need one and the other. And Peter was very strong, and that enabled me to be the daft sod. Almost like that Stan and Ollie thing.

The relationship between Don Maclean and Peter Glaze had been volatile at times. The fact that Don was ultimately billed as *Crackerjack*'s 'star' suggests something of a simmering power struggle between the two. Bernie, as the new resident comic, might have rightly expected top billing. In fact, he was perfectly content to be billed last, after both Peter and Jan:

I don't think that aspect ever occurred to me. Probably because I came in late-ish to the established team.

It was a very happy working relationship. And, though Peter's displays of artistic temperament didn't entirely vanish, Bernie was never at the receiving end:

Peter would get tired. We'd all get tired. And they were heavy days. He could be – a great word – irascible. Maybe I was never a threat. I was very, 'Do what you like with me.' We were pretty at ease with each other. We never fell out, Peter and I.

Beneath all the bluster, there was much to like and admire about Peter Glaze. Ed Stewart, on *Trumpton Riots Again*, said of Peter:

He was one of the old-type vaudeville feeds, and I think that the comedians who were on there, whether it was Leslie Crowther, whether it was Don Maclean or Bernie Clifton, everybody benefited from this experience of his.

Jan Hunt was also impressed by Peter's showbiz pedigree:

Peter was a real pro. I mean, the stories he used to tell us in the breaks between rehearsals, the anecdotes and stories, he was totally fascinating to listen to. He was a very sensitive guy, Peter, and sometimes he used to get a little bit anxious, or a little bit tetchy. There may have been a few words, not an argument as such. But always, after whatever happened, he would always apologise. And he usually came in with a couple of bottles of champagne or something to say, 'I'm really sorry I was a bit off yesterday.' But he was a really lovely man. A very genuine sort of guy.

Bill Wilson returned after a gap of two series, working alternate weeks with Brian Penders, both likeable and capable directors. This time the writing was more collaborative, with Bob Hedley still providing the opening double, then teaming up with Tony Hare for the other sketches.

John Adams was production manager on the series:

About the third day of rehearsals, I said to Bernie, 'Where do you come from?' And he said, 'Chesterfield.' So I said, 'Are you staying in London somewhere?' And he said, 'No, no, I'm commuting.' I said, 'What do you mean – commuting?' He said, 'Well, I drive down and I drive back at the end of the day.' I said, 'How long does that take?' And he said, 'Oh, three or four hours.' I said, 'You can't do that! Why don't you come and stay with us? We're only in Teddington, so it's not very far away.' So he said, 'Well, that will be lovely, but you'll have to ask your wife.' I said, 'Oh, she won't mind.' So Bernie used to stay with us during the week, from about the second week onwards.

And thus a Little-and-Large-type situation of non-stop travel and end-of-series exhaustion was avoided. Energy levels were high throughout the series. Each show kicked off with the usual slick crosstalk routine, with Bernie gatecrashing Pete's lecture accompanied by some bizarre prop. In one show he enters with a hot-dog cart. When Pete enquires whether he has a licence for selling hot dogs, Bernie wonders whether Pete doesn't also need a licence for what he's doing:

PETE: I am selling my talents to the viewers.
BERNIE: Oh, that's all right then, 'cause you don't need a licence for
          selling tripe.
PETE: What do you mean – tripe? I'm telling funny stories.
BERNIE: Oh, tripe and funny 'uns!

A typical musical finale – *When the Yacht Comes In* – is set in the affluent 1920s. Bernie makes his clattering entrance with a large square biscuit tin stuck on each foot (another of his trademark props) and proceeds to woo millionaire's daughter Jan. They attempt to end their beautifully harmonised love song with a kiss, but Peter (the millionaire in question) intercepts the two pairs of lips with his hand. But news has come in from the stock market:

PETE: I'm ruined, ruined! Me money's all gone. I haven't got a penny to me name. It's awful, it's dreadful, it's terrible!

BERNIE: (BRIEFLY STEPS OUT OF CHARACTER) Bit better than last week though, don't you think?

Then all three of them launch into Abba's *Money Money Money*. As sometimes happens, Peter's sense of rhythm is a little approximate. He takes so long over the phrase – 'Aha-ahaa, all the things I could do' – that Jan and Bernie have to cut across him to get to the next line on time. Bernie Clifton recalls a neat trick they developed to deal with such Abba aberrations:

Jan was the master. Every musical item, she'd got it nailed. I remember there was something where Peter could *not* come in on the beat. So he's in the centre, Jan's on one side, I'm on the other. And we both got Pete in the small of his back. And he had to come in on 'four' and we *jolted* him to come in. That's how cliff-edge it was.

In fact, Bernie's whole working week had an atmosphere of chaotic creativity:

On the first morning we'd read the script and realise it needed work. So it was full on! The writers would come in and we'd bang stuff around, kick it around. And sometimes, with respect to Tony and Bob, it would end up unrecognisable because things wouldn't work once you're on the floor. And then the props would arrive on the day and the props would be wrong. You wouldn't see the props until the day of the show. You'd do the tech run and you'd realise the rifle wasn't a rifle, it was a sawn-off something, and we'd have to box round that. It was like rep. Rep on television.

Just like weekly repertory theatre, each new show required new scenery. The sets for *Crackerjack* needed to be planned and designed well in advance, which sometimes placed additional pressure on writer Tony Hare:

The designer was always ringing me up and saying, 'What set do you need for the show after next?' And I always delivered on time, but I was close to the wind. So quite often I used to write the sketch to the set that was going to be built.

A regular strand throughout this series was the *Crackerjack Young Entertainers* competition. This segment of the show was overseen by Colin Farnell who, the previous year, had produced *Pebble Mill Showcase* – in which Don Maclean had introduced a series of acts that were just starting out in television, including magician Paul Daniels. *Crackerjack Young Entertainers* featured the pick of a series of nationwide auditions for young talented amateurs – be they singers, dancers, musicians, impressionists or ventriloquists. One such act was pop trio The Rockettes from Bognor Regis. Gavin Wickham and James Carroll had already had exposure on local TV but, for new recruit, drummer Simon Capes, performing in the Television Theatre was a revelation:

> To a young 13-year-old it was like – oh my goodness – I'd never known anything quite like it! We'd played to children mainly. All of our concerts were to infant schools. And to have such a big troupe of children who'd been geed-up quite a lot by the warm-up act, and Ed Stewart was quite good at geeing everybody up, and then Peter Glaze would mess around. So it would be quite a hyped-up excited audience. So we came on, and our style was energetic, and we had an audience that was cheering along – it was fantastic!

Young Entertainers took a large chunk out of the middle of *Crackerjack*. As a result there was just one pop guest per week, who always performed in the opening moments of the show, thus instantly grabbing the attention of the audience and, on one particular show, the attentions of Simon Capes:

> We got to stay on one side of the stage while the pop act came on. Mike Moran and Lynsey de Paul played on one episode, and did *Rock Bottom* – and I was infatuated with Lynsey de Paul at the time, as a young boy. And it was just nice to be on stage when they were performing.

Each week the audience would vote for their favourite act. The Rockettes made a return appearance in the semi-finals with another self-penned song, winning a place in the end-of-series grand final. For this they performed the Hank Mizell song *Jungle Rock* (a belated chart hit in 1976 of a song originally released in 1958).

In previous appearances the trio had been self-sufficient, but this time Simon and the boys were backed by Bert Hayes and his orchestra:

We went down into this – it wasn't an orchestra pit, it was actually an enclosed soundproofed block – and it was fantastic. I'd never played on such an impressive drum kit. And they worked out some horns, some orchestral stuff to put behind us in the 'fills'. It's quite fun when you hear it – well, it was at the time – the orchestra with their horns and their trumpets going.

During that final show, Simon also learned one of the tricks of the TV trade, as he watched the filming of the 'cowcatcher' opening:

At the beginning of each episode, they had these daft silly pieces. They were green-screen sketches. I remember them putting up this sort of ten foot green board, and wondering what it was. And they did a little sketch in front of the screen with the *Starsky and Hutch* car going past and the opening titles from the show. And you couldn't really see what was going on unless you looked at the monitors. And then you saw the actual video of *Starsky and Hutch*. Whereas otherwise they were just performing in front of this big green screen. It was quite fun to see how it was done.

The Rockettes won the grand final and Ed Stewart presented them with a music centre and ten albums – not the easiest of prizes to split between a trio. Their win resulted in a recording session, though the band subsequently broke up after one boy's family moved out of the area. The trio have remained in touch and one of Simon's lasting souvenirs is a Sheaffer *Crackerjack* pen, a recent upgrade to this most traditional of prizes. During Michael Aspel's era the Burnham propelling pencil had been supplanted by a sleek silvery Conway Stewart ballpoint pen which, when Ed came along, became a Sheaffer fountain pen. But neither Michael nor Ed ever let on. '*Crackerjack* pencil' had become a catchphrase in itself, and *Crackerjack* pencils they remained. Somehow '*Crackerjack* pen' just doesn't have the same ring!

A month after the series ended, in May 1977, Janet Watts of *The Guardian* grabbed hold of that popular stick to beat broadcasters with – 'canned laughter'. Like most emotive terms, it has the woolliest of definitions. And the argument usually boils down to the legitimacy of redistributing the odd laugh from elsewhere in the show to a joke that didn't get much response, perhaps as the result of a retake or two. Her article had been prompted by a letter signed by 13 BBC videotape editors alleging, 'On one notable series practically all the laughter is dubbed on after the show has been edited.' Bill Cotton, Head of BBC TV Light Entertainment, agreed to an interview with the paper, then spoiled everything by singling out *Crackerjack* for special mention:

'Of course there are examples of a producer covering the editing of a track with a laugh on a programme like *Crackerjack*: an audience of children will sometimes react like that' – he dropped his jaw in blank incomprehension – 'and I would imagine that the producer might say, "This programme's going to be improved by the odd addition to an audience that must have been distracted by something or other."'

There's no particular evidence to suggest that *Crackerjack* was a major transgressor in this area. Although a young audience is more likely to be distracted by the workings of a TV studio environment than adults, *Crackerjack* wasn't the type of show to give a gag the time to die. If you didn't like that one, there'd be another along any second. But the odd laugh? Maybe. Ed Stewart admitted as much in his 2005 autobiography:

To guarantee non-stop laughter at all the scenes in the programme, the cast went out filming for a day at a zoo or holiday camp. When the results were edited, they were then speeded up, and played to the audience as a warm-up to the actual recording. The laughter which resulted was then edited in later to any part of the programme which did not have sufficient impact.

*

The *Crackerjack* silent movies had been absent from the last series, largely as a result of the introduction of the *Young Entertainers* competition. *Young Entertainers* made its return in the new series, starting January 1977, and so – thanks to some subtle restructuring of the running order – did the *Crackerjack* silents. There was good reason for this. Alan Bell (who had written and directed the majority of these movies) was now, for the first time, the show's full-time director.

The chain of command ran as follows: Robin Nash remained as executive producer, Brian Penders (previously a director) was now producer, and Alan was director. It may appear a little heavy on the bureaucracy, but Alan Bell was largely left to do things his own, highly efficient, way:

When I first joined the show I was assistant producer. And the assistant producer's either floor managing or doing other jobs, and then sometimes you're elevated to director. And I said to Robin, 'I'm not very good at working *for* people. I'd be much better directing every show.' Because it was well known in the building that *Crackerjack* was getting out of hand. The kids would come in – let's say – at five-thirty and they were there until quarter-to-eight at night. And it was too long. People were getting very worried about the buses, getting transport and things. And I said, 'The reason for that is you've got two directors. One does one week and another one does the second week. And they want to get it perfect. And they'll stop and do retakes. And it actually destroys the spontaneity of the programme.' And Robin said, 'Well, it's impossible to direct every show on your own. And what about the films?' And I said, 'I'll do them as well. Don't worry about that.' So he very reluctantly – fingers crossed – let me direct them all.

And I directed every week. I did the whole show. And I'm not boasting here, but it cut out a lot of the difficulties. Jan Hunt, for example, got on well with one of the directors, but *that* director would not get on well with Peter Glaze. Take that out of it, and you've only got one person to blame and run down behind his back.

And on the first show, halfway through a song, Jan forgot a line and she stopped and looked at the camera. And I said, 'Carry on.' Because it said on the script – 'As live'. And it said in big type – 'NO RETAKES' – as though it was going out on the air. So that was one of the things that didn't make me very popular. But everybody liked it in the end, because you started doing the show at six o'clock and you knew it was going to finish 50 minutes later.

One of the ways in which this efficiency was achieved was by spending part of the rehearsal week filming on location. That meant there was less to shoot live in the studio. In addition to the *Crackerjack* silents, the opening cowcatcher quickie was also done on film, usually with a guest celebrity.

The first show begins with John Noakes doing a piece to camera in front of the crooked spire in Chesterfield (Bernie Clifton's home town). The cameraman stops him in midflow to point out four traffic wardens who are ticketing his car. Then Bernie, Pete, Jan and Ed turn to camera and launch into, 'It's Friday ...'

Other celebrity cameos during the series included Scottish reporter Fyfe Robertson, and boxer Henry Cooper. And, surprisingly, Alan Bell was able to talk them into practically anything. For instance, the host of consumer show *That's Life*, who regularly went out and about, asking members of the public to taste unusual concoctions:

> I wanted *Crackerjack* to be more a variety show than a children's show. And
> I had Esther Rantzen, you know she used to go round the markets and talk

to this little old lady. Well, we had that again and Esther says, 'It's a special brew.' So the old lady took a big breath and sneezed, and of course blew Esther's skirt off. Big laugh from the audience!

Production assistant John Adams also witnessed Alan Bell's persuasive powers with Radio 2 DJ Ray Moore:

It was coming up to Boat Race day. And we were in a rehearsal room in Hammersmith, on the river. And so we thought, 'Well, we'll get a boat, and we'll go onto the landing stage and film it there.' And we got Ray Moore and put him on the landing stage. And we said to him, 'If you can be doing a little broadcast saying, "On Saturday it's Boat Race day, blah blah blah …" And then our team from *Crackerjack* will have this boat, and they'll swing it round and knock you in the water.' So he said, 'Yes, that'll be alright. That'll be fine. I don't mind doing it, but the problem is I don't swim.' So we thought, 'Oh my God!' And the river was quite fast-flowing there. And certainly deep. It's just before Hammersmith Bridge.

So Alan Bell was directing it and he said, 'Oh, that's okay. John, you're a good swimmer, aren't you?' 'Yes, yes.' 'Well, strip off just in case he gets into a problem. And you can jump in and pull him out.' Well, you can imagine that happening *today*, can't you?! So anyway, we knocked him in the water, and luckily we had a lifebelt and we had an oar from the boat. And he grabbed hold of the oar and we pulled him out. Well, we were chatting away to the people at the rehearsal rooms and they said, 'Oh my God! That's so dangerous. Someone recently fell in and got swept underneath the landing stage that you were on!'

Bernie Clifton already had a strong visual element to his stage act, and shared Peter Glaze's ability for physical comedy in the *Crackerjack* silents, even if he didn't quite have Don Maclean's reckless streak when it came to stunts. Jan Hunt was their stooge, together with long-suffering regular Evan Ross. Jan would happily endure any kind of indignity that was required of her – usually as a frumpy old woman getting drenched, before lashing out at Bernie and Pete with her handbag.

Bernie was well aware of the creative powerhouse he was working for:

Alan Bell, he was just a genius. He would make it up on the way to work. He'd ring Geoff Miles up and say, 'Oh, and get a ladder and a biscuit tin, and get some flowers, and I'll see you at the location.' And Geoff would come in half-an-hour later and say, 'I was just getting out of bed and the phone rang and Alan said, "Don't forget you need a ladder, must be a long 'un."' And that was Alan.

Alan's alter ego, Mort Kingsley, continued to write most of the *Crackerjack* silents, but a few were scripted by Johnny Ball, already a familiar face on *Play School*, but also a jobbing comedy writer:

> Alan Bell, he was the guy that recruited me. He would say, 'We want a sketch around an old canal.' So I wrote a sketch where everything happened *except* them going in the water. Because it was winter when they were filming. It was pretty cold. And canals are notoriously dangerous for jumping in, falling in or being knocked in. So I wrote the sketch and he came back and said, 'Great, Johnny. But the stooge is going in.' So whatever I wrote – he loved what I wrote – but he always insisted on it being really tough on the stooge.

As Bernie Clifton recalls, that stooge was invariably Evan Ross:

> He was in all the films. He was a big burly guy from Watford. And he fell in the Thames, in this canal at West London, where we were filming. And, as he went in, he snapped his cruciate ligament. And he went in, screaming with pain. And all I remember from Alan Bell was, 'Keep filming! Keep filming!' And of course Alan was right. Because he had to get the shot.

Not every silent movie involved total immersion, nor serious injury. One week Bernie was a train driver on the Romney, Hythe and Dymchurch miniature railway:

> I remember at the end of that day's filming, racing for a train to see Sinatra at the Festival Hall. I still had soot on my face from the sketch we'd just filmed, and it wouldn't wash off.

Bernie would sometimes liven up location filming with the odd wind-up at Alan Bell's expense:

> We were on a pavement location, some baths in Chiswick, and there was a red phone box right in the middle of the shot. And I rang my mate up and said, 'I want you to keep ringing this number.' And, of course, Alan would say, 'Action!' And next thing – ring-ring. 'Stop! Cut! Somebody pick the phone up! Somebody answer that!' And it was my mate in his house, somewhere in the south of England, saying, 'Listen, mate, I'm trying to get some sleep. I'm in the flat over the shops. All I can hear is your bloody boss

shouting "action". Now, if you don't bloody shut up, mate, I'm gonna …'
Phone down – start again – ring-ring. We did what we could for mischief!

Bernie wasn't the only mischief maker. Another silent movie involved Bernie, Pete and Jan as chefs. It was a remake of the Don and Pete routine from the *Aladdin* pantomime. Only this time, when Peter attempts to carry a massive bowl of freshly mixed cake and falls through the floor, he lands in a bath containing Ed Stewart rather than Les Dennis. The day after filming, they were back rehearsing the final sketch of the show, to be played live in front of the studio audience. But Alan Bell soon realised there was a problem:

> Well, the next day at the rehearsal room, Peter arrives by taxi, and someone says, 'He wants your help getting out of the taxi.' And I go round and he's got a big plaster round his leg, and a crutch. And he says, 'Help me out.' And I say, 'What's this?' 'Well, I broke my leg when I fell down the hole at Ealing Studios yesterday.' And I said, 'What? Why didn't you tell me?' And he says, 'I didn't want to cause any trouble.' And he says, 'I tell you what. I'll sit on the chair, and you do all my bits and I'll watch and remember.' So we did these two scenes, and I'm reading of course, because I hadn't learned it. And on the second runthrough, I got to this bit, and he says, 'No, no, hold on a minute!' And he jumps up and says, 'You do it like this, you see.' And it was just a ruse! I could have murdered him, because it brought the house down at the rehearsal rooms, I can tell you. Because I fell for it.

To accommodate both the *Crackerjack* silents and the *Young Entertainers* feature, the number of studio sketches was reduced from three to two. Instead of the opening double with Bernie and Pete, Bob Hedley now provided a longer sketch, still in crosstalk style, but also featuring Jan. In the first show, Bernie and Peter are in Shakespearean get-up discussing Hamlet, when Jan enters:

BERN: This girl is Glenda Jackson's sit-in.
PETE: You mean 'stand-in'.
BERN: No. She gets tired easily. (TO JAN) Do Hamlet's mother – Gertrude.
JAN: Do you want the lot?
BERN: No. Just do Gert and miss out the rude bit.

They finish the sketch with an original song – *No Wonder Shakespeare Never Gets a Laugh.* The same week's musical finale revisits some familiar territory, and one or two familiar gags, in *Treasure Island*. This time round Peter Glaze takes the role of Short John Silver ('Pity the parrot couldn't get *you* on its shoulder') who makes a thrilling announcement:

PETE: I have Cap'n Flint's map showing the exact location of the treasure.
BAND: DRAMATIC CHORD.
JAN: You know what this means?
BERN: Yes. We've just woken the band up.

As the programme was recorded only a few days before transmission, there was always the opportunity for writers or performers to slip in the odd topical gag, referencing some current news story, at the last minute. Most of the time this did nothing but boost *Crackerjack*'s street cred, but one time it came very close to landing Bernie Clifton and the gang in serious trouble:

I was in digs in Marlow. And it was the day of the show, it was Friday afternoon. And Alan Bell said, 'You've got to come in to White City.' I said, 'Why?' He said, 'Well, there's a line we did.' Peter was playing Logie Baird, the inventor of television. And I was this stupid assistant. And Morecambe and Wise had left the BBC that week and gone to Thames. And during the recording, as rehearsed, Peter said, 'You're hopeless. What's happened to those other people I asked for?' And I said, 'They've gone to Thames with Eric and Ernie.'

Well, on the afternoon it was being transmitted, it hit the fan. And Alan said, 'You've got to come in and dub that line.' So I went and stood in the studio as the show was going out, with a microphone, and somebody with two faders. One was my fader, one was the show fader. And Peter said, 'What's happened to those other people I asked for?' And whereas I said, during the show, 'They've gone to Thames with Eric and Ernie.' He said, 'What's happened to those other people I asked for?' 'They've gone to watch *Everton* play *Burnley*.' And nobody, nobody ever knew.

Halfway through the series, balloon modeller Trevor Little popped up again, having guested on the very first episode of *Crackerjack* a mere 23 years earlier. This series saw a return to physical games rather than questions and answers. An expert gave a brief demonstration of their skill (such as Trevor with his balloons, paper-tearing by Eric Hawkesworth, or cartooning by kids' TV stalwart Tony Hart) which the competitors did their best to copy, in a *Generation Game*-type challenge. *Crackerjack* pens were then distributed by a multi-tasking Jan Hunt. The final game involved assembling a jigsaw of a celebrity's face – a throwback to *Jig-Jak* days, but without the quiz element. Even after all this time, they still didn't seem to have found a decent, permanent replacement for *Double or Drop*.

Speciality acts of all kinds abounded in the *Young Entertainers* competition, which now squeezed in five acts per show. But there was a distinct lack of variety in the series final, when a lone singer competed against *three* impressionists in a virtual plague of Kermits and crowd of Crawfords ('Ooh, Betty!'). Mark Shenton concluded his act by rolling up his trousers, donning a balding wig, and strutting the stage as Max Wall. Jacqueline Fisher's big finish was a wickedly impressive Shirley Bassey. But Tracy Browne outshone them all. Partly because of a superior script:

> My mum was very resourceful. And *The Penguin Book of Jokes* was very useful too. And we kind of conceived the idea that if we structured it around the *Muppet Show*, we could shoehorn in a lot of guests. So that was it really. The spine of the show was always the *Muppet Show* and the guests were whoever was topical at the moment. It was Frank Spencer, of course. It was Margaret Thatcher, Edward Heath, Columbo, The Liver Birds …

A schoolfriend had entered Tracy for the *Crackerjack* competition and she was invited to audition in Southampton:

> I was 12 when I auditioned. Can't really remember much about it other than the huge numbers of kids and their parents bustling about – I seem to remember it was about 900 – in what felt like a huge space, probably a church hall. I was always a bit confused about the 'representing Southampton, but coming from Jersey' spiel that Ed Stewart introduced me with. Perhaps they thought no one would know where the island was! It *was* the 1970s, after all.

Tracy Browne made a total of three appearances during the series, which gave her ample time to soak up the atmosphere of the show:

> I remember them being very jolly. Lots and lots of banter and fun backstage. Jan Hunt and Peter Glaze. It's that weird thing, as a turn, you don't necessarily talk to your fellow performer, but you're connected by just being with each other and watching what's going on. However, they did take their time to allow my family to take photographs with them. Ed Stewpot was probably the most remote of all of them. The others did more in the show. He was probably in his dressing room, waiting.

However, at the semi-final, one particular Browne family photo caused a bit of a rumpus:

> My mum nearly got us into terrible trouble when Mud were rehearsing. You remember those cameras with the little cubes that would – sort of – erupt with a flash? Well, she used a little flash camera like that to take a picture while they were doing a camera rehearsal. And the floor manager held his hands up and said, 'Stop! Who took that picture, please?' Because, apparently, it could ruin thousands of pounds' worth of camera equipment – a humble little flash. So I do remember being mortified by that, and thinking, 'This is a disaster! Are they going to kick us out?'

In the series final, Tracy ended her act with *Swinging on a Star* in the persona of Lena Zavaroni (her idol at the time) and the audience voted her the winner:

> The prize was quite lovely – it was an Aiwa sound system, which still lurks in my parents' attic in Jersey. Also the legendary *Crackerjack* pencil was a lovely Sheaffer fountain pen, which was engraved, which was rather nice.

Unlike previous series winners The Rockettes, Tracy didn't have the problem of splitting the prize three ways!

Alan Bell had a clear vision of what he wanted to do with *Crackerjack* and the confidence that he could achieve it both speedily and efficiently. He was also heavily involved in all aspects of the show, both on film and in the studio, and was a scriptwriter and film editor to boot. But what one person sees as creative input, another may regard as meddling. And writer Tony Hare became increasingly unhappy:

> I'm afraid Alan and I had a conflict of interests. Whether it was because he was changing so much stuff I was writing, I don't know. But I remember ringing up my agent Kenny Earle and saying, 'Sorry, Kenny, I'm going to have to leave *Crackerjack* at the end of this series. I can't work with this guy.' I said, 'I like him, he's a nice bloke, but he's so difficult.' It was funny, because I'd never had any problems with a producer up to that point. Personality-wise there was no problem. But I was so used to the cosy way in which Brian Penders directed, and there was obviously a friction between Alan and me. And I just left at the end of that series.

Tony Hare had been a huge influence on *Crackerjack* over much of the previous decade, and he was responsible for some of the funniest and slickest musical finales the show ever produced. He went on to write TV sketches for Russ Abbot and Keith Harris before turning his attentions to radio, where his highly visual humour found its natural home. With quirky characters and a healthy dose of sound effects, he created a whole galaxy of bizarre worlds on Roy Hudd's topical sketch show *The News Huddlines* and spin-off sitcom *The Newly Discovered Casebook of Sherlock Holmes*.

Tony's name is absent from the credits of the last show in the series. The only writer credited is Bob Hedley. The scene of the cowcatcher opening is strangely familiar. Bob Wellings, presenter of BBC1's early-evening magazine show *Nationwide*, is at Chessington Zoo, standing next to a stretch of open water. There are clear parallels to the Ray Moore boat-race quickie earlier in the series, when the team swung the boat they were carrying and knocked him into the river. As before, we see them approach from the distance, only this time they're carrying a ladder. Bob Wellings' fate is sealed! But, just as they take a swing at him, he ducks. Bob looks down with amusement at the drenched figures of Bernie, Pete, Jan and Ed, before turning back to the camera. 'Well, of all people, they should have known, shouldn't they? Because it's Friday, it's five-to-five and it's *Crackerjack*.'

The last sketch of the show is introduced by Ed Stewart as 'yet another rerun of Robin Hood and his Merry Men'. It was well-trodden territory on *Crackerjack*, and Peter Glaze reprised the role of Friar Tuck, which he previously played opposite Don Maclean's Robin. There are a good few jokes of the 'non-stick friar' and 'deep-fat friar' variety. But most of the gags are at the expense of Ed Stewart, who makes an early entrance still attired in his blue *Crackerjack* jumper:

ED: Ha, ha, ha! I am the Sheriff of Nottingham, and you're under arrest!

PETE: What are you dressed like that for? That's not the Sheriff's get-up.

ED: I've lost me key to the dressing room.

In fact, he's wearing the dressing-room key on a chain around his neck. It's a bit of end-of-series mischief by writer Bob Hedley, who repeatedly pokes fun at Ed's real-life absent-mindedness throughout the sketch. Bernie Clifton (who affectionately describes Ed as having 'a kind of bumbling authority') was very familiar with Ed's casual approach to acting:

Ed wasn't really part of the sketch team, till they got hold of him and shook him and said, 'Listen, you've got to come in at the end of the sketch. And you've got to learn your lines!' Because prior to that he'd just wander in. Lovely Ed.

Later on in the sketch, Bernie (as Robin Hood) says:

I haven't got the heart to tell him that this is the last of the series. If he doesn't get a *Radio Times*, he'll turn up next week in the middle of *Horses Galore*.

(*Horses Galore,* Susan King's series about horses and those who work with them, would gallop into the *Crackerjack* slot the following Friday.)

It's great when a series ends on a high. And when Chris Greener makes his entrance as Little John, you really couldn't get much higher. At seven-foot-six Chris was, at that time, Britain's tallest man and towered above the rest of the cast including Bernie Clifton:

We were mucking about, he tapped me on the chest and knocked me over!

*

Crackerjack returned for its next run, not in its usual start-of-the-year slot, but in Autumn 1978, just five months after the previous series had ended. This was some indication of the popularity of the show in its current format, and boosted its number of episodes over the year to 26 – a total last reached in the late 1960s.

All the old team were back. Peter Glaze had spent late August at the Edinburgh Festival with *A Word in Your Ear* – a one-man miscellany of songs, readings and reminiscences, with music composed by his *Crackerjack* colleague Bert Hayes.

Also in late August, it was announced that Robin Nash had been promoted to BBC TV Head of Variety, replacing Terry Hughes, and leaving an executive vacancy on the *Crackerjack* team. That vacancy was filled by someone who knew the show better than most, having devised *Crackerjack* and produced it for ten years, from its very first episode until his brief relocation in Australia. Since then Johnny Downes had mainly produced the long-running celebrity panel game *Call My Bluff*, in which contestants had to pick the true definition of a word from three implausible contenders. Now Johnny was brought in as *Crackerjack*'s executive producer, while direction remained in the hands of Alan Bell:

If you ever wanted to cast a 1939 BBC producer, you'd have got someone like Johnny. He was articulate and sensibly dressed and upright, and would never do anything wrong. And if somebody dropped a pencil on the floor and it broke the lead, normally you'd pick it up and probably throw it out. But no, he would take it up and dust it and clean it and put in the pot. No, he was very careful about the BBC's budgets.

There seemed some logic in getting the original devisor of the show back to oversee proceedings but, in the 23 years that *Crackerjack* had been onscreen, children's television had changed radically. Had Johnny Downes kept up with those changes? Jan Hunt wasn't convinced:

> Johnny was lovely, but sadly my memory of Johnny was – oh dear – a little bit in the negative. Only because we'd brought a lot more into *Crackerjack*. And you've got to move with the times, haven't you? Even though you've got a successful format there's always room to update it a little bit. So when Johnny came back to produce it, he didn't particularly like all the flamboyant finales. And he said he was going to take *Crackerjack* back to how he wanted it. And that really was the end of the *Crackerjack* team. Because, as a team, we all felt a little bit uncomfortable, and we thought, 'If it ain't broken, why try and mend it?' But it was his prerogative. He was coming in as producer and it was his prerogative to do things as he wanted.

Johnny Downes' first major decision was to bring back *Double or Drop*. Alan Bell wasn't that keen, finding the format 'a bit babyish'. But it had been very popular in its time and, during its 14-year absence, no one had ever found an adequate replacement. When Eamonn Andrews left for ITV in 1964, the game that he had devised went with him. But, as it had never been used since, negotiating the rights was no great problem. So the closing credits of the first show of series 23 were identical in two respects to the closing credits of the first show of series one: '*Double or Drop* was devised by Eamonn Andrews' and 'Producer Johnny Downes'.

The cowcatcher opening to the first episode features another visitor from *Crackerjack*'s past, treated with scant respect by Bernie Clifton and the gang:

> Michael Aspel was sitting at a desk, in a very smart white suit and he said, 'Aeronautical news – and we're about to see a black jet.' And we pressed a button and ink came out of the microphone and just covered him.

The finale to show three is a Western entitled: *What a Cowboy Outfit!* Marshall Peter Glaze gives Bernie Clifton (doing an uncanny Jimmy

Stewart) a masterclass in sharp-shooting. After letting off a deafening volley of shots, he is interrupted by a furious Michael Parkinson, who enters with puffs of smoke still emanating from his jacket:

MIKE: Do you mind? I'm trying to rehearse my show next door!
(STORMS OFF)
PETE: Who was that?
BERN: I don't know. I always go to bed straight after *Match of the Day*.

Recording the show a few days before transmission definitely had its pros and cons. You could slip in a gag at the last minute, even though (as with the 'Eric and Ernie' gag of the previous series) you may be required to slip it straight out again. But in show five of this series, the pros and cons reached truly mammoth proportions.

On the morning of the day of recording, the *Daily Mirror* ran an exclusive interview with madcap comedian Freddie Starr, who *Mirror* journalist Ken Irwin succinctly describes as 'the Jekyll and Hyde superstar'. During the interview Freddie confesses to a succession of rows and bust-ups with fellow performers over the years, including one that took place during the run of a pantomime in Oxford:

'When I arrived at the theatre, I found that nearly all the furniture had been taken from my dressing room,' said Freddie. 'Then I discovered that it had been put in Peter Glaze's dressing room. When I asked him for the furniture he didn't want to know. Eventually I lost my temper, went to his dressing room, and grabbed him by the throat, pinned him up against the wall and threatened to smash him up unless I got my furniture back. Mr Glaze then complained and there was another row before I eventually got some decent furniture in my dressing room.'

Although Peter Glaze suffered any number of Crazy Gang practical jokes with all the fortitude he could muster, you pull a prank on Freddie Starr at your peril! But it is Peter Glaze who gets the last laugh when, at the start of *Crackerjack* (recorded later that same day), he reads out a telegram from Bernie Clifton:

I'm sorry I can't be there, to do the show today.
You'll make my dressing room look quite bare, when you take all the
    furniture away.

Peter does a typical outraged reaction and flounces off. It's a good topical gag and the only shame is Bernie's not there to deliver it in person. Just as the gag was a last-minute addition, it was only discovered on the day of recording that the show would be lacking its principal gagster. All week Bernie Clifton had been rehearsing the show during the day, while fitting in a few club engagements at night:

> I was in Norwich and I had to drive down to somewhere in Essex to do this cabaret. And I was so ill. I'd got my roadie with me, and we were recording *Crackerjack* the following day. And I was so ill, my roadie Andy took me to his mum's, and they put me up there and gave me hot toddies. I had to ring in and say, 'I just can't make it.'

Director Alan Bell had a difficult decision to make and precious little time in which to make it:

> Bernie, on the Tuesday morning, said he wasn't feeling very well, wasn't coming in. And he was getting worse and said, 'I can't possibly do this show.' So the BBC moved in and said, 'We'll just show a repeat – and just tell everybody we're very sorry.' And I said, 'Well, why don't we just do the show?'

Everyone rallied round, scripts were hastily rewritten, and somehow the show went on. Bernie's only appearance is in a pre-filmed 'Bernie and Pete' silent, shot in Knebworth gardens. The middle sketch (moved to later in the show and featuring a robotic UFO) is adapted so that Jan delivers all the funny lines originally intended to be split between her and Bernie. Jan and Peter have great chemistry, particularly in the song at the end, making it all the more surprising that it's the first *Crackerjack* crosstalk double-act ever to feature a female comic.

Another female comedy spot (this one booked well in advance of Bernie's absence) is provided by Tracy Browne, the winning 'young entertainer' from the previous series. Strangely, although auditions for *Young Entertainers* were heavily plugged at the end of the last series, it never returned. It's possible that the shorter gap between the two series made it impossible to organise in time. Whatever the reason, The Rockettes and Tracy Browne are the only two winners this short-lived talent contest ever had.

Tracy's (mostly male) line-up of impressions includes Frankie Howerd, David Bellamy and Magnus Pyke – together with Frank Spencer and his rarely impersonated wife Betty. A return booking was never part of the prize – she was now there on merit alone. But Tracy had started to have misgivings about her choice of career:

> Lena Zavaroni was my idol. I thought she had an amazing voice. She was obviously a little older than me, but she was blazing a trail, having gone on *Opportunity Knocks*. And I started reading reports about Lena Zavaroni. There were the nights in Carnegie Hall with Frank Sinatra, and glorious career highlights which she enjoyed. But then the reports started coming in about this strange thing called 'Ay-nor-ex-eye-a nervous-a'. And literally nobody knew a thing about it. That it was a wasting disease. And she wasn't eating. And it gradually dawned on me that perhaps all might not be well in the house of the child performer generally.
>
> When I won the whole thing, Alan Bell had a sort of quiet talk with mum and I backstage. And he said, 'I just want to assure you there's plenty of time for you to have a career. Be careful. There are a lot of unscrupulous people out there.' He didn't specify. He wasn't particular. But I do remember – perhaps the words aren't exactly the ones that he uttered – but that's the sentiment. Hold back, get your schooling done, and see if it's still a passion for you. And it was really a combination of those two things that made me retire from impressions at about 14.

Happily, Tracy made a return to acting and impressions in adulthood. Now known as Kate O'Sullivan, her TV credits include *Bremner, Bird & Fortune*, *Dead Ringers* and *2DTV*. She was on *The One Show* in early 2017 in a feature celebrating child talent contests. Alongside her were previous *Young Entertainers* winners The Rockettes, whose drummer Simon Capes now works as a recording engineer. Until that meeting, Kate was totally unaware that the two of them had a *Crackerjack* connection:

> We had worked together at various studios. He was engineering and I was doing voiceovers. So he was on the other side of the glass. We're talking mid to late '90s. And we'd never discussed it. It had somehow never cropped up. I had no idea about his other life.

With Bernie Clifton missing from *Crackerjack*, and no time to coach a replacement, the musical finale was going to be hard to pull off. Fortunately, as Alan Bell was driving into work, inspiration struck:

> As I drove in to the Television Centre round Shepherds Bush Green, a circus had come to town, with elephants and things like that. And I said, 'Why don't

we say there's a big star coming to take Bernie's place at the end of the show? And we'll bring an elephant on.' And everyone thought I was crazy. And I went across to the circus man and he had an elephant there. And I said, 'How much would you charge to let us borrow your elephant for half an hour?' And I think it was something silly like £100. And we arranged for the police to stop the traffic at exactly twenty-to. We couldn't have an elephant in the wings, because it would give the game away.

Throughout the show, subtle clues are provided by further telegrams from Bernie, such as:

I've arranged for a star to appear on the show, the audience are certain to
    love him.
He's really quite big in the business, and there's just no one in showbiz
    above him.

Naturally Peter is convinced that Frank Sinatra will be dropping by. Although the show lacks its usual meaty finale, the time is effortlessly filled with guests (two pop acts in addition to Tracy Browne) and a *Double or Drop* that seems to go on forever, with Ed Stewart addressing his questions to three prize-mountains on legs, until the inevitable avalanche.

Just as Ed is about to say goodbye, Jan rushes on with one final telegram for him to read:

Here's the moment you've all been awaiting, he's bigger than all the big
    guns.
He's loads of pure charm and charisma, as for talent this lad has got tons.

As the elephant makes its entrance there is a huge scream of delight from the audience, even louder than the sigh of relief from Alan Bell:

So we timed it to get it exactly right and we had the police there. I'm up in the gallery and I say, 'Is the elephant there yet?' And they say, 'No. We're looking for it.' 'Well get it quickly, because we've only got another four minutes to go.' And eventually they said what this big star was, and it came on. And I discovered later, the reason the police were late was that they'd seen in their duty book – 'Help an elephant across the road at 6.40' – and they didn't believe it!

Bernie Clifton was back at work the following week in a show that took a further sly dig at the Glaze/Starr debacle. In the finale, Peter is the Duke of

Wellington boasting about his beautiful personal furniture. He picks up a chair with a canvas back (the type used in film studios) and turns it round, revealing the name 'FREDDIE STARR' painted in large letters. There had been fewer pop songs in the final sketch since Tony Hare's departure from the writing team, but a rendition by Bernie and Jan of *Summer Nights* is enlivened by Peter periodically crossing the screen in front of them, clutching a wellington boot and singing, 'Welly, welly, welly.'

Mike Giles, the sound supervisor for the series, would attend technical runs in the rehearsal studio a couple of days before the studio recording – along with the lighting director, the technical manager, and sometimes the senior cameraman:

> After the run, each discipline would mark up a floor plan with details of lighting requirements, boom and camera positions – although many directors would pre-empt much of the camera positioning in general, often using cardboard discs with string attached to ensure that camera cables were not going to become hopelessly tangled on the day. But those plans often needed tweaking after the tech run.

The technical crew could also be a valuable morale-booster:

> Comedy programmes placed great importance on the reactions of the technical crew at the outside rehearsal. I well remember a more senior sound supervisor on my sound training course emphasising that it was important to laugh convincingly at anything that seemed like a joke, even if you had to work out what was funny on the way home.
>
> Encouraging the cast and allowing reaction time helped the sound supervisor to maximise audience reaction on the night. The nature of sound is such that the audience mics cannot normally be kept at full volume whilst there is speech from the performers, because of colouration from the public address loudspeakers. So the sound supervisor has a hand permanently on the audience fader to grab laughter or applause, but must then drop the audience mics again immediately more speech occurs.
>
> *Crackerjack* presented a particular problem because the show involved continuous reaction from the kids, whilst Bert and the band were also going full pelt against the excitement from the stage. So this required a sound balance which allowed the stage speech to be heard (and understood) whilst maintaining musical integrity and infectious atmosphere – all within the limits of the meters on the sound desk. Grey hairs appeared by the minute and perfection was often not the order of the day, but the end result was fun!

Val Mitchell was the hostess recruited to pile on the prizes during *Double or Drop*. Like many of her predecessors she was an actress, singer and model – and (unlike many of her predecessors) she was actually given the opportunity to act! Val frequently appeared in the final sketch – the first hostess to do so since Jillian Comber – and was also regularly credited in the *Radio Times*. In *The Scarlet Pimpernel* Val is maidservant Nell, whose every entrance risks exposing Sir Percy Blakeney's secret identity. ('Use a crimper, Nell.' 'Don't whimper, Nell.' 'You little tinker, Nell.') The sketch also includes a topical gag at the expense of Bruce Forsyth, another BBC star who had recently defected to ITV (in this case to front an interminable, and much reviled, Saturday-night show). But, unlike the Eric and Ernie gag of the previous series, this one stayed in:

BERN: Sorry I was late. I was held up by a mad highwayman.

JAN: How did you know he was mad?

BERN: Well, he left my money and he took my ticket for *Brucie's Big Night*.

Val is firmly established as a member of the quartet in the last show of the series which (being the first autumn run of the show since 1969) is a Christmas special. She joins Bernie, Jan and Peter in both the opening sketch and its concluding song *They've Nicked Father Christmas for Speeding*. All four of them then take part in the first game, a far from enviable task, in which they're dressed as babies and spoonfed by a group of blindfolded children.

In the extended final sketch, Pete is invited by Bernie to stay at a luxurious country house for Christmas, only to discover that they are the hired help. In what had become a seasonal tradition, Pete ends up in drag, while Bernie impersonates a crusty butler. At one point Pete boasts to the house guests, 'We've got some lovely food here – untouched by human hand.' Bernie adds, 'The chef's a monkey.' 'Oh yeah, and what's so funny about that?' yells a cleaver-wielding Mickey (*The Monkees*) Dolenz, milking his brief cameo for all it's worth.

At the end of the series, Peter, Ed and Jan made a swift exit and opened in panto shortly afterwards. Perhaps too shortly, judging by *The Stage* review:

All three were unable to get to Bournemouth until four days before the show opened on Christmas Eve and despite the work done beforehand by director

Peter Sontar during those four days, *Dick Whittington* opened badly under-rehearsed.

It wasn't really the fault of the performers that they were in so much demand on both telly and in the theatre. Despite the rough edges on opening night, things rapidly improved. Bernie Clifton fared better as Simple Simon in *Puss in Boots* at Lewisham, though of course he comprised a far smaller percentage of the cast.

*

Everyone was back in Autumn 1979 apart from Alan Bell, though his *Crackerjack* silents still featured throughout the series. Direction was again in the hands of Brian Penders, who made few changes to the format. There were no more celebrity cameos or location filming for the opening quickies. Instead the green-screen came out of storage, placing the cast in a variety of locations – including the control room of a space mission, counting down to take-off. Seconds later the astronauts request an immediate return to earth to watch *Crackerjack.* (Cue: reversed film of rocket launch.)

The first sketch was usually some kind of Peter Glaze lecture, with heckling by both Jan and Bernie, now generally making their entrance together. And the final sketch always incorporated a song or two. Bob Hedley, who had written the previous series single-handed, was helped out by a range of writers who contributed the odd finale – including John Speer, Laurie Rowley and Terry Ravenscroft.

Terry Ravenscroft is a prolific sketch writer, and his *Cissie and Ada* duologues for Les Dawson and Roy Barraclough are still remembered (and frequently quoted) with great affection. But, like other writers before him, Terry didn't find *Crackerjack* the most pleasurable of experiences:

> In one of the sketches I wrote, *The Last of the Mucky 'uns*, Peter Glaze complained to me that he hadn't had any funny lines for a bit. I explained to him that, in that particular part of the sketch, he was acting as the feed for Bernie. Unhappy with this he said, 'That's all right, I can make the feed lines funny.' I explained that if he were to deliver the feed lines as punchlines it would ruin the gags. It didn't make any difference, he still did it. And killed the gags.

At the start of the series, the *Daily Mirror* ran a piece on the show's host:

I have a theory about the kids in Ed Stewart's audience. They seem to have been released after a week in a darkened room with the promise of a cream bun if they scream loud enough. When 'Stewpot' presents *Crackerjack* it's a right old cacophony. But the amiable six-foot giant doesn't mind too much. At 38, he confesses he's still a kid at heart and loves playing the fool.

Ed says: 'I'm a Big Brother in the nicest possible way, and I have a great affinity with children. That's because I still think like a child. *Crackerjack* has been on the air so long, I can tell people's ages by asking who they remember presenting it.' Today's guest Georgie Fame remembers Eamonn.

Pop acts were still eager to appear on the show and give their latest single some extra airplay. Two guest spots a week were filled with big-name acts. Of course, the pop world was Ed's world too. He was totally at ease in this stellar line-up. Not so Bernie Clifton:

> I remember there was a girl called Judie Tzuke and she'd signed up to Elton John's Rocket Records. And she was a big star. She'd got this hit at the time – *Stay with Me till Dawn*. And she came on and sang it. And I was too shy to say, 'Excuse me, you don't know me but I think you're fantastic.' I've always regretted it.

Judie shared a show with Suzi Quatro. Other acts during the series included Lulu, Bonnie Tyler, The Nolan Sisters and Sparks. XTC appeared in October singing *Making Plans for Nigel*. A month later *Crackerjack* repaid the compliment (if it could be called a compliment!) by effortlessly slipping the song into their medieval finale. Peter Glaze's vocal style during that particular number can best be described as a cross between Morrissey and Pavarotti.

The week following Peter Glaze's spirited XTC tribute act, *Crackerjack* hit a problem. It takes inflexibility on both sides to make a dispute, and BBC management and unions had become no strangers to these. And some of these disputes flared up into industrial action. The 'work to rule' ethic was something Bernie Clifton had personally experienced:

> The unions were very strong. And let's say we were going to record at six, so the rehearsal had to finish at five. The lights would go out mid-sentence. Click – that was it!

After pay-regrading talks broke down, BBC technicians pulled the plug on several shows. But (as the *Daily Express* reported) any child who attended the *Crackerjack* recording on Tuesday 20ᵗʰ November 1979 was in for a special, if not exactly cost-effective, treat:

> Last night a *Crackerjack* recording was cancelled but, to avoid disappointing the children, the programme went ahead for the studio audience only.

The strike rumbled on and many other recordings, including further episodes of *Crackerjack*, were cancelled. But, if you enjoy a bit of poetic justice, there is much to relish in this *Express* piece from Friday 7ᵗʰ December:

> Ironically, Arthur Scargill, the militant Yorkshire miners' leader, has been blacked out by an industrial dispute tonight. He was due to take over the chatmaster's seat in the late night BBC2 show *Friday Night … Saturday Morning*, but the show was hit by the recent BBC grading dispute. Instead, tonight at 11.20 we have the endearing bearded Willie Rushton (late of *Celebrity Squares*) introducing his mates The Alberts, Barry Cryer and Peter Glaze.

For Bernie Clifton, the *Crackerjack* shutdown had unexpected benefits:

> I was booked for the Royal Variety Show in November 1979 and for two weeks prior to it there was a strike at the BBC. And we'd rehearsed a show, but we couldn't record it because of a strike. So it was under wraps, bolted down. And I used to go in every day and use the space at Acton to rehearse my Royal Variety spot. And I'd got the whole rehearsal room decked out like the Royal Variety stage. I had a second ostrich – and Jeff Thacker, who was a dancer in Second Generation, he was tucked up inside it. I had a friend, Lesley, she did the choreography, and a pianist. And I used to come in at teatime and use the BBC space. It was just fortuitous that at the very time when I needed all the time in the world, I wasn't needed for rehearsals.

The strike took its toll on the rest of the series, with *Crackerjack* repeats replacing scheduled new episodes. Whether it was the original intention or not, the end-of-series special was a second showing of the previous year's Christmas show. It was a disappointing end to the series and, for many of the cast, there was worse to come. The only person to reap much benefit from all the disruption was Bernie Clifton, whose meticulously rehearsed ostrich routine proved to be one of the highlights of the Royal Variety Performance:

As a result of the Royal Variety, I was inundated – the old joke, isn't it? – 'I was inundated with an offer!' I was inundated with offers from ITV. Jon Scoffield, who produced the Royal Variety, came to me afterwards and said, 'Unbelievable, my boy. I shall be on the phone tomorrow to your manager and I'll guarantee you 13 major dates.' And I went, 'Who is this man?' And as a result of that I did a special from Elstree for ATV, and then went on to do various stuff for ITV.

With Bernie Clifton out of the next series, it was just a matter of recruiting a new comic to join Pete, Jan, Ed and the gang. It was goodbye to the old series – see you in the next. But what nobody saw coming was the *Daily Mirror*'s stark headline of Monday 12th May 1980:

CRACKERSACK!

Children's favourites Ed Stewart, Peter Glaze and Jan Hunt have been given the boot from TV's *Crackerjack*. When Ed – nicknamed 'Stewpot' – heard the news he snapped: 'This has come as a shock to me. I have not been told that I'm being dropped from the show. I'm hurt at the way the BBC has done this to us.'

The axings follow comedian Bernie Clifton's decision to quit the 25-year-old children's series. It will have an entirely new team of 'regulars' when it returns in the autumn.

BBC TV variety chief Robin Nash explained: 'Bernie's departure gave us the chance to rethink and reshape the show. I have several artists in mind for the next series. They are established performers but they may not have been seen much on TV.'

Jan said, 'I have been with the show six years and they have been happy and progressive ones.'

Whatever the merits of the decision, it couldn't have been handled worse. In his autobiography, Ed Stewart gives his own account of how he learnt the news in a late night phone call:

'Hello … Ed Stewart?' I could just make out a crackly and slightly inebriated voice. 'This is the *Mirror* here. I'm just calling to tell you that you won't be presenting *Crackerjack* any more …' and I distinctly heard a loud cry of 'CRACK-ER-JAAACK' in the background.

'How do you know that?' I asked in a shaky voice, not wanting to believe what I was hearing. 'Robin Nash, your producer, has just told me … we're all out here at the Montreux Film Festival. Just a moment, I'll pass him on to you.'

Robin's unmistakeable voice confirmed everything. 'Yessh, darling Ed. You're all too old and we're putting some new blood in.'

So basically Robin Nash got drunk and confided in a journalist. How could that possibly go wrong? Everyone was shaken by the announcement and by the crass way it was made. And everyone I have spoken to says Peter Glaze took it the worst – and that no attempt was ever made to properly thank him for his inestimable contribution to the show over a period spanning almost 20 years. Ed Stewart goes on to suggest the shock of Peter's sacking could have contributed to his early death. Not true. Peter Glaze had a good few years left in him, and his later career is detailed in a potted biography by his wife April Young:

> A kind of completeness occurred when in 1981 he was invited to join the company headed by Roy Hudd and Christopher Timothy, who played Flanagan and Allen in the show *Underneath the Arches*, which was presented at the Chichester Festival Theatre for the season with enormous success. Peter played Charlie Naughton. The show opened in the West End at the Prince of Wales Theatre in February 1982 and it was still running when, on Sunday 20th February 1983, Peter died. He had played the show at the Prince of Wales for almost a year to the day!

The Crazy Gang had helped launch Peter's West End career and were there again (in spirit, at least) at his final performance. Peter had performed both the matinee and evening show on the Saturday, before dying suddenly of a heart attack at home the following day. A particular sadness is that Roy Hudd and Christopher Timothy were shortly to leave the production, to be replaced by Bernie Winters and Leslie Crowther (who had recently starred in their own Flanagan and Allen stage musical *Bud 'n' Ches*). Jean Crowther told me that Leslie had been looking forward to this onstage reunion with his former *Crackerjack* partner.

Peter's son, Tony Glaze, only learned of his father's health difficulties after his death:

> I think he had been ill for some time. He had a heart problem. But I didn't know about that. I think he just decided he was going to work right up to the end, which is what he did basically.

Tony kept in regular contact with Peter's wife, April Young, who continued to run her theatrical agency:

And when she retired at the age of 80, bless her, she really got involved with village affairs. Baking cakes and making jams and chutneys for the fete. Taxi servicing different people hither and thither. She was a very busy lady right up to the end.

At her 90th birthday party, she had a photograph of Peter on the table beside her. And it was her boast that it was the first time she'd managed to get all the living Glazes together around the same table.

In December 1979 Ed Stewart not only hosted his last *Crackerjack* but also said 'Byeee' to *Junior Choice*, which he handed on to Tony Blackburn. In the 1980s Ed put away childish things and moved to Radio 2. In the mid-90s he became probably the first radio DJ ever to climb both Mount Snowdon and Ben Nevis live on air.

Jan Hunt was reluctant to say a permanent goodbye to *Crackerjack*:

> Years after it had finished on television, I went to the BBC because I wanted to do a stage version of it. But they were laying down so many rules and regulations that it became a problem and I dropped the idea.

Perhaps it wouldn't have been as good as the original – we'll never know – but it would certainly have pulled in an audience. Like so many of *Crackerjack*'s stars, Jan recalls the show with enormous affection:

> I used to love going in on the morning and seeing the scripts for the next show and what was going to be my homework, to develop and create the characters that Bob and Tony had written. That was always fun. And because we were allowed to inject the odd thing here and there, you never felt, 'That's the script and I've got to stick to it.'
>
> But then my next favourite part was to get in with Bert Hayes and the musicians. I mean we were very lucky to work with a backing like that in those days. And to hear those orchestrations – it just used to make my heart sing. And I used to enjoy lunchtimes and I always used to have hot sausage roll with brown sauce.
>
> Getting through it was always a bit hairy, because you think, 'Oh, I hope I'm going to remember it. I *do* hope I don't make any mistakes.' And I used to sit with my dad every Friday, because my mum was working, and watch it. Not because I was being narcissistic. Because when you watch yourself, you think, 'Oh, I didn't know it looked like *that* when I did it.' So I think you can be your own good critic. And watch and learn. In show business, the day you think you can't learn anything is the day you should give up. And I'm still learning, and I'm nearly 80, so there you go.

A few months after our interview, Jan abseiled down Portsmouth's Spinnaker Tower for charity. The following year, aged 80, she took to the skies for a sponsored wing-walk! Her music-hall troupe Paper Moon Theatre Company is constantly touring the country, with frequent guest appearances from Jan's *Crackerjack* colleagues Don Maclean and Bernie Clifton.

Bernie Clifton has also never stopped learning. And one of the few things he has taken seriously is singing. In 2016, on *The Voice* (the talent show where the judges turn their backs on you), he confounded expectations with his rendition of *The Impossible Dream.* That early tip Robin Nash gave him about projection clearly paid off!

Bernie's thoughts, looking back on *Crackerjack*, are similarly inspirational:

> I just think it's a treasured time in my life, in my career, to have been pitchforked into an established iconic show as a 'turn', as a club act from the north. And I only wish that, at the time, I'd appreciated it as much as I do now. But because you're up to your armpits in the stresses and the strains of it, you haven't got the opportunity to step back and think, 'Wow, this is great!'
>
> My overall comment would be, 'I'm such a lucky boy to have had that as part of my CV.' Even now, I can go out and do an after-dinner speech and say, 'Good evening, I'll just find out how old you are. It's Friday – it's five to five …' And half the room goes, '*Crackerjack*!' and the other half goes, 'What?' It's a great icebreaker. And so, for those purely selfish reasons, I think I'm so lucky to have been there and done it.

12

Can You Make Your Accent Stronger?

1980 – 1981

THE 1980S WERE JUST five days old when this piece appeared in the *Daily Mirror*:

> A tough new approach to children's television is challenging traditional softies such as *Blue Peter* and *Crackerjack*. The controversial BBC serial *Grange Hill* starts again next Tuesday and coming up is an ITV series which will cause even more fuss.
>
> Southern Television have been fretting over the series *Noah's Castle* for months. The theme is a food shortage in present-day Britain and the series shows riots and thefts from food stores. The violence includes fights between the police and gangs of Punks.

Yes, a new decade had arrived. And five o'clock telly was starting to look distinctly less cheery and comforting. The kid gloves were off. This was tea without the cosy.

Against this background, perhaps it's no great surprise that *Crackerjack* had to shape up or ship out. *Grange Hill* (a schooldays serial set in a boisterous North London comprehensive) began in 1978 – and from 1979 it went out twice a week, frequently barging into the recently vacated *Crackerjack* slot. The harder-hitting storylines were still to come, but the fact that the *Mirror* labelled *Grange Hill* 'controversial' at this early stage indicates it was not everybody's idea of family-friendly TV. (A highly tenuous link between the two shows is that, in its early years, the theme tune to *Grange Hill* was also used for ITV's *Give Us a Clue*, a celebrity charades panel game chaired by Michael Aspel.)

For all true lovers of the BBC, the initials BH signify that magnificent bastion of radio excellence – Broadcasting House. But the new-look *Crackerjack* would also lack two major figures with the initials BH. Bob Hedley had joined the show, together with Don Maclean and Jacqueline Clarke, in 1973. Along with Bob Block and Tony Hare, he was one of the major *Crackerjack* scriptwriters, who put his own stamp on the Peter Glaze lectures and had a gag for every occasion. He went on to write for Dick Emery, amongst others, and continued to do a bit of stand-up himself from time to time.

The other BH was *Crackerjack*'s longest-serving permanent fixture, Bert Hayes, who had been with the show even longer than Peter Glaze. He joined, along with Ronnie Corbett, way back in 1957. He was absent from the Little and Large series (just like Peter Glaze), then stayed on continuously until the end of 1979 (just like Peter Glaze), tackling everything from *Golden Years* to *Summer Nights* with flawless rhythm and musicality (just like ... no, perhaps not). In his later years, Bert Hayes was a mainstay of many local musical productions. He died suddenly, aged 73, having played piano for the Margate Operatic Society only hours earlier.

Crackerjack's new broom was Michael Hurll, an experienced variety producer fresh from *The Two Ronnies*, who had also succeeded where *Crackerjack* had failed by producing a successful series for Syd Little and Eddie Large. He was now installed in the role of executive producer, both of *Crackerjack* and *Top of the Pops*. A BBC spokesman told *The Stage*:

> Like the *Top of the Pops* post, the executive producer of *Crackerjack* will not be just a figurehead but will be very involved in the production.

Michael Hurll is extensively quoted in the BBC's press release for the new series:

> There will be more games, including the ever popular *Double or Drop* and more audience participation. There'll be a good news and a bad news item each week, as well as guest appearances by pop groups and a comedy act

featuring a top comedian. Altogether I hope to make it a funnier and faster moving show, more in keeping with what kids and families want today.

There's not much here that sounds any different from the last series (or even the very first series in 1955) apart from the news items, perhaps an idea he borrowed from *The Two Ronnies*? Fortunately the show was more inspired than its press release, thanks to a tradition as old as *Crackerjack* itself – that of taking a chance on some fresh talent. Later on, in the same press release, Michael says of the new team, 'The other thing about them is that they are all Northerners.'

Maybe the BBC has had a tendency to be a little southern-centric, and you don't have to delve back very far to a time when regional accents were frowned upon. Not that *Crackerjack* ever fell into that category, having showcased the likes of Bernie Clifton, Don Maclean, Little and Large and Edinburgh-born Ronnie Corbett, to name but a few. Michael Hurll goes on to detail his 100 per cent northern line-up:

> The Krankies, who shot to fame when they made the Queen Mother laugh at the Royal Variety Show in 1978, will be joined by comedian Stu Francis and attractive Jan Michelle. The Krankies are Scottish, Stu is Lancastrian and Jan is from Liverpool.

For everyone concerned, this would be a major boost to their careers – provided the new-look *Crackerjack* didn't fail! Former *Crackerjack* sketch writer Johnny Ball had also been considered as a possible host. He declined the offer as, by then, he was fully committed to his *Think of a Number* TV shows. Although not privy to departmental discussions, Stu Francis subsequently learnt of the vital importance of this relaunch:

> I was told, after I got the job, that the powers that be were going to take *Crackerjack* off. They thought it had run its course. And Michael Hurll said to the hierarchy, the people in the ivory tower, 'Well, hang on a minute. It's very popular. Why don't we look at completely changing it? Keep the scaffolding, but let's bring it into the 80s. Give it a facelift.' And they said, 'Alright, go away and come back with your plans.'
>
> And so he went back to the powers that be and said, 'Look, instead of having a full team, we'll have a host, a hostess, change the games. And I think we've got just the guy to front it. It's a guy called Stu Francis, who's done stuff for us before, the likes of *Seaside Special*.'

As producer of *Seaside Special* (the summertime big-top variety series that visited a different coastal resort each week), Michael Hurll had booked Stu Francis once a series for the previous three years:

> And of course the powers that be in the ivory tower had never heard of me. And Michael said, 'Yes, Stu Francis. He has all these silly catchphrases like "Ooh, I could crush a grape!" And I think those catchphrases will catch on with the younger generation, with the kids.' And they said, 'Right. Where can we see him?'
>
> And I was doing a summer season at the Opera House in Scarborough and they came up, the powers that be. Jimmy Gilbert, I believe, who was Head of Light Entertainment, was one of them. And they came up to Scarborough, saw the show, went back to London and said, 'Yeah, we think he's the guy to do it. We saw him, we liked him. Get on with it. Do it.' And I was so relieved that I didn't know they were in the theatre. Because I would've been thinking, 'Oh, goodness me!' Pacing up and down, as you would.

Back in 1959 producer Jimmy Gilbert had given Pip Hinton her big TV break. Since then, he had steadily risen through the ranks, succeeding Bill Cotton as Light Entertainment head in 1977.

All the best catchphrases come about by chance rather than design, and Stu's was a prime example of an inspired adlib:

> I was working a club – it was a long time ago, but I'm sure it was a club called Jollees in Stoke on Trent. It was a Theatre Club and there was a big gang of ladies on a table, at the front, at the side. And I'm working away, and they're laughing and laughing. And one lady, who was a bit older than the others, she's one of these ladies who has a loud, 'Whooooo!' and it sort of sets everybody off.
>
> And I kept looking at this lady, who was laughing and smiling and looking up at me. And I said, 'You're clearly enjoying yourself, aren't you, darling?' 'Ooh,' she said, 'When I were coming tonight I was so excited.' And I said, 'Well, so am I.' And I leant right over the table, looking at this lady, and I said, 'In fact, do you know, I'm so excited, I could … I could …'
>
> And I thought, 'Where am I going with this?' I'd taken myself down a cul-de-sac. I don't know why I said it! And the table went quiet. The room seemed to go quiet, thinking, 'What's he going to say to this old lady?' And I said, 'I'm so excited I could … I could… ooh, I could crush a grape!' And she went, 'Oooh, you fool!' and they were off again. And I don't know where it came from. Literally, to this day, I don't know where it came from.

And I finished, I came off stage. And I walked to the bar at the back. And there was two fellers at the bar, and they'd got a tray of drinks and were going back to their table. And one of these fellers looked at me and he said to his mate, 'Oh aye, here he is – I could crush a grape!' And I thought, 'I've just been on that stage for the best part of an hour. And I've come off stage, and that's the first thing that guy's said to me. That's the only thing he's remembered about me being up there.' And that's how it came about.

Although 'crush a grape' seems the ideal child-friendly catchphrase, *Crackerjack* was totally new territory to this Bolton-born comic:

I came up through the clubs. The social clubs, working men's clubs, then night clubs, then theatre clubs. So my audience had always been an adult audience. I thought, 'How am I going to pitch this?' My catchphrases were 'Ooh, I can crush a grape – I can jump off a doll's house.' And you can't keep saying that for 13 weeks! So we played on that, and I got a couple of writers in as well, who were doing stuff for me. And we sat down and came up with a lot of other silly catchphrases, so we weren't saying the same thing every week.

The Krankies, like Stu Francis, were club performers. Early in her career Janette had appeared in a Glasgow pantomime called *The World of Widow Crankie*. She adopted the surname (with a subtle change of spelling) when she became half of a female double-act calling themselves The Krankie Kids. Subsequently she went into partnership (both professionally and matrimonially) with Ian Tough, and the pair became known as The Krankies.

Janette's mischievous schoolboy character was a later addition to the act. He was called Wee Jimmy following a tradition of such diminutive performers as Wee Georgie Wood and Jimmy Clitheroe. What made The Krankies different from their predecessors was that Wee Jimmy was, in reality, female – which would give rise to the odd naughty gag in their club act.

When Bernie Clifton decided to leave *Crackerjack* it was as a direct result of the impact he had made at the 1979 Royal Variety Performance. The Krankies had made a similarly career-boosting appearance on the 1978 show, attended by the Queen Mother. But, as Ian Tough found, the term 'overnight success' was not to be taken literally:

What launched us was the Royal Variety Show. However, we thought, as you would, 'Oh, next week I'll be on the television every week.' Nothing! Of course, not realising that TV plans well ahead. And that's when Michael

Hurll gave us the *Seaside Specials*, and then the Ronnie Corbett show. And then Michael said, 'I want you to do *Crackerjack*.' And it changed us from a cabaret act into a family theatre act.

Any success in showbiz is reliant on years of hard work topped off with a gentle sprinkling of good fortune. Janette Tough remembers what led up to that pivotal royal show:

We won the Club Act of the year. And it was supposed to be Princess Margaret that presented it and she was ill. And Bernard Delfont came instead and booked us for the Royal Variety. So that's fate! And if it *had* been Princess Margaret – there you are – kiss my astrakhan coat goodbye! But it was lucky that that happened to us. That we got our break that way.

The other new member of the *Crackerjack* team was Jan Michelle:

I'd been not long out of a pop group called Champagne, touring with them. We'd won *Opportunity Knocks* and everything. And I was trying to get into acting. And I was called in for an audition. Well, it was basically an interview, but Michael gave me the job there and then, which was great. It was terrifying for me because I hadn't really done much presenting.

And I was a hostess on *Play Your Cards Right*. Because, as it turned out, all of a sudden both transmissions happened on a Friday evening. So I was going out on the BBC at five o'clock and then going out on ITV as one of the Dolly Dealers. Which the press loved, because of all this controversy about me wearing all these elegant sexy gowns on *Play Your Cards Right* and doing a children's show. It was all publicity!

A big selling-point, in Michael Hurll's own pre-series publicity, had been the Northern roots of the *Crackerjack* team. At one time, those with regional accents would have been required to tone them down. For Jan Michelle it was quite the opposite:

I'm from a normal council estate in Liverpool. And when somebody says to you, 'Can you make your accent stronger?' it's really difficult. It's even more difficult than doing a different accent. They just wanted me to enunciate it a little bit more for the television. Certainly regional accents were becoming more prevalent then and, for some reason, they think it makes you more relatable. I don't know why. But, when I first started, RP – Received Pronunciation – was very important for the BBC.

As Ian Tough recalls, matters such as class and accent were often the cause of friction between *Crackerjack*'s executive producer Michael Hurll, and one of his predecessors (and currently his boss) Robin Nash:

> Michael was a big friend of the variety people. He liked variety. Liked comics. But Robin Nash had been running it up until then. Robin still had his old-fashioned ideas, which I think Michael did not want to know at all. And I could see the clashes coming, because Robin Nash wouldn't allow us to have ordinary schools in. We had to have public schools. Because his excuse was – ordinary children whistle and shout. And Michael said, 'That's what we *want!*' And I said, 'We want the kids from Wimbledon.' And Robin went, 'Dear dear, no. They'll be whistling and shouting at the cameramen, putting them off.' And Robin didn't like our accents. I can remember him arguing with Michael about Stu, saying, 'But it's a *very* strong Northern accent. And they're *Scottish!*'

With all these heated discussions ringing in his ears, the man entrusted with directing the series was John B. Hobbs, whose comedy credentials included the Wendy Craig sitcom *Butterflies*. The portrait that Stu Francis paints of him is hardly unique:

> He was very much what you'd expect a BBC director to be. Every day at rehearsals it was the suit, the collar, the tie, the handkerchief. Like a stick of rock, John Hobbs would have 'BBC' written right through him. If you said, when he walked in, 'What does that guy do?' 'Producer/director BBC.' He was always suited and booted. And lovely manners, lovely etiquette. And he was a great director.

Ian Tough recalls John Hobbs rocking back and forwards in his seat during rehearsals, as everyone went through their lines:

> The more displeased he got, the heavier he started rocking. 'Oh, he's rocking again!'

As the transmission date for the first show loomed, John Hobbs' restless body must have been a positive blur. The BBC was in the midst of a strike of scenery construction workers, which (as *The Times* reported) had rapidly escalated following the filming of a comedy sketch for *The Dawson Watch*:

> The strike arose after the corporation had refused to send a carpenter and an assistant on location because, it said, two people were already on hand from

the visual effects department to cover a stunt by Les Dawson, in which he walked through a glass-panelled door.

In addition to *Crackerjack*, other children's programmes to have recordings cancelled included *Play School* and *Record Breakers*. Fortunately the strike was resolved (and the recording rescheduled) in time for the first transmission on September 26th 1980. The only downside was that viewers were deprived of a song from musical guest Lynda Carter (TV's *Wonder Woman*). She was replaced by Leo Sayer who, for a change, *did* let the show go on.

Harry Parry's *Crackerjack* theme (which hadn't been heard since Eamonn Andrews' departure) was the only signature tune the show had ever known. In the years that followed, *Crackerjack* opened on a brief musical sting, sometimes not even that. The new series has a bright breezy comedy theme tune, played by (and possibly composed by) new musical director Burt Rhodes. Burt had written the theme for sitcom *The Good Life* and much incidental music for *The Benny Hill Show*, so was well qualified to provide a tune that Ian Tough describes as, 'Just like a waterfall – diddle-diddle-diddle!'

The opening of the show is a fine example of multi-tasking, with Stu Francis combining the roles of host and comedian – something that hadn't been attempted since the days of Leslie Crowther. Not by Michael Aspel nor Ed Stewart:

> They were out-and-out presenters, of course. And the likes of Leslie and myself, we were presenters on it, but we were basically comics. We did both jobs. I think it's called a pound of flesh!

But Stu Francis didn't walk out on stage alone. He was accompanied by (and in early shows preceded by) Jan Michelle, who was more than a hostess, she was a co-host. It didn't take Stu long to adapt to this new way of working:

> We used to do the banter, me and Jan Michelle. The presenting bit, she took to that like a duck to water. Having always worked on my own, suddenly to work with somebody else … it's changed, it's different. Then suddenly it sort of becomes natural. But *I* grew up with the Cannon and Balls, and the Little and Larges. If you were paired up in a double act, it'd be two lads. To suddenly be doing this patter, this double act, with a girl felt a bit strange. Then suddenly it was like, 'Here we go, great, love it!'

It's not exactly earth-shattering, but for *Crackerjack* this was a minor revolution – a female co-host. Okay, Jan is largely stooge to Stu's gags, but the previous stooge (and the *only* stooge in many people's living memories) was Peter Glaze. Add to that The Krankies, who consist of a male stooge and a female comic, and it's clear that *Crackerjack* has made a serious attempt to move with the times.

'Meet your hosts – Jan Michelle and Stu Francis,' says the unseen announcer. Jan makes her entrance shouting, 'Hello boys and girls!' while Stu opts for the more informal, 'Hiya kids!' Although performing comedy was new to her, Jan learnt plenty from co-host Stu:

> He was very supportive and he was sort of my mentor, you know, 'You just come out and be yourself.' And I'd done television with the group Champagne all over the world and, of course, we sang live. So I was used to television and cameras and recording studios. But it was electric, the atmosphere in there. The children loved screaming it out – it's five to five and it's *Crackerjack*!

Stu also savoured the buzz of the Television Theatre:

> Although you had a bank of cameras in front of you, between you and the audience, it still had a theatre feel. Far better than a studio. And, of course, you had the balcony as well. So, when you're working, you look up. The balcony's full, the stalls are full. So you've got the atmosphere. And on the left, in a massive soundproof booth, we had the live band. And the whole thing – the band started, the music kicked off at the beginning and it's like 'lights, action' and you felt, 'Oh this is great.'

Ian Tough agrees:

> The atmosphere was great. Mind you, you'd look out and think there was nobody in, because all the little kids weren't big enough to see over the seats.

Most of the writing for the series is credited to Bill Robson, who is something of an enigma. He doesn't have any other obvious writing credits, and when you look at the individual episode archive listings his name doesn't feature at all. Instead there are names like Norman Beedle and Graham Deykin, both experienced comedy writers, but never listed on the end credits or in the *Radio Times*. Perhaps 'Bill Robson' was the name of a writers' collective, just as the writers of *Spitting Image* adopted the pseudonym Katie

Bee for their collaborative sketches. (Katie Bee being KTB or, in full, KTBNDIH – Keep That Bloody Noise Down In Here!)

In a typical opening routine, Stu is demonstrating one of the prizes, a musical computer that plays tunes when you press the buttons – but every time Jan tries it, it just makes a rude buzzing noise:

JAN: That's not a tune!
STU: No, it's an opinion.

Sometimes the routine is themed around that week's guest star – usually a comedian or speciality act, rather than a pop star. When Ali Bongo is the guest, there are jokes about magicians. When Lenny Henry is on, Stu cracks another appropriate gag:

If you're good at impressions, you take people off. If you're not good, the producer takes *you* off.

Lenny Henry was already a familiar face on the Saturday morning ITV kids' show *Tiswas* – a show that Jan Michelle had previously auditioned for. *Tiswas* had actually been running since the mid-1970s. (The BBC responded soon afterwards with *Multi-Coloured Swap Shop* hosted by Noel Edmonds). Chris Tarrant had been with *Tiswas* from the start, though Lenny and regular presenter Sally James were more recent recruits. It was messy, it was anarchic, and it was yet another reminder that *Crackerjack* needed to keep evolving if it was to survive.

Jan and Stu's opening spot is followed by The Krankies. Wee Jimmy is usually showing Ian his latest invention, such as a scarecrow. ('It's so good, the crows brought back all the corn they stole last year.') A colleague of Ian Tough was responsible for many of their best routines:

My drummer said to me – as a drummer would – 'Some of that stuff you're doing is total crap. I can write better.' So I said, 'Oh really? Well write us something.' And he did. He wrote us the town names, the signs. They said, 'Well, if this guy can write stuff like this, get him in.' So he came in – Ron Ottaway.

In Ron's sketch, Wee Jimmy has designed a series of town signs for people who can't read, using drawings rather than words:

JIMMY: That one's great, look! It's a man with his head down a rabbit hole.

IAN: What town's that supposed to be?

JIMMY: That's Edinburgh. You get it? 'Ead-in-burrow!

IAN: But look, that's a picture of me and your headmaster. What town's that?

JIMMY: Berk-n-head.

IAN: Don't be so cheeky!

In fact, that last gag is more than a little cheeky. At one time 'berk' was considered a fairly mild insult and quite suitable for kids' TV. But once it became widely known that it derived from the rhyming-slang phrase 'Berkeley Hunt' it was swiftly outlawed.

Like Stu Francis, The Krankies have a catchphrase that is forever associated with them. Unlike Stu, this wasn't something they brought with them to *Crackerjack*. And, as Janette Tough recalls, it only came about after lengthy debate:

It was Michael Hurll said we should have a catchphrase. We were doing cabaret at the same time as we were doing *Crackerjack*. And we travelled with four dancers and a band. And we were sitting in the car and we told the girls we needed to get a catchphrase. I said, 'Something that means fabulous or something like that. Something excitable.' So this girl, Karen Long was her name, she was just sitting in the back of the car and she went, 'Errm … fandabidozi.' And we went, 'What? What does it mean?' She said, 'I don't know, I just made it up.' So it was actually her.

Travelling between *Crackerjack* rehearsals and engagements up north had taken a severe toll on Little and Large. Thankfully Ian and Janette Tough coped better, though Ian found the weekly routine no less punishing:

Before they said, 'Would you do *Crackerjack*?' we had a two-year diary full that had to be honoured. And we were both completely knacked. We used to get up at seven in the morning, catch the train from Coventry to London, go to rehearsals, finish rehearsals about five, catch the train back to Coventry, grab something quick to eat, get in my car and drive to Manchester or Liverpool, do a ten o'clock or eleven o'clock cabaret, drive back, a couple of hours sleep and we were shattered.

And all the time trying to learn the stuff. So it was like weekly rep. The Two Ronnies were working in the next studio, and I went through on a break to watch them – Michael Hurll was directing it. And I thought, 'Hey look! They've got all their words on the television!' And I thought, 'Right, we've cracked it!' And I said, 'Michael, it was great yesterday. I noticed they used …' 'Yes, that's autocue.' 'Oh. Well, can we have that?' 'No!' 'Why?' 'Because you will learn to do it properly first!' 'Okay, then, I'll learn it properly.'

There was a new elimination game for this series – *Take a Letter*. It was introduced with snazzy graphics – flashing letters against a night-sky background – and a short song with Jan Michelle and the band. You might expect this to be on tape along with the graphics. But no. They performed it live every week. And Jan had to move fast:

> Because I was a singer I used to – just before the games – I used to run down from the stage into the orchestra booth and sing the jingle intro into the game live. Then I used to run back up and push the little horrors' faces into the rice crispies or whatever. I was out of breath because I'd just run down to sing the jingle, then I had to be back in time, before the camera got to the game.

In *Take a Letter,* letters of the alphabet were randomly positioned on a magnetic board. The contestant had to run to the board, pick a letter, and run back to Stu. Stu then searched his clipboard for the relevant letter, which either required answering a general-knowledge question or doing a stunt. As the questions and stunts tended to alternate, and there was no obvious connection between the letter chosen and the question or activity required, the more sceptical viewer may be tempted to ask Stu Francis whether it made any difference which letter they picked:

> Hand on heart – no, it didn't! Because I wanted to balance the skills for each of the kids. So if some kid was unfortunate enough to get a load of questions and think, 'Oh, this is difficult. This is like being on *Mastermind*.' And other kids getting all the stunts that were easy. It's not fair! So I used to try and balance the scales for them.

The scales were less balanced when it came to the sexes. The most popular stunt came in two parts. Firstly the contestant would have to retrieve a marshmallow from a bowl of custard using their mouth. A subsequent stunt would require them to retrieve another marshmallow from a bowl of cocoa, which would form a second coat over the custard still adhering to their face after the previous stunt. A similar two-tone effect could be achieved using treacle and sugar puffs. These bowls of gunk were mounted on wooden trolleys, efficiently wheeled on and off by Jan Michelle, who would encourage the children's efforts:

> It was great fun working with the children. But some children, obviously, were quite difficult. Not instantly likeable. And there was always that temptation – I never did, I was completely professional – but to go 'You're a little devil!' and push their head a little further into the sloppy porridge and rice crispies. Obviously I never did! But, yes, they did test you sometimes.

Other stunts involved donning costumes, doing impressions or bursting balloons. And this type of stunt, Stu freely admits, was invariably given to the girls:

> The girls got the niceties and the boys got the mess. The girls still got the stunts but they were nice stunts. And we also found, after the show, the boys always loved it. The more messed up they got, great! Because I think they got street cred when they went back to their mates. They used to love getting covered in it. Whereas it wouldn't look right on a girl.

Between the boys' round and the girls' round of *Take a Letter* was another new feature – *Good News, Bad News* – featuring Ian, Janette, Stu and Jan telling gags, many of which had been sent in by children:

IAN: From Colin Higginson, aged 9, from Manchester – the good
            news …
JIMMY: I've started taking girls out.
IAN: But the bad news …
JIMMY: I keep forgetting to bring them back.

Although *Crackerjack*'s credits made it no secret that The Krankies were Ian and Janette, it was decided fairly early in the series that whatever character Janette played in the sketches, it would be Jimmy playing the part rather than Janette:

> I was supposed to do the *Good News, Bad News* sometimes as Janette, but it was a bit too confusing for the kids. I think the first week we tried it with me dressed as Janette. But John Hobbs said, 'No, we'll just stick to you being Jimmy.'

The two winners of *Take a Letter* joined the previous week's cap-wearing champion in *Double or Drop*, with Stu Francis asking the questions, just as Eamonn Andrews had a quarter of a century before:

We were still doing *Double or Drop*. And that's when I realised, throughout my childhood I'd been wrong. Those cabbages *weren't* as big as I thought. They weren't the size of pumpkins. When I was doing it, I used to think, 'It's *déjà vu* this.' Watching it, and then suddenly here I am doing it.

And the kids really got into it, because of course, if they didn't drop anything they got more. 'Oh I don't want another cabbage!' It'd be under the chins, under the arms. Any which way but don't drop anything. You could see their faces, really going for it. Stacking up and stacking up. And they were clinging on for dear life. Obviously the longer they went on, the more they got. It was brilliant. And to make things difficult – if they were getting too much – they'd give them a beach ball. As though it's not hard enough to hold all this stuff, then they get a beach ball! Or an umbrella – where do you put an umbrella?

Ian Tough adds:

Stu used to hate *Double or Drop*, because smart-arse kids would say (IN A POSH VOICE), 'I'm sorry I can't understand your accent. What did you say?' I said, 'Stu, I can see you nudging him! Make him drop it!'

After *Double or Drop* came the final sketch, the traditional costume drama with music, which was a particular high point for Jan Michelle:

I think my fondest memory is rehearsing the sketches at the end. They were so silly and it's not every day you get to dress up as a member of the opposite sex. I used to love putting on a moustache and being a man. I played *Greensleeves* on a recorder in one show. I'd learned it as a child in primary school. And they said, 'Can you play the recorder?' And I said, 'Yep.' Then I realised, 'No, you can't Jan, you can only play *Greensleeves*.' I remember being the most terrified about that, having to play *Greensleeves* on my recorder live on television!

A typical finale was *Sinbad the Sailor* with Stu as Sinbad rescuing Jan, the sultan's daughter:

JAN: One day I'll be a sultana.
JIMMY: You'd better be careful – they end up in wedding cakes.
STU: Is that the currant practice?
JIMMY: Yes, but I don't know the raisin.

Every sketch would finish on a song but, as a departure from *Crackerjack* tradition, it didn't come from the pop charts. Quite the contrary, it was a traditional melody with new words. In the case of Sinbad, the tune was the *Eton Boating Song*:

JAN: Now Sinbad once went to Egypt, to see the River Nile.
IAN: He bought a new magic carpet, to travel there in style.
JIMMY: But the carpet got engine failure, and it crashed in the sand and the dust.
ALL: So Sinbad the Sailor had to come back home on the bus.

Like sketch writer Ron Ottaway, the lyricist always received an 'additional material' writer's credit. And (also like Ron) he was a pal of Ian Tough:

The guy who wrote the songs was a friend of mine called Jim Cammell, he was a car salesman. We met him in Blackpool, and we were telling him we were about to do *Crackerjack*. And he said, 'Well, I do a bit of writing.' So I said, 'Yeah, well, submit it.' And from Day One he got a song on every single week.

Sketches for the series include parodies of *Treasure Island*, *Beau Geste* and *Robin Hood* – subjects that *Crackerjack* had tackled time and time again, ever since series two when costume dramas made their first appearance. For Ian Tough, they had no place in the *Crackerjack* of the 1980s:

They were always historical, like the BBC had done for years. It was semi – I suppose – educational. We did Sherlock Holmes – that was awful! I played Moriarty I think. Jimmy was Holmes and Stu was Doctor Watson. But it still felt old-style and it wasn't us. And we used to go home to the flat and say, 'None of this crap. Why can't we do proper sketches? Pretending to be bloody this and that!'

As the series drew to a close there were definite signs that more tweaks were being made to the format. The sketches became less historical and more slapstick. And, for the final Christmas episode, *Double or Drop* was dropped (for good, as it turned out). Instead there was a *Take a Letter* celebrity final, featuring former *Crackerjack* comics Syd Little and Eddie Large.

Changes were afoot, and would continue when the team returned the following year. At least everyone assumed they would return. But, for Jan Michelle, it wasn't to be:

I was, if I'm honest, disappointed not to be asked back. Because at the end-of-series party it had been a success – well that's what they say, isn't it? And Michael Hurll said, 'Obviously we'll be inviting you back.' So when my agent rang and said, 'You won't be,' I was quite disappointed. But it's one of those things in this business. You move on, don't you? But I thoroughly enjoyed my time and I learnt a lot. And it just gave me a lot more confidence.

Whatever the reasons behind the decision, it seems surprisingly harsh and difficult to comprehend. Jan had done everything asked of her and done it well. The crosstalk, the gags, the hostessing, the sketches. She was the first (and last) female co-host on *Crackerjack* and a vital member of that comedy quartet. And, most regrettably, her successors (talented as they were) would return to the traditional supporting role of *Crackerjack* hostesses.

Two months after the series ended, Jan grabbed the headlines as the 'Crackerjack' bride' when she married choreographer Brian Rogers, who graciously accepted second billing in most of the news coverage. She continued to work on stage and in the Bond movie *Octopussy*. Brian and Jan Rogers now run the Performers College in Essex, providing training for future generations of stage and TV stars.

*

In October 1981 *Crackerjack* returned with a new theme song. In fact, its first and only theme song. The cheesy 'diddle-diddle-diddle' instrumental opener of the last series was out. (Well, not completely out. It was still there in the background as play-on music for The Krankies.) In its place was a rumbustious rollicking rock number which, in Ian Tough's opinion, encapsulated the attitude of *Crackerjack*'s new producer:

> That was Paul Ciani. He wanted it today, in your face. He said, 'I want something heavy. Get Chas and Dave to write it.' And they came up with that one.

It was the perfect opener, from the duo responsible for such Cockney classics as *Gertcha* and *Rabbit*. 'Get your voices ready …' The kids were instantly bouncing up and down in their seats and clapping along. Plus plenty of opportunities to respond with a shout every time the show's title got a mention. Lumberjack, steeplejack and Uncle Jack receive a stern 'no'. But *Crackerjack*? Such a lovely word!

Surprisingly, though Chas and Dave wrote it, they didn't sing it. Not yet, anyway. It was Stu, The Krankies and an altogether less gruff vocal ensemble. Stu, Ian and Janette had spent the summer season at the Floral Hall Theatre in Scarborough (with a line-up of dancers that included Jane Leeves, later to achieve global stardom as Daphne Moon in *Frasier*). So it was decided to shoot the opening credits video with the three *Crackerjack* stars plus a bunch of local kids. But, as Ian Tough recalls, Scarborough didn't have quite the same ethnic mix as London:

> They couldn't find a black kid. They found one, a doctor's son. He was in every shot. 'Just move that wee boy there, please!'

Producer Paul Ciani had previously worked on *Rentaghost* and *The Basil Brush Show*. *Crackerjack* writer Tony Hare had been a schoolfriend of Paul, who was known in his younger days as Paul Griffin. After joining the BBC, Paul encouraged Tony to apply for the job of dresser, and both of them steadily worked their way up in their respective professions. Tony Hare has no idea what prompted the change of surname from Griffin to Ciani:

> I think it was just an affected name. It sounded good. He didn't want to use the name Griffin. He did look Italian, and maybe there was background there. Because he was very dark. Quite a good-looking chap. Very slim.

With Paul Ciani in charge, Ian Tough noticed a distinct change in atmosphere:

> I did feel for the first series it was like going to an office. It did not feel like the showbiz we were used to. Second series did. Then we thought, 'Ah!'
>
> I often used to stand in the lifts at Shepherds Bush and nobody smiled or laughed. I used to say, 'Head of comedy department him.' And he'd have a face like a poker!
>
> Paul Ciani was total fun. We had to pull *him* back sometimes. A great inventive brain. He was like a breath of fresh air. He was a great character. And I think, that way he got more out of us. Rather than the BBC stiff-upper-lip brigade, 'Is this funny?' Ciani would just say, 'Oh, we'll make it funny. Don't worry.'

Stu Francis agrees that Paul Ciani made a refreshing change from the traditional old-school BBC producer:

A smart guy but more casual. A bit more like us. I mean, with John Hobbs it wasn't 'me and you'. It wasn't quite like that. But Ciani was more 'us'. He'd listen more, he'd get involved more. Not just directing it. He were a bit more of a wild card. Paul would let you have a go. If I said, 'Paul, why don't I do this instead of that?' He'd say, 'Well, go on then.' He were more, 'Yeah, come on. Here we go. It's rock and roll.' That were Paul. He knew exactly what he was doing. He knew exactly what he wanted from you. But he was still a bit of a loose cannon.

Paul Ciani had a clear vision of what he wanted *Crackerjack* to be – even if, regrettably, that vision didn't include Jan Michelle. Ian Tough could see the logic behind Paul's decision:

> Jan was a lovely girl, but Jan was more model-type than these bouncy, wee cheeky Second Generation dancers. Sally Ann, she was great for sketches. Well, the two were. They had a presence that was totally different.

Sally Ann Triplett had represented the UK at the Eurovision Song Contest the previous year in the band Prima Donna. She had also been in Second Generation, a song-and-dance team formed by experienced choreographer Dougie Squires as a follow-up to his 1960s troupe The Young Generation:

> I was in Tottenham Court Road, Centre Point, and I had this audition for *Crackerjack*. And I was late. And I saw my uncle in a cab, because a lot of my uncles, like four of my uncles, were cabbies. And I saw my uncle Terry, and I flagged him down and I said, 'Uncle Terry, Uncle Terry, can you take me to the BBC?' And he said, 'No!' In true cabby style, he said, 'No, no, Sally, I haven't got time for that!' And he just drove off. So I had to jump on the Central Line and make my way to the Beeb.
>
> They were only auditioning for one. They were auditioning for a girl, like Jan Michelle, the girl before us. They must have seen a bunch of girls and they liked me and they liked Leigh. And we went back again, Leigh and I, and did something together. And then that was it – we both got the part. Leigh and I knew each other really well, and I think it was because we knew each other that Paul just decided he'd go with both of us.

Leigh Miles had worked with Sally Ann on many occasions:

> Sally Ann and I were with the same management, Trends Management. They were a very big theatrical agency at the time. And Dougie Squires was part of that. I used to work with Sally Ann for Dougie Squires' Second Generation.

One of the things I remember vividly was doing a *Generation Game* with Larry Grayson. And I was dancing for Dougie Squires at that time. And Larry announced to the audience that I was going to be doing *Crackerjack*. And I was thinking, 'Oh my goodness!' Because, really, at the time, I was so excited to do it.

The archives listing for the first show of the series talks of, 'New hostesses Sally Ann and Leigh in pink and blue velour tracksuits and legwarmers.' Leigh has fond memories of the outfits they wore:

We used to go clothes shopping with the costume designer. And it was great. I remember the clothes. And, at the time, they were fashionable. I was probably in pink and Sally was probably in blue. The clothes were one of the things we got the most excited about. 'Ooh, we're going to be wearing this!'

The hostesses are less a part of the opening banter for this series. Stu now makes his entrance alone. They pop in during his opening monologue, then pop out again leaving him to conclude it. But while they're there, Stu does most of the set-ups and the girls do most of the gags. Like here, when they've been asked to help with Stu's fan mail:

STU: I suppose they'll all want a photograph.
SALLY: I think it's time you had another one taken.
STU: What's wrong with the one I've got? I think it's very nice.
LEIGH: Oh, it is! Especially the way you're waving your rattle in the pram.

After the girls have left, Stu reflects on his new celebrity status, with a final gag that will strike a chord with anyone who has ever worked for the Corporation:

I can tell I'm getting more famous – even the producer's stopped calling me 'thingy'. But you can always tell when you're doing well at the BBC – the commissionaire lets you in!

Many people have told of prolonged battles with commissionaires to get a place in the BBC car park, though this never concerned Leigh Miles on her weekly trip to the TV Theatre:

In those days you could drive – because I was South-East London – you could drive to West London in about an hour. Or even less, 50 minutes. I remember you used to be able to park your car round the back. In the street. I doubt if you could do that now!

Take a Letter continued much as before. Leigh and Sally Ann sang the theme, though now on tape, so they were spared the lightning dash to the orchestra room that Jan Michelle endured. For Sally Ann, it was bags of messy mayhem at breakneck speed:

I'd say, 'This is Michael, he's ten years old, and he's from Leeds!' And we had like pink blancmange with a cork in it. And Leigh and I would wheel them on and go, 'You've got to get the cork out of the pink blancmange!' And Stu would be like, 'Come on, you can do it. Yes, he's done it!' And Stu was always covered in something. He'd go, 'Let me help you, let me help you!' And he'd go in and get blancmange all over himself.

And we were obviously recording it live. And we got to the end of *Take a Letter* on the very first episode, and I was on one side with a child, Leigh was on the other side with a child, and Stu was in the middle. And he looked down at the scoreboard and he went, 'And at the end of *Take a Letter* Susan has ten points and Andrew has … ten points.' And we had *not* worked out what would happen if it was a tie. We hadn't worked that out! And if you look very closely, you can see me – very, very faintly – I go, 'Oh shit.' You can just see my mouth move, if you watch it back. And Stu is like, 'Um … um … um … I'm going to ask you one more question each.' And he just sort of made it up on the spot.

Crackerjack producers had traditionally avoided retakes at all costs. Because they *did* cost, both time and money. And Stu Francis knew it was expected of him to soldier on whatever happened:

Paul Ciani always said to me, 'Keep it going, keep it going! If you think I'm going to be in an editing booth all day tomorrow, you've got another think coming!' Because it was recorded Thursday evening and went out Friday. So he said, 'You be kind to me, I'll be kind to you.'

Once there was a strike on. And Ciani said, 'I've never lost a show yet, and I'm not starting now.' So we had to do it live on the Friday. And they couldn't change the set because this strike was on. And part of the set was on one side. And where we did the variety stuff was on the other. So when I said, 'Right, it's time for the game,' I had to then – instead of there being a break, and we'd stand on one side and they'd put the set up – I had to duck under the cameras. Then the camera panned round to the other side – and they'd play a little sting of music – while I ducked under the cameras, popped up at the other end – bump – and we were there. And it worked. And Ciani said, 'There! I've never lost a show.'

Ian Tough also rated that show a particular success:

There was one show we had to do live. And it was the best we did. 'Cause we could adlib, like we were used to doing. And we did a decorating sketch. And I went through the ladder by mistake, and there was an adlib there. And when we looked back at it, we thought, 'You see, that's better.' Because that's what we were used to – living on your wits.

The whole team was involved in the *Good News, Bad News* section. This series, some of the kids who'd sent in jokes were invited to tell them live on stage, like Andre Clark from Battersea:

I found out the real difference between Jimmy and Ian Krankie … about three feet.

At the end of *Good News, Bad News*, Ian Krankie would tell the kids how to send their jokes in. A part of the show that Stu Francis always looked forward to:

Ian Krankie always used to say, 'Don't forget, write in to the BBC …' And then he had to give the address and the postcode. And he'll tell you himself, nine times out of ten he got it wrong. He'd have to do it again. And I was stood behind the camera winding him up. And they used to say, 'Stop, you've got it wrong. Do it again.' And sometimes I'd lie on the floor under the camera. And Ciani would come down and say, 'Francis, go away! You're costing us money!'

Guests throughout the series were still the comedy spesh acts, like ventriloquist Ward Allen, pickpocket Andy Mann, and (making one final visit) the comedy band that did wicked impressions of other bands – The Barron Knights. They were popular *Crackerjack* guests, having first appeared on the show back in 1965. Original band member Pete Langford remembers their many visits to the TV Theatre:

It was many, many years ago when we first did *Crackerjack*, and to this day, about teatime on a Friday, I still say, 'It's Friday, it's five o'clock and it's *Crackerjack*!' Leslie Crowther was the same off camera as he was on, and very, very funny. Peter Glaze was again a very friendly guy, as was Bert Hayes. When the show was over, we used to chat in the dressing rooms for ages. We appeared again when Ed Stewart was the presenter, and Ed and I became good friends and used to play golf together.

Of course, such a joyous show is only possible after days and days of arduous rehearsal. Though Sally Ann Triplett didn't find the rehearsal process particularly arduous:

> We used to rehearse in Acton. We used to get there at about ten. And The Krankies were there, and Stu and Leigh and myself and Paul Ciani. And we rehearsed the little scenes and the songs and sketches and stuff for about an hour and a half. And then, at about half eleven, quarter to twelve, Paul Ciani would say, 'Right, I think we're done!'
> We'd go up to the canteen and they would start drinking wine and beer or whatever. I didn't drink, I was also driving. I remember it vividly – every lunchtime, after rehearsals, we would have wine and lunch upstairs in the canteen. And Paul loved a drink! And that was it. And then I'd go home. And then I'd do the same the next day. I think we did that for about three or four days, then we would record an episode.

Sometimes there was more work to do, and Ian Tough had to prise Paul Ciani away from his long liquid lunch:

> We used to say, 'Paul, we should get back!' 'No, have another one.' 'Jesus, I can hardly stand up – we've got to do the sketch!' He said, 'Yes, but you've got to do it in front of me, and *I* can't stand up!'

The songs had now been dropped from the final sketch – possibly the first time in the show's history that the finale lacked any kind of musical content. But earlier in the show there was often a song performed by The Krankies, such as *Jimmy's Gang*, *Krankie Rock* or *Hubbadubbadooby*, with Leigh and Sally Ann either side of them in a synchronised dance routine.

The celebrity *Take a Letter* that had first been tried at the end of the previous series was now a regular feature, replacing *Double or Drop*. Each child was paired with a TV personality, who helped them out with the stunts. Couples included John Inman and Wendy Richard, Torvill and Dean, and newsreaders Richard Whitmore and Jan Leeming. Rampant sexism meant that Jan had to bounce balls and burst balloons, while Richard was required to shove his face first into a bowl of jam, and then into sugar puffs.

New to the writing team was Colin Bostock-Smith, fresh from *The Basil Brush Show* and ITV's *Metal Mickey*. He would go on to script the Richard O'Sullivan sitcom *Me and My Girl*, and have the original idea for the Judi Dench and Geoffrey Palmer series *As Time Goes By*. Colin was particularly responsible for the final sketch, set in the present day rather than the past – with the exception of the futuristic *Star Battleship Strikes Back*.

Ian Tough remembers the odd occasion when the final sketch needed some last-minute adjustment:

> Paul would sit there and go, 'It ain't gonna work. It's rubbish.' But they'd already built the set. Say we had to do a sketch in a schoolroom. They were all built in advance. So even though it was a crap sketch, the scenery had been built and the costumes had been made. So now it's got to be rewritten, but to suit that.

One of the final sketches is set in the Fandabidozi Holiday Camp. It's a thinly veiled parody of *Hi-de-Hi!* with Yellowcoat Jimmy, Stu (in a rabbit costume) as the camp comic, and Ian as the upper-crust entertainments manager. When Stu mentions how refined their new boss is, Jimmy asks, 'Does he carry his fish and chips in a briefcase?'

By the end of the show, Ian is drenched in water and there's not a face that hasn't had a custard pie pushed into it. It's a sketch that's far more about physical comedy than clever wordplay. In many ways, *Crackerjack* has gone right back to its roots. Series two had seen the advent of the historical sketches. But series one had been slapstick pure, simple and unapologetic. Maybe when the show's first producer Johnny Downes came back in the late 1970s, and wanted to return *Crackerjack* to what it had been, this was what he had in mind. There is nothing particularly educational in this sketch, but that was never the intention of the show. As Eamonn Andrews wrote, back in 1957:

> ... the *important* things were catered for, and it was our job to find something *unimportant* ...

After the series finished, Sally Ann Triplett went straight into pantomime, where she met and started dating Stephen Fischer. Soon afterwards they were recruited for Eurovision as twosome Bardo, singing *One Step Further*, which saw her back at the Television Theatre:

I'd also done *Song for Europe* at Shepherds Bush when I was in Prima Donna. And I went back there after *Crackerjack*, the following year, to do Bardo. So weird.

And so I ended up doing Bardo, we represented Britain, we got to number two in the charts, we had a silver disc, and we had a record deal with Epic CBS and did two more singles. And Bardo took up the next couple of years. I don't think I ever thought of doing *Crackerjack* again.

But I remember it being full of happiness. I don't remember it ever feeling anything like a job. It was just fun. Paul Ciani was the most amazing man. I remember him with great affection and love. He was such a lovely kind man. And The Krankies were, of course, The Krankies. They were very, very naughty. They were naughty onscreen, offscreen. And they liked to tell stories about their past. And I got on really well with Stu as well. It was just a really lovely time and it went so quickly. It was 12 episodes – and then it was done.

Sally Ann has continued to have a busy career, starring in numerous stage musicals both in the West End and on Broadway.

Apart from Sally Ann, the rest of the team were expected to return in Autumn 1982. But they didn't. Ian Tough explains:

Michael Grade moved to LWT. And the story we've been told by Laurie Mansfield is that Michael came in one Friday and said to the kids, 'Turn that over.' And the kids said, 'No, we're watching Jimmy.' And he lifted the phone to Mansfield and said, 'You handle The Krankies? Get me them. If my kids won't turn the television over, no kids are turning the television over.'

I remember Mansfield saying to me, 'No, you're not doing *Crackerjack*, you're going to LWT. And you're going out on a Saturday night.' So I don't think the BBC knew we were leaving.

Janette adds:

But then, the BBC's money, when we did *Crackerjack*, was terrible. We were staying at the Shepherds Bush Hilton. And it was dearer than what we were getting. But if we had nae done that, we wouldn't have got on.

My fondest memory of *Crackerjack* was getting to know Stu, and we've been friends ever since. We all liked each other. We weren't jealous of each other. We weren't saying, '*I* want that line.'

Ian agrees:

There was no star in it. No, we were more the opposite. I'd say, 'Stu, you can do that bit if you want to.' 'Bugger off, *you* learn it!'

Ian and Janette returned to the BBC in 1985 with *The Krankies Elektronik Komik*, resuming their working partnership with producer Paul Ciani. Since then they have both appeared on *French and Saunders*, and Janette has had memorable cameo roles in *Absolutely Fabulous* (both the TV show and the movie). They still regularly star in panto with their good friend John Barrowman.

The Krankies' departure from *Crackerjack* came as a shock to many, Stu Francis included:

They didn't come back. Then, shortly after, they went to London Weekend. I was surprised they didn't come back. And that's when we changed again.

13
Swept Away in an Ill-Considered Blast

1982 – 1984

S OME PERFORMERS ARE THEMSELVES on stage – or exaggerated versions of themselves. Others assume totally contrasting personalities. In 1982 Stu Francis and the *Crackerjack* audience were to encounter one such magical metamorphosis:

> He became this character – The Great Soprendo. It's nothing like the real Geoffrey Durham. He'd put the wig on, the glasses on, and you could see him transformed into this larger-than-life wonderful character.

The curly haired, flamboyantly dressed, extrovert magician couldn't be more different from the softly spoken Geoffrey Durham:

Well my act – The Great Soprendo – started out in life as a piss-take of magicians. It was a character that I never came out of, and I never told anyone who I really was. And I never did what people would do now, which was get photographed without the makeup on. But it was sort of ironical. And I didn't do what Tommy Cooper would have done and get the tricks wrong. I used to take the piss out of magicians but then get the tricks *right*, which seemed to be quite a good gimmick.

When I started out as a magician, I looked at the competition – sort of aiming high. And there was David Nixon, who was quintessentially English, and there was Tommy Cooper. And I didn't want to get compared with

249

either of them, so I decided that I'd be foreign. And because I speak Spanish – I've got a degree in it – it seemed quite a good idea. So I'd been going for four or five years.

In the Summer of 1982 Geoffrey and his then wife, the comedian and singer-songwriter Victoria Wood, were appearing at the Duchess Theatre, London in a show called *Funny Turns*:

I did the first half, she did the second half. We'd been doing it actually for years – we were both unknown when we started doing it. And then she got a TV series called *Wood and Walters*, and as a result of that we got a West End run, which was intended to go on from June to about Christmas. And then the Falklands War happened and everything closed in the West End. Because the best entertainment in London was the *News at Ten* every night. There were huge bloody battles going on, miles from anywhere. It was terribly sort of – dare I say it? – exciting. And there was hot news two or three times a day. So everything in London closed. Everybody lost their show. And we closed after seven weeks.

Paul Ciani, the producer of *Crackerjack*, had a problem. He had special guest stars The Krankies suddenly not in his show. He was due to start recording in October. It was now, I suppose, August. And he'd seen the show that we did at the Duchess, but I don't think he knew *then* the extent of the problem that he had.

Because we closed early, we then quickly booked ourselves into the Edinburgh Festival. And we went and did the whole four weeks of the Edinburgh Festival. And Paul came and had lunch with us at Edinburgh and said would I do some shows?

Paul decided to fill the gap left by The Krankies with a rotating bill of special guests. Of the ten shows of the 1982 series, The Great Soprendo did three of them and Bob Carolgees with Spit the Dog (a *Tiswas* favourite who had appeared once the previous series) did two. The other five shows featured ventriloquist Keith Harris, with his two dummies Cuddles the monkey and Orville the duck. Keith had been performing since the 1960s and had made many appearances on *Seaside Special*, *The Black and White Minstrel Show* and *The Good Old Days* – as well as guest appearances on the previous two series of *Crackerjack*.

Regular writer for the series was Mike Radford, who had worked on many sketch shows including *The Little and Large Show*, *The Two Ronnies* and *Three of a Kind* (with Lenny Henry, Tracey Ullman and David

Copperfield). Also contributing to the series was Barry Fairweather, who had provided additional material for the previous two series of *Crackerjack*.

Keith Harris had his own writer, George Martin, who before joining Keith had been scriptwriter for magician David Nixon and then Basil Brush. Early in his career George had worked at the Windmill Theatre, where he billed himself 'The Casual Comedian' and made jokes about the stories in that day's newspaper.

An indication of both George Martin's topicality and his many decades of experience are found in a routine he writes for Keith Harris, Cuddles and Stu Francis in November 1982, referencing a new TV channel that had started broadcasting earlier in the month:

STU: I've just been offered a job on Channel 4. What would you do if you was in my shoes?
CUDDLES: Clean them.
STU: What I mean is – which channel do you think is best for my talents?
CUDDLES: For your talents? I think the English Channel!
KEITH: Never mind all the channels, we're going to stick with the good old BBC!

They then launch into a clap-along rocky number: 'We three, we've got it made – working for the BBC – Stu Francis, Keith Harris and me.' It may have been given an updated tune and orchestration, but those with long memories would have recognised it as a parody of a radio signature tune from the early 1940s (which was, itself, a parody of a song by The Ink Spots): 'We three in *Happidrome* – working for the BBC – Ramsbottom and Enoch and me.'

Another musical makeover is applied to the theme song, now not only written by but also *performed* by Chas and Dave, who briefly appear in cartoon form alongside Stu Francis in the animated opening credits.

New musical director for the series was Nigel Hess, who had to endure many a chilly recording day in late autumn:

I remember the bandbox being incredibly cold. We used to literally sit there in coats and scarves and gloves. And once we did actually complain and somebody from – I don't think it was called Health and Safety then – but somebody came in. And in those days they used to test the temperature of a room with something that looked like a football rattle. And they'd hold it up and wave the rattle around in the air, which would rotate. And then they'd take the reading off this machine, to give the room temperature. So we were all sitting there in coats and gloves and scarves, trying to play. And of course all the instruments were going out of tune because it was so cold. And we got this chap to come in, and he waved this football rattle in the air, looked at it and said, 'No, it's fine.' And walked out again. And left us all speechless.

But the isolation of the band room did have some benefits:

There were these big double doors that opened out into the theatre and – with all the kids they had got in – you opened the doors and suddenly got this wall of sound. But we were soundproofed, so you could see all the kids, you know, ripping up the seats, all very excited. But we were all in our own little cocoon, thank goodness, because we couldn't have operated otherwise – it was just so noisy.

Someone who had to face the crowd without the benefit of soundproofing was Geoffrey Durham:

It was at Shepherds Bush Empire, which was slightly odd actually. Because, if you've got a studio audience who is actually also a theatre audience, you've got nowhere for the cameras to be. Because the cameras ought to be where the audience is. So it, sort of, doesn't work. And so we were onstage with a set facing the side of the stage. The cameras in front of us and the audience to our right. It's really odd, because when you're a performer and somebody laughs, you want to turn to them and say, 'Thank you very much.' But you couldn't, because you were turning to your right and not ahead of you. So I was totally disorientated when I got on there. I found it very, very hard.

There was a warm-up man whose job, as he saw it anyway, was to work the kids up into a mad frenzy. And he did this – because these kids were all from London schools – by saying, 'Who supports Chelsea?' and getting a cheer. And then saying, 'Who supports Arsenal?' and getting a cheer. And then saying, 'All you lot who support Chelsea, what do you think of Arsenal?' And then he'd say, 'Here he is, the Great Soprendo.' So you'd walk on to this rabid bunch of savage kids, all screaming at each other. And I found it really difficult.

The first or second *Crackerjack* I ever did – I can hardly believe it now, everyone was quite happy with it – I did a head chopper. I can't remember whose head was chopped and then magically restored. Whether it was a kid – I think it probably was. And I can't quite believe that ever happened. It's one of those things when you just go, 'Surely I didn't! Surely I wasn't there!'

And there *was* one letter of complaint. And Paul Ciani said, 'It's all nonsense. I support you to the utmost.' But he was wrong. And I was wrong. And it should never have happened.

The third act on the guest rota was Bob Carolgees who, like Keith Harris, had a mischievous (though mute) animal companion. Sound man Mike Giles remembers an incident during rehearsals:

> Bob Carolgees presented us with a precious vinyl disc of the music to accompany his act with Spit the Dog, pleading with us to take great care of it. My gram op duly copied it onto tape and popped it back safely in its sleeve, so that we couldn't damage it. Bob then nearly had a fit when we stopped the rehearsal to sort out shots – at which point my gram op deftly stopped the track and played the classic recording of a stylus swiping across the grooves. Bob had to see the disc to be reassured that it had been a joke!

Alongside the various novelty acts, such as puppets and acrobats, this series marked a return of the pop guests. There was a strong connection between *Crackerjack* and *Top of the Pops*. Producer Paul Ciani had previously worked on the show, as had *Crackerjack*'s new director John Bishop. Dexys Midnight Runners, Suzi Quatro, Toyah and Bad Manners all made an appearance this series. They may have become household names since, but to Geoffrey Durham many were something of an unknown quantity:

> I remember a big conversation about whether it was Depeche Mode or Depechy Mode, because no one had heard of them. We used to do a lot of new bands. And, of course, they all turned out to be huge stars. Which meant that Paul Ciani was very good at choosing them.

The task of booking the pop acts was shared between Paul and assistant floor manager Nick Fiveash:

> We would have an act that was in the charts. Maybe it had done *Top of the Pops* the previous week, so was available for our week. I'd whittle it down to the last three or four and go into Paul's office and say to him, 'Okay, this is what we've got. What do you fancy?' And sometimes he would say, 'Oh, I really like them.' And sometimes he'd say, 'Well, what do *you* want?'

Some of the pop groups would perform live, others would mime. Sometimes musical director Nigel Hess would have to score the orchestral backing purely by listening to the single. But, for Nigel, the variety turns were a particular challenge:

> We had some great players in the band. The drummer was Clem Cattini who was, even then, a legend, and quite why he was doing *Crackerjack* I don't know. He used to play with The Tornados and he was *the* pop session drummer.
>
> And then, of course, we had all the variety acts. And if they came with music it would be almost unusable, because they'd trundled this music around for years and years and years doing their act, and you almost couldn't read it because it was so dog-eared. So we, sort of, had to start again really.
>
> We had to create fanfares or little links to get from one act to another. And it would sometimes change within transmission. I remember one – I think it was a comedy routine which didn't require any music. And they suddenly cut to the end of the routine. I don't know why – whether they were told to by Paul or the floor manager, or they were overrunning. And of course I had been given the cue line at the end of the routine for the music, but we were all sitting reading the papers and having a chat.
>
> And I suddenly heard this cue line and Paul Ciani in my headphones saying, 'Music, music, music!' And so I stood up and gave a downbeat, hoping that somebody would play, and all that we got was a hit from Clem on his bass drum. That's all we got. So this comedy routine finished with a 'boff!' on the bass drum and that was it. And of course all the rest of the band sat and looked at me like I was mad.

At the start of the series the *Radio Times* ran a piece on *Crackerjack*'s newest hostess, who would be working alongside Leigh Miles:

> New *Crackerjack* star Julie Dorne Brown worked in a factory making television sets before she disco-danced her way to fame. So her old workmates in Bridgend, Glamorgan, should have no problem tuning in to watch her first appearance on the show.
>
> Three years ago Julie entered a local heat in a disco-dance contest, won it and went on to become the world champion! Now she's taking time off from being one of the regular dancers in the Zoo team on *Top of the Pops* to work on *Crackerjack*.

As Julie Brown recalls, there were none of the usual job interview formalities:

> I was working as a dancer on *Top of the Pops*. And we were all buzzing around in the same building. And I think that Flick Colby, the choreographer

there, had mentioned there was an opportunity. It was being in the right place at the right time. And I think it was because I'd done the disco dancing championship thing, that I wasn't just a dancer on *Top of the Pops*, I was kind of favoured a little. All of us dancers were picked to do other projects, because we were easy picking. We were right there, and we said 'yes' to everything.

Of course I knew about the show, but to actually go in and be part of the Stu Francis team, 'Like yeah – *I* can crush a grape. That'd be awesome!'

Stu Francis, what an amazing guy for me to get my first real hosting job with! And he was, 'Come on, you just do anything you want to me, I'll be fine. Just do it.' 'I don't *want* to throw it in your face.' 'Just throw it in my face – I don't care.' So after that, it was not only in his face. It was on top of his head, it was down his back, it was down his pants. It was a never-ending gift of giving.

After the opening animated credits, the first camera shot (as had always been the case) is of the enthusiastic theatre audience. The camera closes in on Stu Francis, seated in the midst of them. From there he shouts his usual 'Hiya kids!' before making his way up to the stage. From the very start the message is clear. There's no celebrity mystique surrounding Stu – he's just one of the kids.

As in the previous series, the two girls are introduced midway through Stu's opening spot and exchange a few gags – mainly at Stu's expense. Also unchanged are the elimination rounds of *Take a Letter*, involving Julie Brown in the usual frantic mayhem:

> Leigh and I would be running on with the props – apples in a bowl of runny chocolate sauce or something. And we'd be just dunking a kid's head in there and you'd forget like they've got to breathe! Because you'd be so into the moment. You'd be like, 'Quick, get them out!' And I loved the one where you'd have to run up to the board and he'd be asking questions like, 'What colour is a London bus?' And the kid would be so frustrated. He'd be like, 'Yellow?' thinking of a school bus or something. And the whole show, once it started it didn't stop.

In addition to Cuddles the Monkey, Keith Harris's other companion during the series was a timid green nappy-wearing flightless duck named Orville. Production manager John Adams worked alongside Keith and Orville in a number of shows, and once shared a car with Keith and producer Paul Ciani for what turned out to be a memorable journey:

We were leaving the rehearsal room. I was driving, Paul was in the front with me and Keith Harris was in the back of the car with Orville on his knee. And we're passing where Kensington Palace is, and there's terrific traffic jams both ways. And I suddenly saw Princess Di driving her green Audi. And she had the security man in the front seat. And I said, 'Gosh, there's Princess Di coming towards us.' You know, very, very slowly. So the next minute Keith, in the back, wound his window down and – as she came alongside – stuck Orville out of the window and started talking to Princess Di. And the cars just stopped, and they must have had a conversation for two or three minutes. She was roaring her head off. No one was tooting, because they all knew what was going on.

This was the era of the novelty pop record. And if you had a catchphrase, the next logical step was to record a song cashing in on that catchphrase. *Orville's Song* made the top ten – and Julie Brown danced to it, both on *Crackerjack* and *Top of the Pops*. The Krankies had previously performed their *Fandabidozi* song on the show. So it was inevitable that sooner or later Stu would follow suit. One lunchtime, Nigel Hess, the show's musical director, approached Stu Francis:

Nigel came over and he said, 'You know all your catchphrases? Have you ever thought of a song?' And I said, 'No I haven't, to be honest.' He said, 'How do you fancy, if you write down all your catchphrases, give them to me, and I'll see if I can set them to music.' So I jotted them down. And the following week, he came in and he said, 'Got a minute? Come in.' And I went in, again, lunchtime break. And he played a bit on the piano. 'Do you like that?' 'Yeah.' 'Good, leave it with me.' And the following week. 'Come in.' The week after, a bit more.

And then he said, 'Come in.' And he'd got the bass player and drummer there. And he went, 'One-two-three-four ba-da-ba-baba-ba-ba-baa.' And he went through it with the piano and said, 'Right, sing this.' And we did it about two or three times. And at the end of the series – lunchtime – he went, 'Come in.' And he'd kept the lads back, the band, seven-piece. And he counted the lads in. And the brass came in and everything. I sang it with the band. It blew me away! So from just him messing about on the piano, then the bass player and the drummer, then a seven-piece band and me doing *Crush a Grape*, with all the brass blasting off, absolutely brilliant!

And he wrote the whole thing, manuscript, wrote the seven-piece parts. And at the end I said, 'Nigel, that's unbelievable.' And he said, 'Here you are, that's for you.' So Paul Ciani said, 'What we'll do, instead of a pop section, in a couple of weeks' time we'll do that.' And that's what we did. We did it on telly and it went into the charts – not the top ten, but it got a tickle.

The *Take a Letter* final was the same as before, with a pair of celebrities from sport, children's television or the news paired up with the winning children and sharing the questions and stunts. The women were still spared much of the mess. If it was a female celebrity partnering a boy, it would be the boy who'd have to stick his face in the treacle.

For the entire history of *Crackerjack* the final game had always been followed by the show's finale – initially a singalong and then (from series four) a sketch, usually with songs. This series heralded a break with tradition. Partly because, since the departure of The Krankies, there was no regular comedy team to perform a sketch. And also, possibly, to reflect the ever-changing nature of children's TV. On *Tiswas*, every Saturday morning, flans were flung and buckets of all manner of liquids were lobbed. *Take a Letter* was already pretty sticky and slimy, but Geoffrey Durham was present at that moment in kids' TV history, when Paul Ciani decided to take things to a whole new level:

> I was actually at a meeting in which Paul Ciani invented – and I'm pretty sure no one had done it before him – the gunge drop. Which became an absolute staple of children's television for about ten years. That, if you got the question wrong, you got covered in crap. Things would drop on your head. I always used to be on the set when things dropped on people's heads and I used to wear these awful stupid pink silk suits and things. And even though nothing was dropping on my head, I always presented them with a dry-cleaning bill at the end, which I don't think they were very pleased about. I think I got a reputation for being a bit of an arse.

The *Take a Chance* feature was ostensibly an opportunity for the children to increase their points and win a better prize. The celebrity was given a choice of three booths to sit inside, with Stu Francis occupying one of the others. The booths were not unlike toilet cubicles, with a transparent glass cistern high above, screened off from the audience until both participants were seated. Then the screen was raised, revealing both the contents and the descriptive name they had been given. In early shows, contents included tomatoes, stew and salad cream. The celebrity and Stu Francis had to answer a question. A correct answer got your opponent gunged. A wrong answer got you gunged.

The expression 'getting gunged' has now passed into the language, and gunge has been an ingredient of many TV entertainment shows over the years. In *Not Only ... But Also*, back in the 1960s, Peter Cook and Dudley Moore had catapulted guests from their seats into a vast pool of gunge. Michael Aspel had broken his wrist in a similar gunging stunt on *Crackerjack* in the early 1970s. But Stu Francis believes the use of specially constructed 'gunge tanks' was something new:

> After that, lots of shows got the gunge tanks. Even that Noel Edmonds thing. But it came from Ciani. It was Ciani who came up with the idea of the gunge tanks, because he wanted a big finale that people would remember. And the people we gunged – nobody ever said no. And they tried to do it to suit certain people. They once gunged Les Dawson, and covered him in two gallon of mushy peas. And you can't get more Lancashire than that!

So gunge became top-of-the-bill. For the first time in the history of the show, the game was the finale. And a messy old finale at that. It was generally well received, by the kids certainly. But, as Geoffrey Durham recalls, there were some who were less happy:

> They started off with baked beans and other such items in the gunge drop. And then they got complaints. I remember being told that a letter had come in from a vicar, who had really seriously complained that food was being dropped on people, when people were starving in other countries. And he really objected to it. And so I remember there was a crisis meeting in which Paul Ciani and his associates decided to concoct gunge – I don't know what they made it of – that they would call different things that weren't food. They'd call it Nasty Frogs or Slime. And so slime would drop on people, and that was suddenly acceptable.

If any member of the team could be called the 'gunge chef' it was *Crackerjack*'s assistant floor manager Nick Fiveash:

> The gunge tank was Paul's idea. The content, mostly, was mine. Each week I would ask the props department at the BBC to deliver something in the region of about 12 gallons, times four, of white custard in these dustbins – they literally were plastic dustbins. Four of those would arrive each week and I would then proceed in the afternoon to mix in food colouring and little objects. I remember doing one week – which Paul thought was hilarious – toothpaste. I managed to put a clear pipe into the gunge tank and pour red

food colouring in. And as I pulled the tube out, the red colouring made stripes in the white custard.

I decided as a bit of fun to make them all different, and make them so the kids would think it's horrible! And I had some clear jelly and put plastic spiders in it. Once I started to mix up these concoctions, that's when I'd have to tell the graphics department in advance, 'Okay, this week I'm doing this, this and this.' And they'd come up with the sign they used to stick on the side of the tank.

Sometimes it's impossible to avoid the interviewer's stock-in-trade question. It just has to be asked. So, Stu Francis, as the gunge tank's most frequent recipient, how does it feel to be gunged?

Once it happens, it's alright. It's just that second waiting. You know it's going to come. Sometimes they'd mess about and you'd just be thinking, 'Oh, get it over with. Just do it, just do it.' It's that split-second knowing it's coming. Once you were covered, that were it. It was just finish the number at the end and leg it to the showers.

I remember Bucks Fizz coming on. And, of course, everybody joins in on the finale at the end. And we'd just had the gunge tanks and I'm covered, and everybody tends to go like that – (CLAP!) – to the music at the end. And I always remember Bucks Fizz staying well away. And Mike Nolan going, 'Don't come near me! Don't come near me!' He didn't want to get splashed, because he had a fabulous suede suit on. They were like smiling at the end, dancing around. But one eye on the camera, one eye on us who's covered in gunge, thinking, 'If you come near me, I'm off this set.'

Mike Nolan may have avoided the perils of passive gunging, but any celebrity who signed up for *Take a Chance* knew the risks involved, even though Nick Fiveash did his utmost to minimise those risks:

My favourite, favourite story – and to this day, if ever I see her, she still looks at me in absolute horror – was the week that Floella Benjamin was one of the guest stars that teamed up with one of the kids. And obviously we didn't drop stuff in the dress rehearsal, because we'd never have cleared it up in time for the evening show. So we used to go, 'Okay! Go! Yes, you're covered in gunge!'

And she said, 'I've just had my hair braided and plaited. I'm doing *Play School* tomorrow. So please, please don't drop it on me.' 'Yeah, yeah, yeah,' Paul promised her. So, come the recording in the evening, I was behind the scenes. I used to have a monitor so that I could see once the person was in position. I had a couple of stagehands backstage who could operate the buttons that released the gunge. And we got to the thing, and we'd all said it's the right-hand column – it's the right-hand gunge tank – that's the one we're going to drop. And, for some unknown reason, the guy pressed the wrong button. And poor Floella Benjamin, with her £150 hairdo, suddenly got 12 gallons of custard on top of her head.

So the next day I was in the office and in walked Floella, and her hair was literally an afro. She'd put bows in it and everything, and she just looked at me and went, 'Yeah, you know why I look like this.' And on a number of occasions that I've bumped into her at a function or a do or anything, she always makes the sign of the cross. 'Keep away from me!'

Hostess Leigh Miles left at the end of this, her second series. She has since moved into choreography, including work on comedy shows such as *The Dame Edna Treatment*, *The Armstrong and Miller Show* and *Mrs Brown's Boys*. For Leigh, *Crackerjack* was an invaluable training ground:

> It taught me a lot of skills to take forward. Because I was so young, it gave me a very good grounding in TV. And really that was where I stayed for most of my dancing career – in TV. *Crackerjack* was one of those classic programmes. An iconic programme. And it was an honour to do it. It's a part of history. A programme that people watched and loved.

But for Geoffrey Durham, who had never really thought of himself as a children's entertainer, one series was more than enough:

> I did three shows and I thought, 'I won't be doing that again.' I said to my agent, 'Well, I'm not sure that was the best idea in the world!' They liked me and it seemed to go alright, and I got on very well with Stu Francis and Paul Ciani. It was a lovely, gorgeous group of people, but I thought, 'I'm not sure if I want this.' Then I went off and did a pantomime at the Palace Theatre, Manchester. And when I walked on, I got cheered! And I remember phoning my agent and going, 'I think I was wrong! I think I'd better do *Crackerjack* again if I get asked.'

*

Geoffrey Durham *did* get asked and returned to do four shows out of the 13-show run during autumn 1983. The new hostess for the series, alongside Julie Brown, was Sara Hollamby, who had previously worked in the fashion industry until a trip abroad led to an unexpected change of career:

When I went out to Hong Kong, literally within ten days I got a job as a presenter on the English channel, just by fluke. I came back after three years and, because that was where I'd started in television, I didn't really know the ropes of what to do in the UK. So I just wrote to the BBC and said, 'I've been in Hong Kong, I've just come back and I'd like to work on children's television.' I hadn't even got an agent at this point.

And they came back and said, 'I'll pass your letter on to Paul Ciani, who's the producer of *Crackerjack*.' And I thought, 'Ooh, that'd be good.' In the meantime, someone else said, 'Oh, you've got to have an agent. You've got to have an Equity card.' But anyway, eventually Paul Ciani came back to me and said, 'Let's have a meeting.' So we did, and I met Stu Francis, and that was it. It was pure luck. A letter landing on the desk on the right day at the right time.

Both Sara and Julie Brown feel they got the job through a combination of relevant experience and fortunate timing. The pair of them would make their entrance each week, interrupting Stu's opening routine with a few gags, often poking fun at his diminutive stature:

STU: I should have been a doctor, because only this morning I cured a
         headache, depression and a pain in the neck, all in one go – I
         locked Julie and Sara in the dressing room! (GIRLS ENTER) Hey
         Julie, you're looking all 'keyed up'.
JULIE: And *you* had nothing to do with it?
STU: (WINKS TO CAMERA) As if I would do a thing like that.
SARA: No, I suppose not – you wouldn't reach the keyhole.

There was definitely something of the mischievous schoolboy about Stu Francis. Since the departure of Jimmy Krankie, Stu was now *Crackerjack*'s big kid. It had always been part of his onstage personality, and he was young enough to make it convincing rather than absurd. To the boys who were watching, he was one of them – pulling pranks and moaning about soppy girls. Julie Dorne Brown reveals the truth behind those tales of dressing-room malarkey:

Rehearsals were fun, doing silly things with him backstage. Not just onstage. Always ended up throwing a tub of jelly over him, or something like that, in his dressing room. There was always something going on – you were never safe. I think that was the most fun thing. As soon as you got in there, you better watch yourself! Check behind the door, under your couch, in the dressing room. Make sure before you put your pants on that there was nothing in there. It was just a whole fun bunch of jokers. And I'm glad that the fun actually came from the studio and out into people's homes, exactly as it should have.

Sara Hollamby also recalls the exuberant atmosphere:

Stu had loads of energy, bags of energy. He was the linchpin. He was very motivating for all of us. But also Julie Brown, when she was firing, she was firing on millions of cylinders, I tell you. And what was nice was, when we recorded it, lots of people from the BBC, from different shows, used to come and watch.

Sara believes a major boost to the show's energy levels came from the Chas and Dave theme song:

All the audience, the kids, used to sing it as well. And it was deafening. It was absolutely deafening. It made the hairs on your neck stand up on end. And you know what kids are like – if they get the opportunity to shout and scream as loud as they can, they're going to go for it. So they did. It not only got the audience going and motivated, it was good for us as well. It just set the scene for the whole show. And I think the energy of the show all came from that. Because everybody is suddenly into it, and in that mood. You didn't need a warmup guy with that. The kids warmed us up. It was brilliant in that respect. It was a work of genius, that signature tune.

As if there wasn't already a surfeit of slime in *Crackerjack*, this series notched up the 'yuck' quota even further. But, far worse than a gunge drop, there was an apostrophe drop in the graphics heralding *Crackerjack*'s newest game: *Its in the Box*. This replaced the elimination rounds of *Take a Letter*. Each week Stu introduced it by saying, 'Yes, it's time for us to find out what's …' To which the audience shouted back, '… in the box!'

Instead of running to a board of magnetised letters, the contestants ran to a board with a series of hand-sized hinged compartments. They had to push their arm through one of the holes and feel into a container for a cube or ball, coloured yellow or orange, then return to answer a question from Stu before dropping it into its appropriate plastic tube. There were a few other refinements – the child nominated a colour and shape for their 'joker' (which scored double) and each cube or ball had a number printed on it, to indicate how many points it was worth. But, of course, the most fun was to be had from discovering the contents of the boxes that the contestants had to rummage through. As far as Stu Francis was concerned, it was a game just made for television:

> The great thing about it was, they had a camera at the back. So the hand came through and – at home watching the telly – you could see what they were putting their hand in. Which made it better, because the *kids* didn't know what they were putting their hand in. But there was no like, 'That's a girl's box, that's a boy's box.' It was up to them. They just dived in wherever.

Sexual equality (of a sort!) had finally arrived. *Crackerjack* had always been guilty of tailoring the games to the gender of the contestant. Even in *Take a Letter* the boys always got the messiest stunts. Now, whether boy or girl, you could be guaranteed to finish the game with an arm liberally coated in Martian Swamp, Moon Mousse and Pink Plunder. The downside was that the runners-up would then have precious autographed pop albums and annuals thrust into their messy, sticky little hands – a hazard that Stu and the production team were not completely insensitive to:

> I think what they did was, if they were really messed up, they'd replace them afterwards. 'Oh, that's covered in treacle – here, have a new one.'

There was a new comedy guest in show one, and in four later episodes. He was particularly keen to be working with Sara Hollamby, telling the *Radio Times*, 'If someone could lend me a fiver I wouldn't mind taking her out to supper!'

Sara also remembers him affectionately as, 'The nicest man you could ever hope to meet. He was an absolute gentleman.' But just as it seems we're heading for our first *Crackerjack* romance, Sara breaks the mood by adding, 'He was an old guy then and he used to get in this tiny little box.' This only starts to make any kind of sense when one learns that *Crackerjack*'s newest guest star was Basil Brush.

Basil Brush was hardly a newcomer to television. He wasn't even a newcomer to *Crackerjack*, having appeared as a guest as early as 1968. This book has been peppered with references to Basil throughout. Paul Ciani and Jacqueline Clarke both worked on *The Basil Brush Show*. And Basil's creator Ivan Owen (in his early acting career) had regularly appeared as Detective Inspector Bruce on *Crackerjack*'s sister programme *Playbox*, as well as guesting in a *Crackerjack* sketch with Ronnie Corbett in the late 1950s.

Basil, the glove-puppet fox with the vocal tones of Terry-Thomas, got his own show after regular appearances on magician David Nixon's TV series. But he hadn't been seen on the BBC for the past few years, as journalist Michael Richardson explained in the *Daily Express*:

> Basil Brush, the fox with the infectious laugh, is back in his old lair at the BBC TV studios. After a three-year absence, he is to help comedian Stu Francis present the early evening *Crackerjack* show. Basil – catchphrase 'Boom, boom' – was a BBC viewers' favourite for 16 years before he suddenly vanished in a row over programme timings.
>
> Basil, who lately had strayed to ITV, had an audience of 10 million in his previous reign at the BBC. His creator and mouthpiece, Ivan Owen, said last night: 'We had been happy at the BBC and never really wanted to leave.'

The row with the BBC had come about because Ivan Owen felt Basil's show deserved an early-evening timeslot, rather than the usual 'children's hour' scheduling. The outcome did not go in Basil's favour. His next job was on ITV, presenting *Let's Read with Basil Brush* in the mid-morning.

But now Basil was back on the Beeb with a new sparring partner. Here Basil is attired in a pilot's jacket and goggles:

BASIL: Tally-ho Red Leader, Angels One-Five, Mayday-Mayday, August Bank Holiday and Pancake Tuesday! I've just started my own airline. I'm doing holiday tours all over the world. How much have you got?

STU: One pound fifty.

BASIL: For that I can transport you at lightning speed as far as Shepherds Bush.

STU: Shepherds Bush? But we're already here.

BASIL: I said it was quick. That's one pound fifty you owe me.

Despite his early years as an actor, once Ivan Owen became the voice of Basil he did everything possible to stay out of the limelight. Basil would happily pose for photographs, but never Ivan. He believed it would destroy the illusion, and preferred to stay out of sight, inside a box with his hand in the air. Stu Francis quickly got to know Ivan's idiosyncrasies:

> I used to sit next to the box, and Basil would be there next to me. And they said, 'Stop! Cut!' And I remember Ivan saying to me, 'Stu! Stu! What's happening?' Because he's underneath, in the box, on a little stool. And I

looked down and said to Ivan, 'Oh, I've just been given a signal. There's something wrong with the lighting. They've got to adjust it.' And Basil would go to me, 'What are you doing? Who are you talking to?' I said, 'You what?' And he said, 'You talk to *me*.' And Ivan meant it! You always talk to the fox. Don't look in the box and go, 'Ivan, we've got a lighting problem.' You had to talk to the fox all the time.

I had so much fun with him. I used to throw lines in that weren't scripted. We were doing this thing, and Basil had this foil jacket. He was going to be a spaceman or something. And he said something to me, having a go at me. And I looked at him for a split second, and I said, 'Listen, you oven-ready ferret!' And I could see Ivan laughing. And 'cause he's laughing, his hand shakes a bit. And afterwards Ciani said, 'Brilliant! Leave it in!' But the fox, you could see him shaking. He weren't meant to. But because Ivan was laughing, the hand was shaking.

At the end of the show, when it was all finished, 'Right, see you, Ivan.' And we used to get gangs outside the stage door for autographs. It would take us half an hour to get out of the stage door. And Ivan would walk out and Basil was in a violin case. And he'd just walk straight through. Everybody thinks he must just be one of the musicians going out. And I used to say, 'Look at that. It's the only fox I know who goes home in a Rolls Royce.' And there he is in a violin case. A very nice violin case, I should say.

Basil's routines were scripted by his current writer Peter Robinson, who had previously worked on *Crackerjack* during Don Maclean's final series. The other series writer was Graham Deykin (returning after a two-series break), an experienced gagman who had written for Dick Emery and *The Two Ronnies*. The director for the series was David Taylor, who had previously worked on sitcom *Terry and June* and who Stu remembers simply as 'a very quiet guy'. Overall control was still in the hands of Paul Ciani – though, to musical director Nigel Hess, he seldom gave the impression of being in control:

A lot of the time on production, Paul used to walk round with a knitted sweater on. It was in beautiful crocheted knitting – I think it might have been done by his mother, or I might have made that up – and it actually said on the back, 'Will Somebody Please Tell Me What The Fuck Is Going On?' And it was all in beautiful crochet! And he used to wear it on production days – because he was always up in the box, so the kids never saw it. I thought that kind of summed up the day really.

The *Radio Times* heralded The Great Soprendo's return in the second show of the series:

Crazy illusionist The Great Soprendo (Trique-Traque-Jaque to his friends – that's Spanish for *Crackerjack*!!) comes back to amaze everyone with his tricks.

Of course it isn't Spanish for anything! It's just one of those fortuitous catchphrases that Geoffrey Durham thought up more by accident than design:

I improvised something on the rehearsal-room floor. And I used to do everything in a Spanish accent. So I did something about 'Trique-Traque-Jaque' with a reference to the J-A-C-K of *Crackerjack*. And Stu Francis fell about laughing, and from that moment called me Tricky-Tracky-Hacky, which caught on a bit with the kids.

There was something faintly risqué about The Great Soprendo's other triple-barrelled catchphrase – Piff-Paff-Poof! – despite the fact that it can be dated back to an operatic chorus by Jacques Offenbach. But Stu and The Great Soprendo always greeted each other affectionately as Stewey and Soppy. Whereas Stu's relationship with Basil was a little more combative – Basil would call him Mr Hotpot or, on one occasion, Mr Meat-and-Two-Veg!

With Basil Brush and The Great Soprendo taking care of nine of the shows, the remaining four had one-off guest appearances by comedians Bobby Davro, Jimmy Cricket and Gary Wilmot – plus a return visit from Keith Harris who, by then, had his own BBC series, also produced by Paul Ciani.

Pop guests during this series of *Crackerjack* included Haircut 100, The Thompson Twins, Kim Wilde and Kajagoogoo; and among the exotically named variety turns were balancing act Los Martinos, jugglers Les Diaboliques, and plate-spinner Bartschelly who appeared the same week as Geoffrey Durham:

He was wonderful. One of those spesh acts that just does it and goes home. I remember him packing his plates up, and I said to him, 'What are you doing?' And he said, 'I'm flying to Brussels, because I'm there tomorrow.' And that was life for these people. And it's all really gone now.

The celebrity gunging continued apace, with astrologer Russell Grant, strongman Geoff Capes and recent *Saturday Superstore* recruit Sarah Greene all on the receiving end. The supposed premise of *Take a Chance* was that, if the celebrity answered the question correctly, they escaped the gunging and the child they were paired with got a better prize. In reality, everyone got a prize and everyone got gunged. Especially Stu, as Sara Hollamby remembers:

> Afterwards perhaps we'd all go to the Bush pub for a drink. And Stu would still have tealeaves in his ears, having had two showers and goodness knows what else.

The end-of-series Christmas special opens with Stu, dressed as Buttons, flying in on a sleigh on wires and boasting, 'Ooh, I could wrestle a reindeer.' The Great Soprendo levitates Stu:

SOPRENDO: Have you ever done anything like this before?
STU: No.
SOPRENDO: Neither have I.

DJs Richard Skinner and Simon Bates and *Saturday Superstore*'s John Craven and Mike Read are the four celebrities who are given just seconds to complete totally impossible tasks (like singing *The Twelve Days of Christmas*) before being deluged in such seasonal delights as Mouldy Cranberry Sauce and Soggy Stuffing. The number of gunge cubicles for this series was reduced from three to two. So (with double the number of celebrity gungees for this Christmas special) Stu largely, but not totally, escapes a drenching.

Julie Dorne Brown left at the end of the series and promptly metamorphosed into Downtown Julie Brown, becoming a DJ on Music Box, the first UK cable music channel:

> And that's when MTV saw me and asked me to fly over to the States for an audition, and I never came back. I currently do a daily radio show on Sirius XM. So I'm the 90s chick. They have no idea I grew up in the 80s!

Like all the *Crackerjack* hostesses I've spoken to, Julie speaks warmly of her time working on the show:

> I loved running on that stage and standing next to Stu because, even though we'd got the show planned down and we'd rehearsed it, he would always

change it when we went on stage. And it just became like it *could* go the way we'd planned it, but anything could happen. And you knew it would be something better. And you just knew it was going to be safe. I mean he never, ever, missed a beat. Never missed a line. You never had that feeling of, 'Oh my gosh, I don't know how this is going to end.' But with someone that's such a pro, and so fun and so kind, that you went on stage going, 'Oh my gosh, this is going to be another great day!'

*

Series 29 of *Crackerjack*, another 13-week run, began in late September 1984. Stu Francis told the *Radio Times*:

> People who gave up watching *Crackerjack* five years ago because they thought they had outgrown it should take another look. They are in for a big surprise. The image is very free and easy now, in keeping with the 80s.

Unlike many other start-of-series interviews, there was no talk of new games, or any other radical revamp, shake-up or makeover. In fact, there was little in this series that was any different from the last. Basil Brush and The Great Soprendo were back, plus Keith Harris (who had only made one appearance in the previous series), and the three of them rotated as special guests. Graham Deykin returned as series writer and Peter Robinson continued to provide Basil's material. Keith Harris's scriptwriter for this series was Wally Malston, a hugely prolific writer for performers such as Jim Davidson, Reg Varney, Marti Caine, and Little and Large.

Musical director Nigel Hess left the show in the capable hands of his deputy Barry Francis, and went on to carve out a career as a composer for television and the theatre, including a number of recent Royal Shakespeare Company productions. New director for the series was Tony Newman, who came to the show after a lengthy apprenticeship as production manager on *The Two Ronnies*.

The only other new performer was hostess Ling Tai, an actress born in Hong Kong, whose TV credits included the *Doctor Who* adventure *Warriors of the Deep*, broadcast earlier in the year. Regrettably the role of the hostess was now further reduced. They no longer made their entrance during Stu's opening routine – it carried on uninterrupted until he introduced the comedy guest. Sara and Ling Tai didn't appear until the first game, when they had little to say except for the child's name and geographical location.

Given the opening routine entirely to himself, Stu Francis shows what he has steadily learned through the past few series – how to make kids laugh. Many comedians would keep it loud, keep it fast. Don't wait for the laugh, just press on to the next gag. Stu is quiet. Very low-key. But talking directly to the kids. And, as a result, every gag scores. To Stu, it made perfect sense:

> Get over the footlights. In other words, 'Come here.' It's not me and you, or you and me. We're all in this together. We're in the same gang. That was my attitude. Talk to them, instead of just shouting. Talk to them. And they're not stupid. They either laugh or they don't. It's either funny or it's not. And that's when I nailed it. You don't have to be shouting at them all the time. They're on it! If they like you, they'll go with you. If they don't like you, no matter what you do, they won't go with you. Nobody will.

They weren't always the most original gags, but they were gags the kids laughed at because they understood them – rather than responding automatically because it *sounds* like a joke. A typical routine is all about food:

> We had potatoes so often, I used to call my mum 'Sunburn' – 'cos she was always peeling. In fact, the only time I ever had meat was when I bit me tongue.

By and large, the material is unsophisticated and inoffensive. Though to crack a gag like 'We were so poor, my little brother was made in Hong Kong,' when one of your hostesses had worked there and the other one was born there, is a regrettable and uncharacteristic blunder by all concerned.

International speciality acts during the series included tightrope walker Brian Andro, knife balancers The Wazyrs and comedy acrobats The Dingbats. Amongst the pop guests were Alvin Stardust, Hazell Dean, Slade and (for the third consecutive series) Modern Romance. *Crackerjack*'s long-standing association with pop is reflected in a bit of Keith Harris and Orville crosstalk:

> KEITH: Do you like Duran Duran?
> ORVILLE: I do, I do.
> KEITH: UB40?
> ORVILLE: *You* be 40 soon!

Crackerjack, being born in 1955, was rapidly heading towards its 30th birthday. Particularly in its later years it had done much to change with the times. But had it changed enough? This piece by Stafford Hildred – headlined

Simply Crackers! – appeared in the *Daily Star* on Friday14[th] December 1984, the day of the penultimate show in the series:

> Is nothing sacred? I have discovered a sinister plot, hatched in the darkest recesses of the BBC. It's more terrible than a fourth series of *Juliet Bravo* … more controversial than turning *Terry and June* into a comedy show.
>
> Whirlwind new BBC boss Michael Grade is considering scrapping *Crackerjack*. Just because the one BBC children's show that doesn't look like a lesson from the Open University has been smashed in the ratings by ITV's kids' quiz *Blockbusters*. So, after almost 30 years of success, it looks like curtains for *Crackerjack*.
>
> Now I understand Mr Grade – the man they call Hurricane Michael at the BBC – thinks the series is too dated to continue. Hurricane Michael has axed lots of shows that needed axing – like the pretentious *Hot Shoe Show*, awful *Ask the Family*, corny *Cold Warrior*, those dreadful Strongest Men contests and so on. But it would be tragic if gifted presenter Stu Francis and *Crackerjack* were swept away in an ill-considered blast by the hurricane.
>
> Please think again, Michael.

The previous series of *Crackerjack* had started at, or around, five o'clock. This series started at 5.15. The *Radio Times* had said, back in September:

> As it's at a later time than last year, there's now more chance that a wider audience – mums and dads, older brothers and sisters perhaps – will be able to see that *Crackerjack* is a family show.

The problem was that 5.15 was also the starting time for ITV's *Blockbusters*. This children's quiz, hosted by Bob Holness, was currently running every weekday, so there was the additional attraction of tuning in to see how yesterday's game (which may have been halted midway) would resolve. There were some similarities between the quiz elements of the two shows. They both involved taking a letter. In the case of *Blockbusters* the contestant had to give an answer beginning with the appropriate letter ('I'll have a P please, Bob!') to form a continuous line of illuminated hexagons, either horizontally or vertically. The down path was shorter than the across path, which was why one contestant was pitted against a team of two.

Although *Crackerjack* had always pitched itself as a show for the whole family, the kids in the studio audience now seemed younger than ever. Much of the comedy material, particularly that of Keith Harris, was clearly tailored for the pre-teens. And, if you were after a good quiz, it wasn't easy to catch the questions amidst all the rush and the frenzy, the shouting and the screaming, the slime and the gunge.

Blockbusters was, by comparison, sedate. It was a more mature show, because the contestants were sixth-formers. The kids on *Crackerjack* were hurtling round the studio like billy-o, in the hope of winning a Scalextric set and a *Crackerjack* pen. But, on *Blockbusters*, stand stock-still and come up with a few answers and you could be jetting off to America. There was a simple reason for this. *Crackerjack* was an expensive show with cheap prizes – whereas *Blockbusters* gave away expensive prizes but was far cheaper to make.

Michael Grade previously appeared in the *Crackerjack* story after successfully luring The Krankies to London Weekend Television. He had only been Controller of BBC1 for a matter of months, but had very quickly made his presence felt. Former assistant floor manager and gunge mixer Nick Fiveash believes that Michael wasn't particularly predisposed to programmes like *Crackerjack*:

> Any entertainment show, for some reason Michael Grade didn't want to know. Anything that had music in, he axed. He axed the variety shows. He seemed to have a bit of a beef with music.

Like Stafford Hildred of the *Daily Star*, Stu Francis was only really made aware of *Crackerjack*'s fate in the final weeks of the series:

> I found out towards the end. It was an in-house thing, and it was crazy. What I was told was Michael Grade decided that *Crackerjack* was to finish. And *Crackerjack* was under Light Entertainment, not Children's Television. But Michael Grade said, 'It's costing too much on our budget.' Edward Barnes, who was Head of Children's Television, said, 'Well, we want to keep it.' Michael Grade said, 'Right, well, keep it, but *you* do it. It comes out of your budget.' Edward Barnes said, 'But we can't. It's too expensive for us. Children's Television hasn't got that budget with everything else we're doing. That's why Light Entertainment do it.' So Michael Grade says, 'Well, I'm telling you we're not doing it.'
>
> So *Crackerjack* did go off, because Light Entertainment weren't prepared to pay for it. Because it went out at around five o'clock. And Light Entertainment really kicks in after six. So he classed it as children's TV. Edward Barnes said, 'Well, it might look that way, but it comes under the Light Entertainment budget.' So it was an in-house thing that nobody could settle.

And I only found out towards the end, with about two shows to go. No long official warning – just, sort of, that's it! Switch the light off on your way out.

Putting sentiment aside, if any programme needed to be axed, then one that was costly to make and struggling in the ratings battle would be an obvious choice. When (in 1964) *Crackerjack* made the move from Children's Television to Light Entertainment, it held its own against evening variety shows, because it had a similar level of talent on both sides of the camera, and a respectable amount of money thrown at it too. But, at this point in its life, being part of the Light Entertainment department had become a distinct disadvantage.

It's easy to portray Michael Grade as the villain of the piece. But, as Controller of BBC1, he had to manage his budget efficiently and many difficult decisions had to be made. Early the following year he decided to give *Doctor Who* 'a long rest' (his words) and received an avalanche of hate mail in response. But there are many levels of management within the BBC, so it wasn't necessarily Michael who single-handedly pulled the plug on *Crackerjack*. When I contacted Michael Grade (now Baron Grade of Yarmouth) I was told by his PA:

> Lord Grade has no recollection at all of ending *Crackerjack*. He's not sure it was actually him.

She subsequently added:

> I have to say, the fact that he has no recollection of axing the show doesn't mean he didn't! He must have had at least fifteen other jobs since leaving BBC1 and it is a very long time ago.

Whatever the internal politics behind the decision, when it came to the final show of the series, everyone knew that it was just that – the final show. And they gave it all they'd got!

It was the traditional end-of-series Christmas show, transmitted on 21st December 1984. The *Radio Times* promised 'surprises galore in this very special *Crackerjack*'. Instead of the usual opening shot of the studio audience, the camera is trained on the street outside the Television Theatre (the home of *Crackerjack* for the majority of its run, from the very first edition). A coach arrives, pulled by four white horses. Coachman Stu ushers Sara, Ling Tai and Father Christmas out of the coach and through the large doors leading to the backstage area, where all the performers are waiting, before the cameras follow him into the auditorium.

Stu Francis remembers the special atmosphere of that final show:

> Cameramen are always concentrating so much. They've got to get the shots right. When the camera's not on, you get a nod and a smile. But when they're actually working, you don't get the feedback. But on that show the camera lads were great and always smiling. And I always remember our Christmas special. I walked in and the lads had dressed the cameras up. They'd got tinsel all round the cameras. Round the front and the side. And some had tinsel round their necks and on their heads. And that was the atmosphere of it. It was great!

After Stu has greeted the kids he casts off his heavy coat, revealing a cosier Christmassy jumper:

> Ooh, I could squash a snowflake! It's cold now, isn't it? In fact, last night I saw a dog froze to a lamppost. I was at London Zoo last week, and the penguins were so cold you couldn't get the wrappers off.

Two out of the series' three special guests make an appearance – Keith Harris who, together with Orville, performs the song *Superduck* – and The Great Soprendo who, naturally, does a trick:

> This is one of the oldest tricks in the world. This trick comes from before BC. It's true! In fact, it comes from before A.

The show allows itself just two moments of nostalgia. The first is when Chas and Dave (writers/performers of the theme song and frequent guests on the show) sing *Harry was a Champion* with a group of dancers dressed as pearly kings and queens. Harry Champion, the singer of *Any Old Iron* and many other music-hall standards, was hardly a household name to the children in the audience. However, he had performed on that very stage in the theatre's early days, when it was known as the Shepherds Bush Empire. The song also references a Rudyard Kipling quote: 'Music halls are a necessary part of our civilisation.' Not only is it a ringing endorsement of this show's variety heritage, it's also a rare instance of *Crackerjack* being infinitely more esoteric than *Blockbusters*.

The second blast from *Crackerjack*'s past comes in *Take a Chance*. Richard Skinner, Simon Bates and John Craven (who all appeared in last year's seasonal special) are joined by old friend of the show Bernie Clifton. Bernie performs all his stunts with wild abandon, squirting far more cream down Stu's trousers than is strictly necessary and, after juggling some eggs, playfully breaks one over Stu's head. His gunge tank contains Santa Surprise – a coating of red sludge followed by a heavy fall of artificial snow. He vigorously rubs much of it into Stu's hair and pokes it into his ears.

In the closing moments of the show, with the entire cast gathered around him, Stu says to camera, 'That's about the end of the show – it's certainly the end of the gunge.' At that moment the heavens open, and anyone who has so far escaped a drenching is now coated in colourful gunk. A succession of footballers (mainly from Tottenham Hotspur) then enter, each carrying a custard pie destined for Stu's face.

The *Radio Times* promised a 'very special *Crackerjack*'. But this was to be expected from a Christmas show. There was no mention during the programme that this would be the last ever *Crackerjack*. The only clue is in Stu's final words. At the end of the previous Christmas show, those words were, 'See you next year.' This time he simply says:

Thanks for watching us. Bye-bye. God bless. See ya!

If there were a few moist eyes, no one could tell. Everyone and everything was moist, not to say sodden. It was farewell to *Crackerjack*. And Stu Francis was just one amongst the many who were going to miss it:

You'd go to work with a spring in your step. It was never like, 'Here we go again.' It just had one big feelgood factor. I really enjoyed it. And it was a sad day when it finished.

14
The Audience Loves to Get Wet

W HEN *CRACKERJACK* WAS UNLEASHED upon Children's Hour in 1955, it was the first – and the only – variety show for children. As the decades rolled by, plenty more children's variety shows came along. They stayed for a while then left. *Crackerjack* outlasted them all. But nothing lasts forever.

In 1988, just four years after *Crackerjack* had ended its run, the BBC1 teatime slot was occupied by daily instalments of Australian soap *Neighbours.* In 1991 the BBC said goodbye to the Television Theatre, which has since reverted to its former name of the Shepherds Bush Empire and presents music acts of a rather more contemporary nature than Harry Champion. Early in the new millennium the BBC launched two digital children's channels – and all its children's programming, including *Blue Peter*, is now found there. At the time of writing, both BBC1 and ITV offer quiz shows at teatime, and the big Saturday-morning spectaculars have been replaced by cookery chat shows.

It is now a rare occurrence to find the whole family gathered round the television set. Most rooms in the house will have a device (from massive to miniature) that can receive TV, and you can watch it on the move too. And, with an ever-increasing choice of channels, you can pick and choose, totally avoiding children's programmes and pop music if they are not to your taste.

After *Crackerjack* finished, hostess Ling Tai appeared in a whole range of TV shows, from *Coronation Street* to *Soldier Soldier*. In 1989 she played Shou Yuing in *Doctor Who*, her third role in the series. Sara Hollamby worked with Stu Francis again in the TVS show *Ultraquiz*. She later presented travel shows and is a regular face on shopping channel QVC. Basil Brush continues to this day – there may now be a different man under the desk, but few can tell the difference. Keith Harris made two further series of *The Keith Harris Show* with Paul Ciani as producer – together with numerous other TV appearances, including celebrity editions of teatime quizzes *The Weakest Link* and *Pointless*. One other major star of the series, the gunge tank, subsequently had a long and fruitful working relationship with Noel Edmonds.

Geoffrey Durham (aka The Great Soprendo) also continued his association with Paul Ciani, plus two other former *Crackerjack* stars, in *The Krankies Elektronik Komik*. Having been part of *Crackerjack's* radical revamp in its final years, Geoffrey was quick to notice that children's television was still swiftly evolving:

> I remember saying to my agent in about 1989, 'I've just seen a presenter who appears not to be much older than the target audience. He's called Phillip Schofield. And I think he's the future. And all us middle-aged old gits doing light entertainment for kids are going to be very old-fashioned, very quickly. And I'm not going to be The Great Soprendo any more.' And I prepared it very carefully and in 1990 I stopped.
>
> Other people weren't as lucky as me. There were some people who didn't have that luck, or that foresight, or couldn't quite move away the way I could. Because I could just take off the makeup. But they couldn't. They'd been branded and so they couldn't quite move anywhere else. It was a great shame for them. Because actually I'd been lucky, or right, or something, in noticing that it was changing and that everything was going to get much, much, much younger.

This was far from retirement. Geoffrey continued to perform as a magician, but now as himself – less manic and far less hirsute. He also provided entertainment for the other end of the age range, with frequent appearances in Dictionary Corner on Channel 4's *Countdown*.

*

For anyone fascinated by anniversaries, *Crackerjack* manages to disappoint on almost every level. It ran for 29 series over 29 years. There are just over 450 billed episodes, but a few of those were repeats or compilations, largely due to industrial action. So the actual total is a little short of 450. But if we bend the rules a little and include the *Crackerjack* stage shows, we can proudly celebrate 30 glorious years of *Crackerjack*!

In between the last few series of *Crackerjack*, Stu Francis took some of his co-stars and went out to meet their public:

> A theatre tour. One-day stands. A variety show. We actually did the gunge thing on the road. We had a band and carried our own crew, to help with the set and the gunge and everything. It was literally a roadshow – we're coming to *you* now.

Hostesses Leigh Miles, Julie Dorne Brown, Sara Hollamby and Ling Tai all took part in various of these tours. Julie and Sara were involved in the 1984 tour – a show called *Take a Chance*. Julie Brown has happy (though hardly 'rock and roll') memories of the tour:

> Of course going out on the road is a lot different than being in the studio where everything's done for you. I remember Sara taught me how to knit on that tour – that was awesome! She knitted a sweater and like, 'I want to do that.' And a lot of the theatres were really cold. So when we went out on stage we'd really be jumping up and down. Like going backstage and being able to see our breath in the wings. Sara and I got together and went shopping, to pick our outfits for the tour, which was fun.

Sara Hollamby also enjoyed the experience:

> The stage show was great fun. It was bloomin' hard work, because we had a coach and we used to go from one venue straight on to the next one. And we only did a day in each place. We did two shows, a matinee and an evening. And then afterwards we'd pack up and go on to the next venue. And I seem to remember we used to mix up the gunge, Julie and I. Yes, it was all hands on deck. We had some stage hands, but we all helped, we all mucked in. Blowing up balloons. God, how many balloons have I blown up? Millions! It was hard work but fun. And we were young!

Although the TV version was cancelled at the end of 1984, the stage show continued into 1985 with a new title: *Stu Francis and the Stars of Crackerjack*. Peter Brown of *The Stage* found it to be good honest entertainment:

Stu Francis was hardly off the stage for the whole two hours, spearheading an unruly mixture of circus, pantomime, crazy games and music. The accent was very firmly on audience participation, where the audience were encouraged to make as much noise as they could – and they did. No sophisticated humour; no blue jokes; no hidden messages to ponder over. Just plenty of good clean fun, noise, knockabout comedy and mess.

The audience participation extended to a tear-off strip in the theatre programme, on which children could volunteer themselves for the games and a 'parent or other adult over 18 to go under the gunge tubes with Stu'.

Alongside Stu were Ling Tai and newcomer hostess Fiona Fox. Clowning of the circus variety was provided by Charlie Cairoli Junior and Co, who had made a couple of TV appearances in the final years of *Crackerjack*. The bill was completed by an act that had never been on *Crackerjack* but was on the very brink of an enduring career on children's television. Their names were Paul and Barry Elliott and, as their biography in the programme accurately predicts, 'You'll be seeing a lot of the Chuckle Brothers in the future.'

Paul Chuckle and brother Barry had their own comedy spot, but also popped up throughout the show, which wasn't just about the gunge:

> We had water pistols as well, which we were attacking the audience with. The audience loves to get wet. And we used to have fun when the curtain went down as well – shooting at each other. We just enjoyed ourselves. We really did. Stu was a great guy. He was like a little boy. A very funny naughty little boy. And it came across the footlights. Kids loved him as well as mums and dads.
>
> Stu used to repeat himself all the time. 'Here's another question, here's another question.' I remember it vividly. And they weren't allowed to call it *Crackerjack*, because the BBC had got the name and it's *their* name. So they got away with it by calling it *The Stars of Crackerjack*. Clever!

Stu Francis was still touring with a *Crackerjack* show in 1986, again joined by Charlie Cairoli and Co, with singers Linda Nolan and Paula Ann Bland also doubling as hostesses. Nowadays he is a pantomime favourite and one of the regular cast members of *The Dressing Room*, a touring comedy show written by Bobby Ball, who stars in it with partner Tommy Cannon. It's part stand-up, part backstage drama – a cross between a play and a variety show, which Bobby describes as 'playriety'.

*

Anyone with personal memories of *Crackerjack* will have their own favour-ite period of the show. And some people reading this will doubtless despair at what it had become by 1984 – a dystopian nightmare beyond even George Orwell's imaginings – with Stu Francis covered from head to toe in gunk and slime. How different from 1955 and the suave, smart-suited subtlety of Eamonn Andrews.

But was it really so different? From the very start *Crackerjack* prided itself on its slapstick, its explosions, its general undercurrent of anarchy. You might think that *Double or Drop* and *Take a Chance* were poles apart. But the seeds of the gunge drop – of the host getting his come-uppance – were all there in Eamonn Andrews' original format for *Double or Drop*. The very last paragraph of that format – headed 'Finale' – was never used. But, had it been, Eamonn (as both devisor and *Crackerjack* host) would surely have been its willing victim:

> The winner asks the Quiz Master a question. He fails to answer and the whole set falls down on him.

Acknowledgements

I N THE PROCESS OF researching the *Crackerjack* story I have interviewed a great many people. My grateful thanks to all of the following who kindly shared their memories with me:

John Adams, Phil Appleton, Michael Aspel, Johnny Ball, Alan J. W. Bell, Maggie Bernstein, Downtown Julie Brown, Simon Capes, Paul Chuckle, Jacqueline Clarke, Bernie Clifton, Jillian Comber, Googie Cooney, Jean Crowther, Geoffrey Durham, Alan Fenton, Nick Fiveash, Stu Francis, Mike Giles, Tony Glaze, Sue Gregson, Tony Hare, Patrick Heigham, Nigel Hess, Pip Hinton, Winifred Hodge, Sara Hollamby, Christine Holmes, Jan Hunt, Teddy Johnson, Peter Kindred, Marina Lambrou, Pete Langford, Eddie Large, Syd Little, Reg Livermore, Don Maclean, Margaret McGrath, Sheelagh McGrath, Rod McLennan, Leigh Miles, Lesley North, Kate O'Sullivan, Christine Ozanne, Ron Prentice, Terry Ravenscroft, Jan Rogers, James Smillie, Barbara Speake, Eddie Stuart, Ian & Janette Tough, Sally Ann Triplett, Eric Wallis and Valerie Walsh.

Thanks also to: Bob Bain, Geoff Bowden, Jo Burt, Paul Burton, Baron Grade of Yarmouth, Terry Hardy, Rob McMicking, Muriel Mars, Murray Melvin, Bernard Newnham, Alan Ramshaw, Jill Millard Shapiro, Ros Sloboda, J. D. Sobol, David Sztypuljak, Rowan Wiltshire and Graeme Wood.

Two of Britain's finest institutions were of particular help with my research – the British Broadcasting Corporation and the British Film Institute. My thanks to Samantha Blake, Kate O'Brien and Tom Hercock at the BBC Written Archives Centre, and Jonny Davies at the BFI Reuben Library.

Digital newspapers and magazines and other online information were accessed courtesy of The BBC Genome Project, The British Newspaper Archive, Google, YouTube, Proquest, *The Times* digital archive and UK Press Online.

I am especially grateful to all those who loaned scripts, recordings, photos and general *Crackerjack* memorabilia, including Jon Anton, Phil Appleton, Alan J. W. Bell, Maggie Bernstein, Chris Boxall, David Bryceson, Simon Capes, Jean Crowther, Stu Francis, Lynda George, Tony Glaze, Tony Hare, Patrick Heigham, Sara Hollamby, Christine Holmes, Jan Hunt, Marina Lambrou, Reg Livermore, Don Maclean, Leigh Miles, David Moore, Kate O'Sullivan, Christine Ozanne, Neil Pearson Rare Books, Peter Raggett, James Smillie and Ian Tough.

Apologies for any names I have inadvertently missed from these lists.

Thanks also to Dexter O'Neill, Paul Ballard, Phil Reynolds, Will Brooks and the team at Fantom Publishing for all their support, encouragement and guidance. And for, yet again, putting their money where my mouth is.

Lastly, my gratitude to family and friends – particularly to Lynda George, for her digital wizardry on a good few shabby photos. But chiefly … (and I can guarantee she'll get the reference!) … to my wife Andrea, who somehow manages to be my constant sounding board without ever sounding bored.

Bibliography

The following books have been invaluable in my research:

A Twitch in Time by Sue Benwell with Jack Douglas (Able Publishing 2002)

Bestseller! by Andrew Marshall and David Renwick (George Allen and Unwin 1981)

Fandabidozi by Ian and Janette Tough with Matt Bendoris (John Blake Publishing 2004)

Flying High by Don Maclean and Chris Gidney (Hodder and Stoughton 2003)

High Hopes by Ronnie Corbett with Oliver Pritchett (Ebury Press 2000)

Hullawrerr China! by Rikki Fulton and Stan Mars (Black and White Publishing 2005)

Into the Box of Delights by Anna Home (BBC Books 1993)

It Seemed Like a Good Idea at the Time by Michael Grade (Macmillan 1999)

Larger Than Life by Eddie Large with Stafford Hildred (John Blake Publishing 2005)

Laughter in the Air by Barry Took (Robson Books 1976)

Listen Very Carefully, I Shall Say This Only Once by Jeremy Lloyd (BBC Books 1993)

Little Goes a Long Way by Syd Little (Harper Collins 1999)

My Turn by Norman Wisdom with William Hall (Century 1992)

Out of the Stewpot by Ed Stewart (John Blake Publishing 2005)

Polly Wants a Zebra by Michael Aspel (Weidenfeld and Nicholson 1974)

Radio Comedy 1938-1968 by Andy Foster and Steve Furst (Virgin Publishing 1996)

Raymond Rollett: The Forgotten Actor by Chris Boxall (King's Lynn Press 1987)

Round the Horne: The Complete and Utter History by Barry Took (Boxtree 1998)

The Bonus of Laughter by Leslie and Jean Crowther (Hodder and Stoughton 1994)

The Tome of the Unknown Actor by Christine Ozanne (Avocado Books 2016)

This is My Life by Eamonn Andrews (Macdonald & Co 1963)

I have also drawn information from the following children's books and annuals:

Eamonn Andrews' Book for Boys and Girls (Adprint 1956)

BBC Children's Annual edited by Freda Lingstrom (Burke, London 1957)

BBC Children's Annual edited by Freda Lingstrom (Burke, London 1958)

The Television Annual edited by Kenneth Bailey (Odhams Press 1958)

The Eamonn Andrews Crackerjack Book (Daily Mirror 1962)

BBC Book of Crackerjack edited by Richard Evans (British Broadcasting Corporation 1966)

Crackerjack Book of Games (British Broadcasting Corporation 1968)

Crackerjack Annual (Atlas Publishing Company 1969)

Crackerjack Annual (World Distributors 1970)

Crackerjack Annual 1972 by Richard Evans and others (World Distributors 1971)

Crackerjack Annual 1977 (Stafford Pemberton Publishing 1976)

Crackerjack Annual 1978 (Stafford Pemberton Publishing 1977)

Crackerjack Annual 1982 (Stafford Pemberton Publishing 1981)

Crackerjack Annual 1983 (Stafford Pemberton Publishing 1982)

Crackerjack Annual (Purnell Publishers 1984)

Index

Alan Stafford

Too Naked for the Nazis

The untold story of sand dancing legends
Wilson, Keppel and Betty

They sound like a firm of solicitors and look like a bunch of Tutankhamen's hiero-glyphs that suddenly fancied a boogie. To many Wilson, Keppel and Betty are the epitome of the bizarre speciality act, shuffling through silver sands during the golden era of British variety. They inspired Morecambe and Wise, Legs & Co, the Chuckle Brothers. But what do we know about the Englishman and Irishman who clog-danced round America, returned home with two fezzes and a Cleopatra from Kansas, and proceeded to walk like three Egyptians? Precious little.

Until now. This lovingly pieced together story of their lives, onstage and off, reveals for the first time the flirtatious Irish dandy with the dicky ticker, the scruffy Liverpudlian party animal, and the teenage tearaway turned tap-shoed temptress who abruptly changed career and became a frequently outspoken war reporter. Their dancing outraged Hermann Goering; years later, in Nuremberg, Goering performed while Betty wrote the reviews.

Alan Stafford has ransacked dusty attics, thumbed crumbling newspapers and buttonholed countless experts and colleagues to discover the trio's hidden past. He's unearthed rare photos, and movies that were presumed lost. And he's tracked down and interviewed three women from the long dynasty of Wilson and Keppel's subsequent Bettys.

ISBN 978-1-78196-149-0

Available in hardback from
www.fantompublishing.co.uk